Questions for AP Exam Practice and Review

Surviving Chemistry AP Exam - 2013

One Day at a Time

20 Days of AP Practice Question Sets

With

Answers, Explanations and Scoring Guidelines

e3Chemistry

E3 Scholastic Publishing

Effiong Eyo

Surviving Chemistry Book Series

Family of High School chemistry books that are certain to:

★ **Excite** students to study

★ **Engage** students in learning

★ **Enhance** students' understanding

For more information and to order

e3chemistry.com   (877) 224 – 0484

info@e3chemistry.com

Acknowledgements:

The author acknowledges and thanks the following individuals for their contributions to this Edition of the AP Chemistry book. With a combined 30 years of AP experience, their contributions have certainly made this book better.

Veronica O'Donnell, NBCT: AP Chemistry Teacher – Cornwall Central HS, NY. Primary Editor, who also offered suggestions on amending and improving on questions.

John Hines: Student – Cornwall Central High School, NY.
Assisted with editing, as well as providing a student perspective on questions and other aspects of the book.

Ruben Steiner: Retired Chemistry Teacher. Currently a coordinator of AP tutoring programs for a test prep agency.
Offered suggestions on amending and improving on Scoring Guidelines to the Free Response questions.

Surviving Chemistry AP Exam - 2013

Questions for AP Exam Practice and Review

© 2012 by E3 Scholastic Publishing.

ISBN-13:   978-1479160730

ISBN-10:   1479160733

Printed in the United States of America

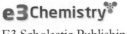

E3 Scholastic Publishing

e3chemistry.com

(877) 224 – 0484

info@e3chemistry.com

Format of this book:

This book contains sets of AP Chemistry exam practice questions organized into days. There are a total of 20 days of question sets.

Questions on the AP Chemistry exam are separated into three categories in two major sections. These categories are listed below.

Multiple Choice Questions: Section I Part A and Part B: *No Calculators*

In this book there are 7 sets of multiple choice questions for Section I Part A and Part B practice.

On Day 1, 4, and 7 sets, 25 AP exam quality multiple choice questions are available for practice on each of these days.

On Day 10, 13, 16 sets, 50 AP exam quality multiple choice questions are available for practice on each of these days.

On Day 19, as part of a full practice exam, 75 more AP exam quality multiple choice questions are also available for practice on this day.

There are a total of 300 AP quality multiple choice questions (enough for 4 exams) available for Section I Part A and Part B practice in this book.

Only the Periodic Table is allowed as a Reference Material for answering questions on this days. Although there are questions that require mathematical setups and calculations, the use of a calculator is not allowed for answering the multiple choice questions.

Free Response Questions: Section II Part A: *Calculators allowed*

In this book there are 6 sets of Free Response questions for Section II Part A practice .

On Day 2, 5, 8, 11, 14, and 17 sets, 2 AP exam quality Free Response questions are available for practice on each of these days.

On Day 20, as part of a full practice exam, 3 more AP quality Free Response questions are also available for practice.

Questions on these days have multiple parts and are math-heavy, and so the use of a calculator and all Reference Materials are allowed.

There are a total of 15 AP quality and challenging Free Response questions (enough for 5 exams) available for Section II Part A Practice in this book.

Free Response Questions: Section II Part B: *No Calculators*

In this book, there are 6 sets of Free Response questions for Section II Part B practice.

On Day 3, 6, 9, 12, 15, and 18 sets, 2 AP exam quality Free Response questions are available for practice on each of these days.

On Day 20, as part of a full practice exam, 3 more AP quality Free Response questions are also available for Section II Part B practice.

Questions on these days have multiple parts. The math in this section is light, and so the use of a calculator is not allowed. All Reference Materials provided are allowed for answering questions in this category.

There a total of 15 AP quality and challenging Free Response questions (enough for 5 exams) available for Section II Part B Practice in this book.

Answers and Explanations.

Answers are given to all questions in this book. Answer explanations are given to all questions (except for those on day 19 and 20). Unlike many other books, this book *does not just explain why* the answer given to a question is the correct one. Instead, with the cleanest, clearest, most simplified, and easiest-to-follow steps ever, this book *shows you how to pick out key information* from a question, *how to think through the question*, and (if necessary) *how to setup and calculate* the problem to arrive at the correct answer given. This method of explanations offer you a better review of how to solve many AP chemistry problems. It is highly recommended that you read up and study the steps given in the explanations to questions you did not get correct.

Scoring Guidelines.

AP exam scorers are provided with Scoring Guidelines on what and how to award points to Section II Free Response questions. Scoring of free response questions is very subjective, and not every AP exam scorers will score the same question exactly the same. However, it is still very important that you are aware of what important information and setup most AP scorers will look for when grading your test. In this book, clean, clear, and easy-to-follow Scoring Guidelines are provided for all Section II practice questions. It is highly recommended, once you start work on any of the Free Response question set, that you work on that question thoroughly as you would if the question was on the actual AP exam. Then use the Scoring Guidelines provided to score your answers carefully. Since the Scoring Guidelines in this book were provided by an expert AP exam grader, with over 16 years experience teaching, tutoring, and scoring old and new format AP exams for a well-established exam prep agency, you are certain to learn which information and setup will earn you the all-important partial and full credits in many different types of free response questions.

Keeping Track of Points and Progress

At the end of each question set, you are provided with a space to note the number of correct points after grading. This is a very important, often overlooked, element in preparing for a test like this. By making a note of your points after each set:

. You'll be able to easily see and keep track of your progress and improvement from one multiple choice (or free response) set to the next.

. You'll be able to easily see and tract which category of questions you are doing great on, and which category you are struggling with

. You'll be to see if what you are doing is getting you better prepared for the exam as the exam date draws near

It is almost pointless to study day-after-day without knowing whether your studying and effort are getting you better prepared for the test. This book allows you to quickly and easily keep track of your points, which allows you to see progress, improvement, and readiness for your chemistry AP exam.

Preparing for Chemistry AP Exam

Months, weeks, and days before the exam

Pay attention and listen to your teacher.
Your teacher knows you better than authors of AP books.
Pay attention in class, do what she or he says and recommends.

Attend review sessions.
Bring specific questions on concepts that you need the most help with.
You'll get more out of a review session if your questions to specific problems are answered.

Practice exam quality questions: Use this book.
Start early (a month or so) and practice a set of questions a day at a time.
Correct your answers and read up on explanations.
Keep note of points of each set to track your progress and improvement.

Study notes and review packages
Focus your studying on concepts you have problems with because you may not have enough time to study everything.
Make notes of concepts that are not clear, and bring them to your teacher.

Alternate between studying and practicing questions. It is highly recommended that you spend a little more time practicing questions and a little less time reading books and studying review packages.

Familiarize yourself with the current exam and scoring formats
The full Practice Exam on Day 19 and Day 20 in this book is based on the most current AP exam format. The Scoring Guidelines for all Free Response questions, as well as the Scoring Worksheet to determine your practice exam AP Score (page 278) are all based on the most current formats. Being aware of these formats is a very important element in preparing for your AP exam.

Night before the exam
Get a good night sleep. Relax!

Day of the exam
Eat a good meal. Relax!
Bring pencils, pens, and a calculator.

During the exam
Relax! Read and think through each question and choice thoroughly, and take your time. You know the answer to that question because you've worked hard and you've been taught well. And most of all,

You got Chem ☺

Good Luck !

Table of Contents

Easy does it

. Practice a set of questions one day at a time. You'll feel less overwhelmed.

Quality over Quantity

. Take your time to complete a set, correct a set, read up on explanations, and compare your performance to previous set of the same category. You'll learn more.

Day 1: 25 Multiple Choice questions

25 points ***Section I Part A and B Practice***

Start: Answer all questions on this day before stopping.

Note: **NO CALCULATORS may be used for questions on this day. You may use ONLY the Periodic Table provided on page 337**

Note: For all questions, assume that the temperature is 298 K, the pressure is 1.00 atmosphere and solutions are aqueous unless otherwise noted.

Questions 1 through 3 refer to the following gases:

(A) HCl
(B) O_2
(C) NO
(D) NO_2
(E) CO

1. This gas diffuses at the slowest rate.

2. This gas has the weakest intermolecular forces.

3. At any given temperature and pressure, this gas has particles with the highest average velocity.

Questions 4 through 7 refer to the following hybridizations:

(A) sp
(B) sp^2
(C) sp^3
(D) sp^3d
(E) sp^3d^2

4. SO_2

5. I_3^-

6. IF_5

7. CH_3OH

8. $Zn(s) + 2AgNO_3(aq) \ ------> 2Ag(s) + Zn(NO_3)_2(aq)$

According to the reaction represented above, about how many grams of zinc must go into this reaction to produce 1.0 mol of silver?

(A) 17 g
(B) 25 g
(C) 33 g
(D) 65 g
(E) 130 g

9. The standard enthalpy of combustion of methanol CH_3OH is
-711 kJ $\cdot mol^{-1}$. What mass of methanol must be completely burned in oxygen in order to produce 355.5 kJ of energy?

(A) 711 g
(B) 355.5 g
(C) 32 g
(D) 16 g
(E) Cannot be determined from information given.

10. According to Raoult's Law, which statement is incorrect?

(A) The vapor pressure of a solvent decreases as its mole fraction increases.
(B) Ionic solids ionize in water, increasing the effects of all colligative properties.
(C) The vapor pressure of a solvent over a solution is less than that of the pure solvent
(D) The solubility of a gas increases as the temperature decreases.
(E) The solubility of a gas in solution increases as the pressure of the gas increases.

11. A molecule of H–Cl contains how many lone electron pairs?
(A) one
(B) two
(C) three
(D) four
(E) six

12. $MgO(s) + H_2(g) <--> Mg(s) + H_2O(g)$ ΔH = -14.0 kilojoules

When the substances in the equation above are at equilibrium at pressure (P) and temperature (T), the equilibrium can be shifted to favor the products by

(A) increasing the pressure in the reaction vessel while keeping the temperature constant.
(B) increasing the pressure by adding an inert gas such as argon.
(C) allowing some hydrogen gas to escape at constant P and T
(D) decreasing the temperature.
(E) adding a catalyst.

13. Which of the following solutions has the highest boiling point?

(A) 0.10 m oxalic acid, $H_2C_2O_4$
(B) 0.10 m potassium chloride, KCl
(C) 0.10 m ammonium nitrate, NH_4NO_3
(D) 0.10 m sucrose, $C_{12}H_{22}O_{11}$
(E) 0.10 m calcium nitrate, $Ca(NO_3)_2$

14. 100 grams of $O_2(g)$ and 100 grams of He(g) are in separate containers of equal volume. Both gases are at 100°C. Which one of the following statements is true?

(A) Both gases would have the same pressure.
(B) The average kinetic energy of the O_2 molecules is greater than that of the He molecules.
(C) The average kinetic energy of the He molecules is greater than that of the O_2 molecules.
(D) There are equal numbers of He molecules and O_2 molecules.
(E) The pressure of the He(g) would be greater than that of the $O_2(g)$.

15. Which of the following species is not isoelectronic with the others?

(A) S^{2-}
(B) Cl^-
(C) Ar
(D) K^+
(E) Mg^{2+}

16. A 1-molar solution of a very weak monoprotic acid has a pH of 5.
What is the value of k_a for the acid?

(A) $K_a = 1 \times 10^{-10}$
(B) $K_a = 1 \times 10^{-7}$
(C) $K_a = 1 \times 10^{-5}$
(D) $K_a = 1 \times 10^{-2}$
(E) $K_a = 1 \times 10^{-1}$

17. Carbon-14 has a half-life of 5730 years. Approximately what percent of
the original radioactivity would be present after 34,480 years?

(A) 1.56%
(B) 3.13%
(C) 6.26%
(D) 12.5%
(E) 25.0%

18. Which of the following statements is true regarding magnesium and
calcium?

(A) Magnesium has a larger first ionization energy and a larger atomic
radius
(B) Magnesium has a larger first ionization energy and a smaller atomic
radius
(C) Magnesium has a smaller first ionization energy and a larger atomic
radius
(D) Magnesium has a smaller first ionization energy and a smaller atomic
radius
(E) Magnesium and calcium have identical first ionization energies and
atomic radii

19. What are the oxidation numbers of chromium in chromate and
dichromate anions, respectively?

(A) +8, +14
(B) +8, +7
(C) +7, +7
(D) +6, +6
(E) +4, +7

20. For which of the following processes would ΔS have a positive value?

$$\text{I.} \quad MgCO_3(s) \ \text{------>} \ MgO(s) + CO_2(g)$$

$$\text{II.} \quad Ba^{2+}(aq) + SO_4^{2-}(aq) \ \text{------->} \ BaSO_4(s)$$

$$\text{III.} \quad Cl_2(g) + C_3H_6(g) \ \text{---------->} \ C_3H_6Cl_2(g)$$

(A) I only
(B) I and II only
(C) I and III only
(D) II and III only
(E) I, II, and III

21. At 37°C and 1.00 atm of pressure, nitrogen gas dissolves in the blood at a solubility of 6.0×10^{-4} M. If a diver breathes compressed air where nitrogen gas constitutes 80. mole % of the gas mixture, and the total pressure at this dept is 3.0 atm, what is the concentration of nitrogen gas in her blood?

(A) 1.4×10^{-4} M
(B) 6.0×10^{-4} M
(C) 1.0×10^{-3} M
(D) 1.4×10^{-3} M
(E) 6.0×10^{-3} M

22. The rate law for a chemical reaction between substances A and B is

$$\text{rate} = k\,[A]^2[B]$$

where k is constant. The concentration of A is reduced to half its original. To make the reaction proceed at 50% of its original rate, the concentration of B should be

(A) decreased by ¼
(B) halved
(C) kept constant
(D) doubled
(E) increased by a factor of 4

23. In the titration of a weak base of unknown concentration with a solution of a strong acid, a pH meter was used to follow the progress of the titration. Which of the following graphs best represents the data collected for this experiment?

(A)

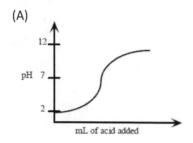

(B)

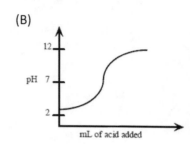

(C)

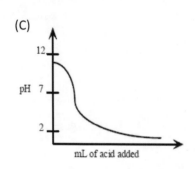

(D)

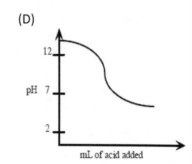

(E)

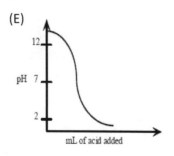

24. Which correctly represents the electron configuration of an oxide ion?

(A) $1s^2 2s^2 2p^2$
(B) $1s^2 2s^2 2p^4$
(C) $1s^2 2s^2 2p^6$
(D) $1s^2 2s^2 2p^6 3s^2$
(E) $1s^2 2s^2 2p^6 3s^2 3p^6$

25.

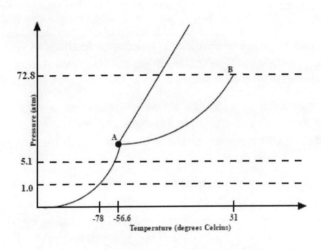

The normal boiling point of the substance represented by the phase diagram above is

(A) -78°C
(B) -56.6°C
(C) 31°C
(D) greater than 31°C
(E) not determinable from the diagram

Day 1

STOP. Correct your answers and note how many correct **points**

Day 1: Answers and Explanations

Answers: Quick Check

1. D	2. B	3. E	4. B	5. D	6. E	7. C	8. C	9. D	10. A
11. C	12. D	13. E	14. E	15. E	16. A	17. A	18. B	19. D	20. A
21. D	22. D	23. C	24. C	25. E					

Answers and explanations

Major concepts tested by the question.

1. D Molecular size-rate of diffusion relationship, Graham's Law
Recall: Greatest mass molecules diffuse at the slowest rate.
Determine: NO_2 has the greatest molar mass (46g/mol) of those listed.

2. B Molecular polarity-molecular attraction relationship
Recall: Nonpolar molecules have the weakest interacting molecules.
Determine: O_2 (nonpolar bond and symmetrical) is the only nonpolar molecule listed.

3. E Molecular size-rate of diffusion relationship, Graham's Law
Recall: Kinetic energy = ½ (mass) (velocity)^2
Interpret: Velocity is relative to the mass of the moving molecules. Smallest Mass molecules have the greatest velocity.
Determine: CO has the smallest molar mass (24 g/mol) of those listed.

Questions 4 through 7: hybridization, molecular geometry, electron pairs
  Step 1: Determine number of electron pairs around the central atom in the given molecules

  Step 2: Determine or recall electron geometry associated with the number of electron pairs you determined in step 1

  Step 3: Determine or recall hybridization associated with the number of electron pair or geometry you determine

		Molecule	electron pairs	electron geometry	hybridization
4.	B	SO_2	3	trigonal planer	sp^2
5.	D	I_3-	5	trigonal bipyramidal	sp^3d
6.	E	IF_5	6	octahedral	sp^3d^2
7.	C	CH_3OH	4	tetrahedral	sp^3

8

Copyright © 2012 E3 Scholastic Publishing. All Rights Reserved

8. C   Mole concept, mass calculation

Determine grams of Zn by utilizing mole ratio from the balanced equation in factor labeling.

$$1 \; Zn(s) \; ------> \; 2 \; Ag(s)$$

$$1.0 \; mol \; Ag \; \times \; \frac{1 \; mol \; Zn}{2 \; mol \; Ag} \; \times \; \frac{65.4 \; g \; Zn}{1 \; mol \; Zn} \; = \; \mathbf{33 \; g \; Zn}$$

9. D   Thermodynamic, Standard enthalpy of reaction

Recall: Standard enthalpy of a reaction is the energy involved in reacting 1 mole of the substance.

Note: 711 KJ is energy produced from combustion of 1 mole (32 g) of methanol

To produce 355.5 KJ (half of 711 KJ), half a mole (16 g) of methanol must combust.

Note: You can also determine the answer with proportion setup

$$355.5 \; KJ \; \times \; \frac{1 \; mole \; CH_3OH}{711 \; KJ} \; \times \; \frac{32 \; g \; CH_3OH}{1 \; mole \; CH_3OH} \; = \; \mathbf{16 \; g \; CH_3OH}$$

10. A   Raoult's Law, partial pressure, mole fraction

Recall Raoult's Law Equation:

$$P_A = P_A^{\circ} X_A$$

P_A = Vapor pressure of solvent A in solution
P_A° = Vapor pressure of pure solvent A
X_A = mole fraction of solvent A in solution

Note: When information given in each choice is considered in terms of the Raoult's law, Choice A is false. Opposite will be true.

11. C   Lewis structure, molecular structure, lone pair electrons

Draw Lewis structure for HCl

H – Cl :   There are 3 lone pairs (nonbonding pairs) of electrons

12. D   Equilibrium, Le Chatelier's principle

$$MgO(s) + H_2(g) \; ---- > \; Mg(s) + H_2O(g) \qquad \Delta H = -14.0 \text{ kilojoules}$$

Note: Reaction is exothermic b/c ΔH is negative.

Recall: A decrease in heat temperature (Choice D) forces the
reaction in the exothermic direction (favors products)

Note: ↑[MgO], ↑[H₂], ↓[Mg] and ↓[H₂O] will also favor
products. But none of these is given as a choice.

13. E   Colligative property, boiling point elevation, Van't Hoff factor.

Recall equation: $\Delta T = k_b \times m \times i$

Note: All three solutions have that same m (molality) and kb (boiling
point elevation constant)

Therefore, solution with the greatest i (Van't Hoff factor,
number of dissolved particles) value will have the greatest
change in temperature (ΔT) and also the highest boiling point.

Determine: **Ca(NO₃)₂**, (an ionic compound) produces the most (3)
dissolved particles:

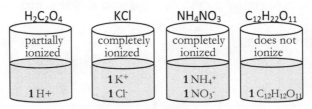

14. E   Mole concept, mole interpretation

Note: The true statement to this problem is best determined by
calculating and comparing number of moles (number of
molecules) of O₂ and He

Recall equation: $\text{mole} = \dfrac{\text{mass given}}{\text{molar mass}}$

Calculate moles of O₂ and He:

$$\text{moles of } O_2 = \frac{100 \text{ g}}{32 \text{ g} \cdot \text{mole}^{-1}} \qquad \text{moles of He} = \frac{100 \text{ g}}{4 \text{ g} \cdot \text{mole}^{-1}}$$

$$\text{moles of } O_2 = 3.1 \text{ mole } O_2 \qquad \text{moles of He} = 25 \text{ mole He}$$

Relate: Choice E is the only true statement since there are
a greater moles (more molecules) of He than O₂.

15. E   Isoelectronic, ions, determining number of electrons

Recall: Isoelectronic refers to particles with the same number of electrons

Determine and compare number of electrons in each particle.

$$S^{2-} (18\ e^-)\quad Cl^- (18\ e^-)\quad Ar (18\ e^-)\quad K^+ (18\ e^-)\quad \textbf{Mg}^{2+} \textbf{(10 e}^-\textbf{)}$$

Note: All, except Mg^{2+}, have the same number of electrons

16. A   Acid dissociation constant, K$_a$, calculation

Step 1: Assume that HX is the monoprotic acid, write the dissociation equation

$$HX \dashrightarrow H^+ + X^-$$

Step 2: Write K_a expression based on equation in step 1

$$K_a = \frac{[H^+]\ [X^-]}{[HX]}$$

Step 3: Determine concentrations to put into equation:

$[H^+] = 1.0 \times 10^{-5}\,M$ because pH = 5

$[X^-] = 1.0 \times 10^{-5}\,M$ because for monoprotic acids, $[H^+] = [X^-]$

$[HX] = 1\ M$ because weak acids dissociate very little. Therefore [HX] stays relatively unchanged.

Step 4: Substitute factors into Ka equation and solve

$$K_a = \frac{(1 \times 10^{-5}\,M)(1 \times 10^{-5}\,M)}{1\ M} = \textbf{1} \times \textbf{10}^{\textbf{-10}}$$

17. A   Half-life, nuclear decay

Step 1: Determine number of half-life periods (n) from length of time (t) and half-life (T)

$$n = \frac{t}{T} = \frac{34480}{5730} \approx 6$$

Step 2: Determine fraction remaining using equation

$$\text{Fraction remaining} = \frac{1}{2^n} = \frac{1}{2 \times 2 \times 2 \times 2 \times 2 \times 2} = \frac{1}{64}$$

Step 3: Change fraction to percent

$$\frac{1}{64} \times 100 = \textbf{1.56 \%}$$

Day 1: Answers and Explanations

18. **B**   **Periodic Trend**

Note: Magnesium (Mg) and calcium (Ca) are in the same Group

Recall these Periodic Table trends **from Top to Bottom** of a Group:
     Ionization Energy decreases
     Atomic Radius increases

Relate: Mg (higher up on the Table than Ca) will have a larger ionization energy BUT a smaller atomic radius

19. **D**   **Ions, Oxidation number**

Note: The correct formula of each ion must be known in order to correctly determine the charge of Cr in each ion

Recall: The sum of all charges (+ and -) in each formula must equal the overall charge of the ion **(-2)**

Step 1: Write the correct formulas for both ions
     chromate: CrO_4^{2-}

     dichromate: $Cr_2O_7^{2-}$

Step 2: Calculate total – charge from O in each formula
     Recall: Oxygen has a charge of -2 in most formulas

     Total negative in CrO_4^{2-} = -8   (4 x -2)

     Total negative in $Cr_2O_7^{2-}$ = -14   (7 x -2)

Step 3: Determine charge of Cr needed so that sum of all charges in each formula = **-2**

   CrO_4^{2-} Cr = +6   check: (+6   +   -8   = -2)

   $Cr_2O_7^{2-}$ Cr = +6   check: (2(+6)   +   -14   = -2)

20. **A**   **Entropy Change in reactions**

Note: ΔS is entropy (disorder) change of a system

Recall: +ΔS means that a system entropy is increasing (it is becoming more disorder)

     Example of a +ΔS change :   solid ------------ > gas

Note: Of the reactions listed, only Choice A reaction

     $MgCO_3(s)$ -------- > $Mg (s)$ + $CO_2(g)$

     is changing from a solid reactant to a gaseous product

21. D   Henry's law, Partial Pressure, Calculation

Recognize that, based on information given in question, concentration (C) of N_2 can be calculated using Henry's law equation:

$$C = k\,P \qquad \text{where } k \text{ is constant}$$

Step 1: Determine k from initial pressure (P_i) and concentration $[N_2]_i$

$$k = \frac{[N_2]_i}{P_i} = \frac{6.0 \times 10^{-4}\ M}{1\ atm} = 6.0 \times 10^{-4}\ M \cdot atm^{-1}$$

Step 2: Calculate Partial pressure (P) of N_2 based on mole % and total pressure

$$P = 0.80 \times 3.0\ atm = 2.4\ atm$$

Step 3: Substitute factors into Henry's law and solve for C

$$C = k\,P = (6.0 \times 10^{-4}\ M \cdot atm^{-1})(\,2.4\ atm\,) = \mathbf{14 \times 10^{-3}\ M}$$

22. D   Rate, Order of reaction

Step 1: Assume that X represents the change to [B] you are asked to determine.

Step 2: Write rate quotient based on the rate law given and the fact that the new rate (Rate $_f$) is proceeding at 50% ($^1/_2$) that of the initial rate (Rate $_i$) .

$$\frac{Rate_f}{Rate_i} = \frac{1}{2} = \frac{k[A/2]^2 \cdot X[B]}{k[A]^2 \cdot [B]} = \frac{X}{4}$$

Step 3: Solve for X: When all factors are crossed-out

$$X = 2\ (double)$$

23. **C   Titration curve**

   Recall: A weak base will a pH less than 12 but greater than 7.

   A strong acid have pH of 2 or less.

   Note: Choice C curve shows:

   The starting pH is slightly lower than 12. This reflects the pH of the weak base.

   The ending pH is lower than 2. This reflect the fact that at the end of the titration, all of the base have been neutralized, and the solution is of a strong acid.

24. **C   Electron configuration, quantum numbers**

   Recall: Symbol of an oxide ion is O^{2-}

   Determine number of electrons in O^{2-} = 10 e$^-$

   Determine correct electron configuration for 10e- **($1s^2 2s^2 2p^6$)**

25. **E   Phase change diagram**

   Recall that the normal boiling point of a substance is the point (or temperature) at which liquid and vapor coexist at equilibrium at normal (standard) atmospheric pressure (1 atm).

   Note: line AB of the graph is the transition line from liquid to vapor (boiling). For normal boiling point to be determined from the graph, AB must cross the 1 atm dash line. This is NOT the case, therefore, normal boiling point can't be determined.

START: Answer all questions on this day before stopping.

Note: You may use a calculator for answering questions on this day
You may use any of the Reference Material provided on pg 337-340

CLEARLY SHOW THE METHOD USED AND THE STEPS INVOLVED IN ARRIVING AT YOUR ANSWERS. It is to your advantage to do this, since you may obtain partial credit if you do and you will receive little or no credit if you do not. Attention should be paid to significant figures.

---

1.   **10 points**
Formic acid, HCOOH is a significant component of bee venom. Also known as methanoic acid, formic acid has an acid dissociation constant, K_a, of 1.80×10^{-4}.

a) If a bottle contains 0.25M solution of formic acid.
   (i) Write the equilibrium expression for the dissociation of the acid.

   (ii) Calculate the pOH of the solution.

b) Calculate the percent dissociation of the solution in part (a).

c) Calculate the pH of a solution prepared by mixing equal 1.00L volumes of 0.25M formic acid and 0.20M sodium methanoate, NaHCOO,

d) Calculate the mass of NaHCOO needed to produce the optimal buffering capacity.

Day 2 Question 1: Space for Work and Answers

2.   **10 points**

Refer to the following equation.

$$2Mg(s) + 2CuSO_4(aq) + H_2O(l) ---- > 2MgSO_4(aq) + Cu_2O(s) + H_2(g)$$

(a) If 1.46 grams of Mg(s) are added to 500 mL of a 0.200 M solution of $CuSO_4$, what is the maximum moles of $H_2(g)$ that is produced?

b) When all the limiting reagent has been consumed in (a), how many grams of the other reactant (not water) remain?

c) What is the mass of the Cu_2O produced in (a)

d) What is the concentration of Mg^{2+} in the solution at the end of the experiment? Assume that the volume of the solution remains unchanged.

Day 2

STOP. Correct your answers and note how many correct **points**

Day 2 Question 2: Space for Work and Answers

1.   **(10 points)**

Formic acid is a significant component of bee venom. Also known as methanoic acid, formic acid has an acid dissociation constant, K_a, of 1.80×10^{-4}.

a) If a bottle contains $0.25M$ solution of formic acid.

   (i) Write the equilibrium expression for the dissociation of the acid.

$$\text{Recall:}\quad K_a = \frac{[\text{products}]}{[\text{reactants}]}$$

Write dissociation equation $HCOOH \;<===>\; H^+ + \; HCOO^-$ *Write equilibrium expression from your equation* $K_a = \dfrac{[\text{products}]}{[\text{reactants}]} = \dfrac{[H^+]\,[HCOO^-]}{[HCOOH]}$	**1 point** is earned for writing the correct equilibrium expression

(ii) Calculate the pOH of the solution.

Recall: pOH = 14 − pH   or   pOH = -log[OH⁻]

Note: pH or [OH⁻] must be determine from known information

Determine concentrations at equilibrium	
[HCOOH] = 0.25M - X ≈ 0.25 M (weak acid dissociates very little)	
[H⁺] = X	
[HCOO⁻] = [H⁺] = X (1 : 1 mole ratio in equation)	
Substitute [ ] into K_a expression and solve for X	
$K_a = \dfrac{[H^+][HCOO^-]}{[HCOOH]}$	
$1.80 \times 10^{-4} = \dfrac{(X)(X)}{0.25} = \dfrac{X^2}{0.25}$	**1 point** is earned for calculating [H⁺] or [OH⁻]
$X^2 = 4.5 \times 10^{-5}$	
X = 6.7 × 10⁻³ M = [H⁺]	
Determine [OH⁻]	
$[OH^-] = \dfrac{kw}{[H^+]} = \dfrac{1.0 \times 10^{-14}}{6.7 \times 10^{-3}} = \mathbf{1.49 \times 10^{-12}\ M}$	
Determine pOH from pH	
pH = -log [H⁺] = -log (6.7 × 10⁻³) = 2.17	
pOH = 14 - pH = 14 - 2.17 = **11.83**	**1 point** is earned for correctly calculating the pOH (11.83)
or	
Determine pOH from [OH⁻]	
pOH = -log [OH⁻] = -log (1.49 × 10⁻¹²) = **11.83**	

(b) Calculate the percent dissociation of the solution in part (a).

Note: [HCOO⁻] = [H⁺] = 6.7 x 10⁻³ M % dissociation = $\dfrac{\text{[HCOO}^-]}{\text{[HCOOH] + [HCOO}^-]}$ x 100 % dissociation = $\dfrac{6.7 \times 10^{-3}}{0.25 + (6.7 \times 10^{-3})}$ x 100 % dissociation = **2.6%**	**1 point** is earned for setup **1 point** is earned for correctly calculating the percent dissociation.

(c) Calculate the pH of a solution prepared by mixing equal 1.00L volumes of 0.25*M* formic acid and 0.20*M* sodium methanoate.

   Note: This is a buffer problem in which the pH can be calculated using Henderson-Hasselbalch equation.

$pH = pka + \log \dfrac{\text{[base]}}{\text{[acid]}}$ $pH = -\log (1.8 \times 10^{-4}) + \log \dfrac{.20}{.25}$ $pH = \qquad 3.74 \qquad + (-0.096) = \mathbf{3.64}$	**1 point** is earned for setup with Henderson-Hasselbalch equation. **1 point** is earned for correctly calculating the pH

d) Calculate the mass of NaHCOO needed to produce the optimal buffering capacity.

> Before solving: *Note* the following important information .
>
> > Maximum buffering occurs when the solution contains equal concentration of the conjugate acid (HCOOH, formic) and conjugate base (HCOO⁻, formate ion).
>
> > The total volume of the solution is 2 L
>
> *Note:* Moles of formate to be added must be calculated before mass can be determined.

Determine initial [formic acid] and [formate ion] $[\text{formic}] = \dfrac{.25 \text{ mole}}{2 \text{ L}} = \mathbf{0.13\ mol/L}$ **formic acid** $[\text{formate}] = \dfrac{.20 \text{ mol}}{2 \text{ L}} = \mathbf{0.10\ mol/L}$ **formate** *Note* that more formate must be added to bring its [ ] to 0.13 mol/L (equal to that of the conjugate acid as *noted* above) *Determine moles of formate (X) to be added:* $\dfrac{(0.10 \text{ mol } + \text{ X mol})}{2 \text{ L}} = \dfrac{0.13 \text{ mol}}{\text{L}}$ $\quad$ **X** $=$ **0.16 mol of formate** $\qquad$ must be added in the $\qquad$ form of sodium formate $\qquad$ (MW: 68 g/mol) *Calculate mass of 0.16 moles of sodium formate:* Mass = moles $\quad$ x molar mass **Mass** = 0.16 mol x 68 g/mol = **11 g**	**1 point** is earned for calculating initial concentrations of formic and formate. **1 point** is earned for calculating moles of formate to be added **1 point** is earned for correctly calculating mass of sodium formate to be added.

2.   **(10 points)**

Refer to the following equation.

2 Mg(s) + **2** $CuSO_4$(aq) + H_2O(l) ----> **2** $MgSO_4$(aq) + Cu_2O + H_2(g)

(a) If 1.46 grams of Mg(s) are added to 500 mL of a 0.200 M solution of $CuSO_4$, what is the maximum moles of H_2(g) that is produced?

Note: Molar yield of H_2 depends on the number of moles of the limiting reagent in the reaction.

Determine the limiting reagent	
Moles of Mg $= \dfrac{\text{mass of Mg}}{\text{MW Mg}} = \dfrac{1.46 \text{ g}}{24 \text{ g/mol}} =$ **0.060 mol Mg**	**1 point** is earned for calculating moles of Mg and $CuSO_4$
Moles of $CuSO_4$ = Molarity x volume **Moles of $CuSO_4$** = (0.200 moles/L) x (0.500 L) = **0.100 mol**	
Note: Water is always in excess *Therefore:* **Limiting reagent is Mg(s)** since its moles is the smaller of the two.	**1 point** is earned for correctly identifying the limiting reagent.
Determine moles of H_2 using mole ratio of Mg to H_2 in the equation. 0.060 mol Mg x $\dfrac{1 \text{ mol } H_2}{2 \text{ mol Mg}} =$ **0.030 moles H_2**	**1 point** is earned for correctly calculating moles of H_2 produced.

(b) When all the limiting reagent has been consumed in (a), how many grams of the other reactant (not water) remain?

Note: The other reactant is $CuSO_4$

Determine moles of CuSO₄ that reacted with Mg $0.060 \text{ mol Mg} \times \dfrac{2 \text{ mol CuSO}_4}{2 \text{ mol Mg}} = \mathbf{0.060 \text{ mol CuSO}_4}$	**1 point** is earned calculating moles of $CuSO_4$ that reacted
Determine moles of CuSO₄ that remained Moles remaining = moles at start (a) - moles reacted (b) moles remaining = 0.100 mol - 0.060 mol Moles remaining = **0.040 moles CuSO₄**	**1 point** is earned for correctly calculating moles of $CuSO_4$ that remained
Determine mass of CuSO₄ that remained Mass = moles x molar Weight **Mass** = 0.040 mol x 160 g/mol = **6.4 g CuSO₄**	**1 point** is earned for correctly calculating the mass of $CuSO_4$ that remained

(c) What is the mass of the Cu_2O produced in (a)

Determine moles of Cu₂O using mole ratio in equation $0.060 \text{ mol Mg} \times \dfrac{1 \text{ mol Cu}_2O}{2 \text{ mol Mg}} = \mathbf{0.030 \text{ mol Cu}_2O}$	**1 point** is earned for calculating moles of Cu_2O
Calculate mass of Cu₂O from moles Mass = moles x Molar weight **Mass** = 0.030 mol x 143 g/mol = **4.29 g**	**1 point** is earned for correctly calculating the mass of Cu_2O

(d) What is the concentration of Mg^{2+} in the solution at the end of the experiment? Assume that the volume of the solution remains unchanged.

Note: Moles of Mg(s) = moles of Mg^{2+} = 0.060 mol $[Mg^{2+}]$ = $\dfrac{\text{moles Mg}^{2+}}{\text{L of solution}}$ $[Mg^{2+}]$ = $\dfrac{\textbf{0.060 mol}}{\textbf{0.500 L}}$ $[Mg^{2+}]$ = **0.120 M**	**1 point** is earned for correct setup **1 point** is earned for $[Mg^{2+}]$ that corresponds to your setup

Day 3:   2 Free Response Questions
23 points   *Section II Part B practice*

START: Answer all questions on this day before stopping.

Note: **NO CALCULATORS should be used for questions on this day.**
   You may use any of the Reference Materials provided on Pg 337-340

1. For each of the following three reactions, write a balanced equation for the reaction in part (i) and answer the question about the reaction in part (ii). In part (i), coefficients should be in terms of lowest whole numbers. Assume that solutions are aqueous unless otherwise indicated. Represent substances in solutions as ions if the substances are extensively ionized. Omit formulas for any ions or molecules that are unchanged by the reaction.

15 points

(a) A piece of solid tin is heated in the presence of chlorine gas.

   (i) Balanced equation:

   (ii) What is the oxidation number of the tin before and after the reaction?

_____

_____

_____

(b) Ethane is burned completely in air.

   (i) Balanced equation:

   (ii) How many liters of carbon dioxide will be produced from completely burning 2.0 moles of ethane at STP?

_____

_____

_____

(c) A pellet of zinc is dropped into a test tube containing 30 mL of 6M HCl.

   (i) Balanced equation:

   (ii) Indicate two observable changes that will be noted as the reaction proceeds in the test tube.

_____

_____

Your response to question 2 will be scored on the basis of the accuracy and relevance of the information cited. Explanations should be clear and well organized. Examples and equations may be included in your responses where appropriate. Specific answers are preferable to broad, diffuse responses.   **8 points**

2. A set of three vials contains three different organic compounds. Each compound contains only one kind of functional group, and each functional group is different from the others. None of the compounds has an ester or amide linkage, and none is an alkene or alkyne.

   (a) All of the compounds possess a carbonyl group. What kinds of compounds are these three?

   (b) Assuming that each of the three compounds contains four carbon atoms, and is linear (not branched), draw Lewis structures for the three compounds.

   (c) Ethanol is added to each of the three vials. With which of the three compounds is ethanol most likely to react to produce an ester?

   (d) Draw the Lewis structure and name the ester that would be produced in the reaction described in part (c).

Day 3

STOP. Correct your answers and note how many correct **points**

Day 3 Question 2: Space for Work and Answers

1.	15 points

(a) A piece of solid tin is heated in the presence of chlorine gas.

> *Note:*   This is a combination reaction

(i) Balanced equation	**1 point** is earned for correct reactants
$Sn + 2Cl_2 ------> SnCl_4$	**2 points** are earned for correct products
	1 point is earned for correctly balancing the equation

(ii) What is the oxidation number of the tin before and after the reaction.

> *Recall:* Charge of a free element is 0.
> Sum of charges in a neutral formula must equal zero

0 before reaction *(tin is free element)* **+4** after reaction *(allows total charge in SnCl₄ to equal 0)*	**1 point** is earned for correct charges before and after the reaction

(b) Ethane is burned completely in air.

> *Recall:* Burning (combustion) requires oxygen.
> Carbon dioxide and water are produced from combustion.

(i) Balanced equation	**1 point** is earned for correct reactants
$2C_2H_6 + 7O_2 -------> 4CO_2 + 6H_2O$	**2 point** are earned for correct products
	1 point is earned for correctly balancing the equation

(ii) How many liters of carbon dioxide will be produced from completely burning 2.0 moles of ethane at STP?

Volume = 2.0 mol C_2H_6 x $\dfrac{4\ mol\ CO_2}{2\ mol\ C_2H_6}$ x $\dfrac{22.4\ L\ CO_2}{1\ mol\ CO_2}$ **Volume = 89.6 L** CO_2	**1 point** is earned for correctly calculating the liters of CO_2

(c) A pellet of zinc is dropped into a test containing 30 mL of 6M HCl.

   Note: This is a single replacement (or redox) reaction.
       The chlorine is unchanged (oxidation number stays the same) in
       the reaction. Cl should not be included in the equation.

(i) Balanced equation: Zn + $2H^+$ ------ > H_2 + Zn^{2+}	**1 point** is earned for correct reactants **2 points** are earned for correct products **1 point** is earned for correctly balancing the equation

(ii) Indicate two observable changes that will be noted as the reaction proceeds in the test tube.

The liquid mixture will bubble. **Gas escaping from the test tube.** **The test will feel much hotter than before the reaction .**	**1 point is** earned for correctly listing two observations that are typical for this reaction.

2. A set of three vials contains three different organic compounds. Each compound contains only one kind of functional group, and each functional group is different from the others. None of the compounds has an ester or amide functional group, and none is an alkene or alkyne. **8 points**

(a) All of the compounds possess a carbonyl group. What kinds of compounds are these three?

Aldehyde	$\begin{matrix} O \\ \| \\ -C-H \end{matrix}$	
Organic acid	$\begin{matrix} O \\ \| \\ -C-OH \end{matrix}$	**1 point** is earned for each correctly identified each compound (**3 points** total)
Ketone	$\begin{matrix} O \\ \| \\ -C- \end{matrix}$	

(b) Assuming that each of the three compounds contains four carbon atoms, and is linear (not branched), draw Lewis structures for the three compounds.

$\begin{matrix} H & H & H & O \\ \| & \| & \| & \| \| \\ H-C-C-C-C-H \\ \| & \| & \| \\ H & H & H \end{matrix}$	butanal	
$\begin{matrix} H & H & H & O \\ \| & \| & \| & \| \| \\ H-C-C-C-C-OH \\ \| & \| & \| \\ H & H & H \end{matrix}$	butanoic acid	**1 point** is earned for correctly drawing the Lewis structure for each compound (**3 points** total)
$\begin{matrix} H & H & O & H \\ \| & \| & \| \| & \| \\ H-C-C-C-C-H \\ \| & \| & \| \\ H & H & H \end{matrix}$	butanone	

Day 3: Answers and Scoring Guidelines

(c) Ethanol is added to each of the three vials. With which of the three compounds is ethanol most likely to react to produce an ester?

Recall: An ester can be synthesize through condensation polymerization reactions between an organic acid and alcohol

Organic acid	**1 point** is earned for correctly identifying organic acid

(d) Draw the Lewis structure and name the ester that would be produced in the reaction described in part (c).

Note: The complete equation to the reaction described in (c)

$$C-C-C-\overset{\overset{O}{\|}}{C}-OH \ + \ HO-C-C \ --> \ C-C-C-\overset{\overset{O}{\|}}{C}-O-C-C \ + \ H_2O$$

   organic acid   *alcohol*   *ester*   *water*

   (butanoic)   *(ethanol)*   *(ethyl butanoate)*

H H H O   H H
  | | | || | |
H – C – C – C – C – O – C – C – H
  | | | | |
  H H H   H H
 	
ethyl butanoate
	1 point is earned for correctly drawing and naming the ester that is produced.

Day 4:   25 Multiple Choice questions
25 points   *Section I Part A and B Practice*

Start: Answer all questions on this day before stopping.

Note: NO CALCULATORS may be used for questions on this day.
You may use ONLY the Periodic Table provided on page 337

Note: For all questions, assume that the temperature is 298 K, the pressure is 1.00 atmosphere and solutions are aqueous unless otherwise noted.

Questions 1 through 4 refer to the following elements.

(A) K
(B) Mn
(C) Cr
(D) Zn
(E) Ag

1. Which element reacts exothermically with cold water to form basic solutions?

2. Which element exhibits the greatest number of different oxidation states?

3. Which element has the lowest electronegativity?

4. Which element is diamagnetic in the ground state?

Questions 5 through 8 refer to the following change in entropy.

(A) Entropy change will be positive.
(B) Entropy change will be zero.
(C) Entropy change will be negative.
(D) Entropy change can be either positive or negative.
(E) Entropy change cannot be determined from the information given.

5. $F_2(g)$ --------> $2F(g)$

6. $H_2(g)$ at 5.0 atm ----------> $H_2(g)$ at 1.0 atm

7. $2H_2(g)$ + $O_2(g)$ --------> $2H_2O(g)$

8. $PCl_5(g)$ < ===== > $PCl_3(g)$ + $Cl_2(g)$

9. Which of the following substances would be least soluble in water?

   (A) $Zn(NO_3)_2$
   (B) $Na_2[Zn(OH)_4]$
   (C) $ZnCl_2 \cdot x\ H_2O$
   (D) $Zn(OH)_2$
   (E) $ZnCl_2$

10. When a solid melts, which of the following is true?

   (A) $\Delta H > 0$, $\Delta S > 0$
   (B) $\Delta H < 0$, $\Delta S < 0$
   (C) $\Delta H > 0$, $\Delta S < 0$
   (D) $\Delta H < 0$, $\Delta S > 0$
   (E) More information is required in order to determine the signs of ΔH and ΔS.

11. Which of the following is an isomer of n-hexane?

   (A) 2,3-dimethylbutane
   (B) 2-methylbutane
   (C) 2,2-dimethylpropane
   (D) 2,3-dimethylpentane
   (E) 3-ethyl-2-methylpentane

12. Approximately how much distilled water should be *added* to 20.0 mL of 6 M HCl(aq) in order to prepare 0.500 M HCl(aq) solution?
   (A)   60 mL
   (B) 120 Ml ml
   (C) 220 mL
   (D) 240 mL
   (E) 260 mL

Questions 13 and 14: The phase diagram of an unknown substance is shown below.

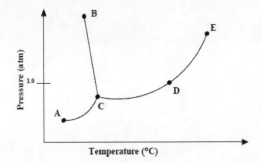

13. The lowest temperature above which this substance cannot be liquefied at any applied pressure is located at point

    (A) A
    (B) B
    (C) C
    (D) D
    (E) E

14. Which point represents the normal boiling point for this substance?

    (A) A
    (B) B
    (C) C
    (D) D
    (E) E

15. Which of the following changes will decrease the rate of collisions between gaseous molecules of type X and Y in a closed container?

    (A) decrease the volume of the container
    (B) increase the temperature of the system
    (C) add molecules of X
    (D) take away molecules of Y
    (E) add a catalyst

16. A student placed three moles of hydrogen gas and three moles of iodine gas into a 1-liter flask and heated the flask to 298°C. The equilibrium expression would be equal to

(A) $K_c = \dfrac{(2x)^2}{(3-x)^2}$

(B) $K_c = \dfrac{(2x)^2}{(2-x)^3}$

(C) $K_c = \dfrac{x^2}{(2-x)^2}$

(D) $K_c = \dfrac{(2x-2)^2}{3-x}$

(E) $K_c = \dfrac{(2x)^2}{x-2}$

17. When $^{238}_{92}U$ decays, the emission consists consecutively of a beta particle, then two alpha particles, and finally another beta particle. The resulting stable nucleus is

(A) $^{230}_{91}Pa$

(B) $^{234}_{91}Pa$

(C) $^{230}_{90}Th$

(D) $^{232}_{90}Th$

(E) $^{234}_{89}Ac$

18. Which of the following represents a process in which a species is reduced?
(A) Mg ----> Mg^{2+}
(B) $2Cl_2$ ----> $2Cl^-$
(C) Ni^{3+} ----> Ni^{4+}
(D) CO ----> CO_2
(E) NO^{2-} ----> NO^{3-}

19. An aqueous solution of silver nitrate ($AgNO_3$, molar mass 169.9 g) is prepared by adding 200.0 g of $AgNO_3$ to 1000 g H_2O. If K_f for H_2O is $1.86°C·m^{-1}$, the freezing point of the solution should be

    (A) 0.00°C
    (B) -0.219°C
    (C) -0.438°C
    (D) -2.19°C
    (E) -4.38°C

20. Frequency of a photon was determined to be 3.00×10^{14} / sec . Calculate the wavelength of the photon.
    (Speed of light = 3.00×10^8 m/s and 1 meter = 10^9 nanometers.)

    (A) 1.00×10^{-6} nm
    (B) 3.00×10^{-3} nm
    (C) 1.00×10^3 nm
    (D) 3.00×10^3 nm
    (E) 3.00×10^{22} nm

21. Photoelectric effect is most easily detected in which elements?

    (A) noble gases
    (B) alkali metals
    (C) halogen elements
    (D) transition metals
    (E) the chalcogens

22. Copper (II) chloride will be least soluble in a 0.1 M solution of which of the following compound?

    (A) NaCl
    (B) $CuNO_3$
    (C) $CaCl_2$
    (D) $NaCO_3$
    (E) KI

23. Pi bonding occurs in each of the following species except

   (A) N_2F_2
   (B) C_2H_2
   (C) HCN
   (D) C_6H_6
   (E) CCl_4

24. You can prepare 0.75 molal NaCl by dissolving 15 g NaCl in what amount of water?

   (A) 0.40kg
   (B) 0.34kg
   (C) 0.27kg
   (D) 0.20kg
   (E) 0.26kg

25. The formulas CH_3CH_2COOH and CH_3COCH_2OH would be expected to have the same values for which of the following? (Assume ideal behavior.)

   (A) Freezing points
   (B) Boiling points
   (C) Specific heat capacity
   (D) Percent composition
   (E) Heats of combustion

Day 4

STOP. Correct your answers and note how many correct **points**

Day 4: Answers and Explanations

Answers: Quick Check

1. A	2. B	3. A	4. D	5. A	6. A	7. C	8. A	9. D	10. A
11. A	12. C	13. E	14. D	15. D	16. A	17. C	18. B	19. E	20. C
21. B	22. C	23. E	24. B	25. D					

Answers and Explanations

Question 1 through 4: Properties of metals, atomic structure

1. **A** *Note:* The list includes all metals. However, only K will react vigorously in cold water because K, an alkali (Group 1) metal, is the most reactive of all the metals listed.

   K + H$_2$O ----- >   H$_2$ + KOH + heat

2. **B** *Note:* Mn, Cr, Zn and Ag are all transitional metals

   Recall: Transition metals tend to form multiple oxidation numbers. Common oxidation states of the four metals are listed below.
   Mn: +2 +3 +4 +7   Cr: +3 +4 +6   Zn: +2   Ag: +1

   Note: Mn has the most oxidation states. You do need to memorize oxidation states of some common elements.

3. **A** *Recall:* Electronegativity values (a measure of atom's attraction to electrons) are lowest for elements to the left of the Periodic Table.

   K (farthest left) will have the lowest electronegative value of those listed. In general, alkali metals tends to have the the lowest electronegativity values.

4. **D** *Note:* An element with no unpaired electrons will have an even number of electrons in all of its sublevels.

   Recognize that of all elements listed, the electron configuration of Zn: [Ar] 4s^2 3d^{10} , is the only one with even number of electrons in all of its sublevels.

Questions 5 through 8:   Entropy changes in reactions

5. **A**   *Note:*   In this system, the number of particles is increasing from
1 F_2 molecule ----- > **2 F** atoms

Recall: Increase in number of particles indicates an increase in
entropy (+ΔS)   Choice A.

6. **A**   *Note:*   In this system, pressure is decreasing from 5 atm to 1 atm.
Therefore, more space for the He particles to move more
freely (show more chaos).
Relate: Decrease in pressure means increase in entropy (+ΔS)

7. **C**   *Note:*   In this system, the number of particles is decreasing from
3 particles (**2** H_2 + **1** O_2) on the left to 2 particles (**2** H_2O) on
the right.

Recall: Decrease in number of particles indicates a decrease in
entropy (-ΔS)   Choice C.

8. **A**   *Note:*   In this system, the number of particles is increasing
from **1** mole of substance (PCl_5) to 2 moles of substances
(**1** PCl_3 + **1** Cl_2)

Recall: Increase in number of particles indicates an increase in
entropy (+ΔS)   Choice A.

9. **D**   **Solubility rules, soluble and insoluble compounds**

Recall: The solubility rules for the ions in compounds.

Note: $Zn(OH)_2$ contains hydroxide ion (**OH⁻**) which forms mostly
insoluble compounds, except when it combines with a
Group 1 ion or an ammonium ion (NH_4^+)

Note: All other choices contain soluble ions (Cl^-, NO_3^- and Na)

10. **A**   **Enthalpy and Entropy change in a physical change**

Recall: When a solid melts, it changes from solid ---- > liquid

Relate: Melting releases heat, exothermic (-ΔH or H < 0)

Relate: Melting results in increase in entropy (+ΔS or ΔS > 0)

11. A   Isomers, hydrocarbons, IUPAC names

Recall: Isomers are compounds with same percent composition (same molecular formula)

Note:

$$H-\overset{\displaystyle H}{\underset{\displaystyle H}{C}}-\overset{\displaystyle H}{\underset{\displaystyle H}{C}}-\overset{\displaystyle H}{\underset{\displaystyle H}{C}}-\overset{\displaystyle H}{\underset{\displaystyle H}{C}}-\overset{\displaystyle H}{\underset{\displaystyle H}{C}}-\overset{\displaystyle H}{\underset{\displaystyle H}{C}}-H \quad and \quad H-\overset{\displaystyle H}{\underset{\displaystyle H}{C}}-\overset{\displaystyle CH_3}{\underset{\displaystyle H}{C}}-\overset{\displaystyle CH_3}{\underset{\displaystyle H}{C}}-\overset{\displaystyle H}{\underset{\displaystyle H}{C}}-H$$

n-hexane   and   2,3-dimethybutane
have the same molecular formula (C_6H_{14})

12. C   Dilution

Use $M_1V_1 = M_2V_2$ to determine volume of the diluted acid (V_2)

$(6)(20) = (.500)V_2$

$V_2 = 240 \text{ mL}$

Determine volume of water (V_{H2O}) added

$V_{H2O} = V_2 - V_1$

$V_{H2O} = 240 \text{ mL} - 20 \text{ ml} = \textbf{220 mL}$

13. E   Phase diagram, critical point

Recall: Critical point of a phase diagram is the point at which no amount of pressure can cause a substance in the gas state to change back to a liquid.

Note: The critical point (Point E) of phase diagram is always located farthest right of all the points on the diagram.

14. D   Phase diagram, normal boiling point

Recall: Normal boiling point of a substance is the temperature at which vapor pressure equals the normal atmospheric pressure (1 atm).

Note: Point D is the transitional point from liquid to gas (boiling) at 1 atm

Day 4: Answers and Explanations

15. D **Behavior of gases, Collision theory, rate of reaction.**

Note: Taking away molecules Y (decreasing [Y]) means fewer opportunity (decrease rate) of collision between X and Y

16. A **Writing reaction equation, equilibrium expression**

Step 1: Write equation for the reaction: $H_2 + I_2 <----> 2HI$

Step 2: Use x to represent moles of the substances that reacted

Let x = moles of H_2

x = moles of I_2 (because of 1 : 1 ratio in equation)

Step 3: Determine moles (concentration) of substances at equilibrium

$3 - x$ = moles of H_2

$3 - x$ = moles of I_2

$2x$ = moles HI moles H_2 reacted (x) + moles I_2 reacted (x) = 2x

Step 4: Write equilibrium expression using above equilibrium [ ]

$$K_c = \frac{[products]}{[reactants]} = \frac{[HI]^2}{[H_2] \cdot [I_2]} = \frac{2x^2}{(3-x)^2}$$

17. C **Nuclear decay, particle symbols**

Step 1: Write the symbols of emitted particles in the order given in question

beta	alpha	alpha	beta
$_{-1}^{0}e$	$_{2}^{4}He$	$_{2}^{4}He$	$_{-1}^{0}e$

Step 2: To get the top (mass) # of the stable nucleus:
Subtract the sum of top #s of particles (8) from 238. = **230**

To get the bottom (atomic) # of the stable nucleus: **Th**
Subtract the sum of bottom #s of particles (2) from 92 = **90**

18. B **Half-reaction, reduction, oxidation number changes**

Recall: During reduction, there is a decrease in oxidation state of the particle being reduced.

Note: Half-equation for choice B is the only one that shows a decrease in oxidation number (Cl goes from 0 to -1)

48

19. **E**   **Freezing point depression, molality, van't Hoff factor**

Recognize that based on information given, change in temperature, ΔT, must first be determined using the equation

$$\Delta T = i \cdot Kf \cdot m$$

before the freezing point of the solution ($FP_{solution}$) can be determined.

Step 1: Calculate moles of solute, $AgNO_3$

$$moles = \frac{200\ g}{169.9\ g \cdot mol^{-1}} = 1.177\ mol$$

Step 2: Calculate molality (m)

$$m = \frac{moles}{kg\ of\ solution} = \frac{1.177\ mol}{1\ kg} = 1.177\ m$$

Step 2: Determine i (van't Hoff) factor for the solute, $AgNO_3$.

$$AgNO_3 \longrightarrow 1\ Ag^+ \text{ and } 1\ NO_3^- = 2$$

Step 3: Calculate ΔT

$$\Delta T = i \cdot k_f \cdot m$$
$$\Delta T = 2\ (1.86\ ^\circ C \cdot m^{-1})(1.177\ m) = 4.38^\circ C$$

Step 4: Calculate $FP_{solution}$

$$FP_{solution} = FP_{water} - \Delta T$$
$$FP_{solution} = 0 - 4.38^\circ C = -4.38^\circ C$$

20. **C**   **Wavelength in calculation, factor conversion**

Calculate wavelength using factor labeling as shown

Recall: $\lambda = \dfrac{c}{f}$

$$\lambda = \frac{3.00 \times 10^8\ m \cdot s^{-1}}{3.00 \times 10^{14} \cdot s^{-1}} \times \frac{1.0 \times 10^9\ nm}{1\ m}$$

$$\lambda = 1.0 \times 10^3\ nm$$

Day 4: Answers and Explanations

21. B. **Photoelectric effect, properties of elements**

Recall: Photoelectric is observed when the surface of a metal emits electrons as light shines on it.

Recall: Alkali metals, with one loosely held valance electron, most readily experience photoelectric effect

22. C **Solution, common-ion effect, van't Hoff factor**

Recall: If a solute containing a common-ion as a solution is placed in the solution, the solubility of the solute will be inhibited (common-ion effect)

Note: Na**Cl**, **Cu**NO_3, and Ca**Cl**$_2$ solutions each contain the same ion as $CuCl_2$ solute.

However, **CuCl$_2$** will be least soluble in the solution with the greatest number of moles of the common-ion

Determine number of moles of the common-ion in each solution

0.02 m NaCl ------ > 0.02 moles Cl$^-$

0.02 m CuNO$_3$ ---- > 0.02 moles Cu$^+$

0.02 m CaCl$_2$ ----- > 2(0.02 moles Cl$^-$) = **0.04 moles Cl$^-$**

Note: CaCl$_2$ has the greatest moles of the common-ion.

23. E **Molecular structure, molecular bonding, hybridization**

Note: Pi bonding occurs in molecules where there are multiple bonding.

Note: CCl_4 is the only molecule listed with no multiple bonding

---

24. B   Solution, molarity , moles, and mass in calculations

Step 1: Determine moles of NaCl

$$\text{moles} = \frac{15\ g}{58\ g.mol^{-1}} = 0.26\ mol$$

Step 2: Substitute into molarity equation and solve for Kg H_2O

$$\text{molarity} = \frac{\text{moles solute}}{\text{Kg of } H_2O}$$

$$0.75 = \frac{0.26}{X} \qquad \text{X} = \textbf{0.34 Kg}$$

25. D   Hydrocarbons, molecular formulas, isomers, properties

Note: The two formulas have the same number of atoms, therefore, are isomers.

Recall: Isomers are compounds with same molecular formula (same molar mass and same percent composition)
                    BUT
different structural formula (different compounds, different properties)

START: Answer all questions on this day before stopping.

Note: You may use a calculator for questions on this day.
You may use any of the reference material provided on pg 337-340

CLEARLY SHOW THE METHOD USED AND THE STEPS INVOLVED IN ARRIVING AT YOUR ANSWERS. It is to your advantage to do this, since you may obtain partial credit if you do and you will receive little or no credit if you do not. Attention should be paid to significant figures.

---

1.   **10 points**

Fluorine gas, $F_2(g)$, and a solid oxide, X_2O_8, are combined and heated in a 2.5 L flask to 721°C. The equilibrium reaction is shown in the balanced equation below.

$$X_3O_8(s) + 3F_2(g) < ========= > 3XO_2F_2(g) + O_2(g)$$

At equilibrium, the partial pressure of $F_2(g)$ is 0.83 atm and the partial pressure of $XO_2F_2(g)$ is 2.64×10^{-5} atm.

a) At 721°C, calculate the partial pressure of $O_2(g)$

b) What is the value of equilibrium constant, K_p, for this reaction?

c) Calculate the Gibb's Free energy change, $\Delta G°$, for the reaction at 721°C.

d) What will be the sign for the entropy change, $\Delta S°$, for the reaction at 721°C. Explain your answer.

e) What will be the sign for the enthalpy change, $\Delta H°$, for the reaction at 721°C. Justify your answer.

---

2.   **(10 points)**
A pure sample of a nonvolatile compound containing only carbon, hydrogen and oxygen is analyzed. It is found to be a nonelectrolyte. Data from a combustion reaction of the compound was analyzed, and it is determined that the compound has mass percents of 31.57% C and 5.30% H.

a) Determine the empirical formula of the compound.

b) A 30.0 g sample of the compound is dissolved in 250.0 g of benzene C_6H_6. The freezing point of this solution is 1.46 °C. (The freezing point of benzene is 5.51 °C and K_f is 5.12 °C $\cdot$ kg^{-1} $\cdot$ mol^{-1})

(i) Determine the molecular mass of the substance.

(ii) Determine the molecular formula for the compound.

(iii) Determine the mole fraction of the solute.

c) Determine the osmotic pressure of the solution if its density is 1.15 g/mL at 25.0 °C.

d) Determine the vapor pressure of the solution at 25.0 °C. (The equilibrium vapor pressure of benzene is 95 mm Hg at 25.0 °C)

Day 5

STOP. Correct your answers and note how many correct **points**

Day 5 Question 2: Space for Work and Answers

Day 5: Answers and Scoring Guidelines
(see important scoring guideline information on on page i)

---

1.   **(10 points)**

Fluorine gas, $F_2(g)$, and a solid oxide, X_2O_8, are combined and heated in a 2.5 L flask to 721°C. The equilibrium reaction is shown in the balanced equation below.

$$X_3O_8(s) + 3F_2(g) <========> 3XO_2F_2(g) + O_2(g)$$

At equilibrium, the partial pressure of $F_2(g)$ is 0.83 atm and the partial pressure of $XO_2F_2(g)$ is 2.64×10^{-5} atm.

a) Calculate the partial pressure of $O_2(g)$ at 721°C,

Note: Since the partial pressure of the other product is given, use mole proportion to determine partial pressure of $O_2(g)$ (P_{O2})

P_{O2} = 2.64 x 10⁻⁵ atm XO₂F₂ x $\dfrac{1 \text{ mol } O_2}{3 \text{ mol } XO_2F_2}$	**1 point** is earned for setup
P_{O2} = 8.80 x 10⁻⁶ atm O₂	**1 point** for the correct P_{O2}

b) Write the equilibrium expression, K_p, and calculate the value of the equilibrium constant for this reaction?

Recall: $K_p = \dfrac{(P_{products})}{(P_{reactants})}$

Write equilibrium expression from the equation	**1 point** is earned for writing equilibrium expression
$K_p = \dfrac{(P_{XO_2F_2})^3 (P_{O_2})}{(P_{F_2})^3}$	
Substitute factors into expression and solve	
$K_p = \dfrac{(2.64 \times 10^{-5})^3 (8.8 \times 10^{-6})}{(0.83)^3}$	**1 point** is earned for substitution
$K_p = \dfrac{1.62 \times 10^{-19}}{5.71 \times 10^{-1}}$	
$K_p = 2.83 \times 10^{-19}$	**1 point** is earned for the correct K_p

c) Calculate the Gibb's Free energy change, $\Delta G°$, for the reaction at 721°C.

Note: $\Delta G° = -RT \ln Kp$ (See References Materials on Pg 340)

Note: T must be in Kelvin: 721°C + 273 = 994 K

$\Delta G° = R \quad T \quad \ln Kp$ $\Delta G° = (-8.31 \text{ J mol}^{-1} \text{ K}^{-1}) (994 \text{ K}) (\ln 2.83 \times 10^{-19})$	**1 point** is earned for setup
$\Delta G° = (-8.31 \text{ J mol}^{-1} \text{ K}^{-1}) (994 \text{ K}) (-42.7)$ $\Delta G° = 3.53 \times 10^5 \text{ J/mol} \text{ or } 353 \text{ KJ/mol}$	**1 point** for the correct $\Delta G°$

d) What will be the sign for the entropy change, $\Delta S°$, for the reaction at 721°C. Explain your answer.

Recall: When entropy (disorder) increases , $\Delta S°$ is +

When entropy (disorder) decreases, $\Delta S°$ is -

$\Delta S°$ will be positive (+). According to the equation, entropy of the reaction increases because **4 moles of gaseous products are formed from 3 moles of reactants.**	**1 point** is earned for correct sign of $\Delta S°$ and explanation

e) What will be the sign for the enthalpy change, $\Delta H°$, for the reaction at 721°C. Justify your answer.

Note: $\Delta H° = \Delta G° + T\Delta S°$ (See References Materials on Pg 340)

$\Delta H°$ will always be positive (+) because	**1 point** is earned for correct sign of $\Delta H°$
both $\Delta G°$ and $T\Delta S°$ are positive	**1 point** is earned for correct explanation

2.   **(10 points)**

A pure sample of a nonvolatile compound containing only carbon, hydrogen and oxygen is analyzed. It is found to be a nonelectrolyte. Data from a combustion reaction of the compound was analyzed, and it is determined that the compound has mass percents of 31.57% C and 5.30% H.

(a) Determine the empirical formula of the compound.

Assume 100 g of the nonvolatile compound, Determine mass of each element	
Mass of C = 31.7 g Mass of H = 5.30 g Mass of O = 63.0 g (100 g – (31.7 g + 5.30 g)	
Convert mass of each element to moles	
moles = mass / molar mass	
moles of C = 31.7 g / 12 g·mol^{-1} = **2.639 mol C**	**1 point** is earned for calculating moles of the elements.
mole of H = 5.30 g / 1.01 g·mol^{-1} = **5.2475 mol H**	
mole of O = 63.0 g / 16 g·mol^{-1} = **3.9375 mol O**	
Determine mole ratio (subscript) of the elements by dividing each calculated mole above by the smallest of the moles (2.639 mol)	
$\dfrac{2.639 \text{ mol C}}{2.639 \text{ mol}}$ $\dfrac{5.2475 \text{ mol H}}{2.639 \text{ mol}}$ $\dfrac{3.9375 \text{ mol O}}{2.639 \text{ mol}}$ C = 1 H = 2 O = 1.49 Multiply each mole by 2 to get whole number subscripts $C_2H_4O_3$	**1 point** is earned for correctly calculating the empirical formula

(b) A 30.0 g sample of the compound is dissolved in 250.0 g of benzene C_6H_6. The freezing point of this solution is 1.46 °C. (The freezing point of benzene is 5.51 °C and K_f is 5.12 °C.kg^{-1}. mol^{-1})

(i) Determine the molecular mass of the substance.

Note: Based on information given, it is clear that moles of the nonvolatile compound must be determine in other to calculate the molecular mass (g/mol)

Determine change in freezing temperature from information given: ΔT_f = FP $_{benzene}$ − FP $_{solution}$ ΔT_f = 5.51°C − 1.46°C = 4.05°C *Calculate molality (m) using equation below:* ΔT_f = i · k_f · m (note: i (van't Hoff factor) is 1 because the solute is a nonelectrolyte) $m = \dfrac{T_f}{K_f} = \dfrac{4.05°C}{5.12\ C\cdot m^{-1}} = 0.791$ m or 0.791 mol/Kg	
Calculate moles of solute $m = \dfrac{\text{moles of solute}}{\text{Kg of solvent}}$ moles = molality x Kg of solvent moles = 0.791 mol/kg x .250 kg = **.198 mol solute**	**1 point** is earned for calculating moles of the solute
Calculate molecular mass of the substance Molecular mass = $\dfrac{\text{mass of solute}}{\text{moles of solute}}$ **Molecular mass** = $\dfrac{30\ g}{.198\ mol}$ = **152 g/mol**	**1 point** is earned for correctly calculating the molecular mass of the solute

(ii) Determine the molecular formula for the compound.

> *Note:* To calculate molecular formula, you need to know how many units of the empirical formula there are.

Determine mass of empirical formula (from part a) $C_2H_4O_3$ = 2(C) + 4(H) + 3(O) 2(12) + 4(1) + 3(16) = 76 g *Find units of empirical* $\dfrac{\text{Molecular mass}}{\text{Empirical mass}}$ = $\dfrac{152\ g}{76\ g}$ = 2 *Determine molecular formula by multiplying each subscript of the empirical formula by 2* $2(C_2H_4O_3)$ = $C_4H_8O_6$	**1 point** is earned for correctly determining the molecular formula

(iii) Determine the mole fraction of the solute

> *Note:* To determine mole fraction (X) of solute, you need to divide mole of solute ($C_4H_8O_6$) by moles of solvent (C_6H_6)

Calculate moles of solute ($C_4H_8O_6$) and of solvent (C_6H_6) moles of $C_4H_8O_6$ = .197 mol $C_4H_8O_6$ see previous calculation for b(i) mole of C_6H_6 = $\dfrac{250.0\ g}{78\ g.\ mol^{-1}}$ = 3.205 mol C_6H_6 *Determine mole fraction (X) of solute $C_4H_8O_6$* X solute = $\dfrac{\text{moles of solute}}{\text{Total moles in solution}}$ = $\dfrac{0.198}{(0.198 + 3.205)}$ X solute = $\dfrac{0.198}{3.403}$ = **0.058**	**1 point** is earned for setup **1 point** is earned for correctly calculating the mole fraction of solute.

(c) Determine the osmotic pressure of the solution if its density is 1.15 g/mL at 25.0 °C.

> Note: Based on information known, osmotic pressure (Π), can be calculated using equation Π = iMRT   (Note i = 1)

Calculate Volume (V) from known information $V = \dfrac{\text{gram of solution}}{\text{density}} = \dfrac{280 \text{ g}}{1.15 \text{ g·mL}^{-1}} = 243 \text{ mL}$ *Calculate Molarity (M)* $M = \dfrac{\text{moles}}{\text{Volume}} = \dfrac{0.198 \text{ moles}}{.243 \text{ L}} = \mathbf{0.815 \text{ M}}$	**1 point** is earned for calculating molarity
Calculate osmotic pressure (Π) using equation $\Pi = $ MRT $\Pi = \left(\dfrac{0.815 \text{ mol}}{L}\right)\left(\dfrac{0.0821 \text{ L. atm}}{\text{mol · K}}\right)\left(\dfrac{298 \text{ K}}{1}\right) = \mathbf{19.9 \text{ atm}}$	**1 point** is earned for correctly calculating the osmotic pressure

(d) Determine the vapor pressure (VP) of the solution at 25.0 °C. (The equilibrium vapor pressure of benzene is 95 mm Hg at 25.0 °C.)

Determine change in pressure of solvent using using Raoult's Law equation: $\Delta P_{\text{solvent}} = $ (X solute) (Psolvent) $\Delta p_{\text{solvent}} = $ (0.058) (95 mmHg) $= 5.51$ mm Hg *Determine vapor pressure of the solution:* $VP_{\text{solution}} = P_{\text{solvent}} - P_{\text{solvent}}$ $\mathbf{VP_{solution}} = 95 \text{ mmHg} - 5.51 \text{ mmHg} = \mathbf{90. \text{ mmHg}}$	**1 point** is earned for correctly calculating the vapor pressure

Day 6:   2 Free Response Questions.

23 points   *Section II Part B practice*

START: Answer all questions on this day before stopping.

Note: NO CALCULATORS should be used for questions on this day.
You may use any of the Reference Materials provided on Pg 337-340

1. For each of the following three reactions, write a balanced equation for the reaction in part (i) and answer the question about the reaction in part (ii). In part (i), coefficients should be in terms of lowest whole numbers. Assume that solutions are aqueous unless otherwise indicated. Represent substances in solutions as ions if the substances are extensively ionized. Omit formulas for any ions or molecules that are unchanged by the reaction.
(15 points)

(a) Sulfur trioxide gas is heated in the presence of solid calcium oxide.

(i) Balanced equation:

(ii) Draw the Lewis-dot structure for the product that forms?

(b) Copper sulfate pentahydrate is heated over high heat.

(i) Balanced equation:

(ii) If 25 grams of the hydrate was heated in a crucible to a constant mass, calculate the mass of the solid substance in the crucible.

(c) Equal molar and volume of barium chloride and sodium carbonate solutions are mixed, resulting in the formation of a precipitate.

(i) Balanced equation:

(ii) Describe what will occur if the precipitate is dried and a few drops of a dilute hydrochloric acid are added.

Your responses to question 2 will be scored on the basis of the accuracy and relevance of the information cited. Explanations should be clear and well organized. Examples and equations may be included in your responses where appropriate. Specific answers are preferable to broad, diffuse responses.   **(8 points)**

2. The reaction represented below is a reversible reaction.

$$HBr(g) + NH_3(g) <=======> NH_4Br(s)$$

(a) Predict the sign of the entropy change, ΔS, for the forward reaction. Explain your reasoning.

(b) Predict the sign of the free energy change when the reaction reaches equilibrium.

(c) The forward reaction is spontaneous at low temperatures. When the temperature of the reaction is increased, the sign of ΔG changes. Explain.

(d) Write an expression for calculating the value of the specific temperature referred to in part (c).

(e) The system is allowed to reach equilibrium at the low temperature described in part (c). Additional solid NH_4Br is added to the reaction vessel. How will the value of the equilibrium constant be affected? Explain.

Day 6

STOP. Correct your answers and note how many correct **points**

Day 6 Question 2: Space for Work and Answers

1.	**(15 points)**

(a) Sulfur trioxide gas is heated in the presence of solid calcium oxide.

Note: This is a combination (synthesis) reaction

(i) Balanced equation	**1 point** is earned for correct reactants
SO_3 + CaO -------> $CaSO_4$	**2 points are** earned for correct products
	1 point is earned for correctly balancing the equation

(ii) Draw the Lewis-dot structure for the product that forms

Ca^{2+} $\left[\begin{matrix} :\ddot{O}: \\ :\ddot{O}:\ddot{S}:\ddot{O}: \\ :\ddot{O}: \end{matrix} \right]^{2-}$	**1 point** is earned for the correct Lewis structure

(b) Copper sulfate pentahydrate is heated over high heat.

Recall: Hydrates are ionic substances with attached water molecules.

Note: When heated, hydrates decompose to anhydrous and water.

(i) Balanced equation	**1 point** is earned for correct reactants
$CuSO_4 \cdot 5H_2O$ ------> $CuSO_4$ + $5H_2O$	**2 points are** earned for correct products
	1 point is earned for correctly balancing the equation

(ii) If 5 grams of the hydrate was heated in a crucible to a constant mass, calculate the mass of the solid substance in the crucible.

Note: The solid substance in the crucible is the anhydrous, $CuSO_4$. To determine its mass in a 25-gram sample, you need to know the following: Molar mass of $CuSO_4 \cdot 5H_2O$ = 250 g/mol

Mass of $CuSO_4$ in 250 g   = 160 g $CuSO_4$

25 g $CuSO_4 \cdot 5H_2O$ x $\dfrac{160 \text{ g } CuSO_4}{250 \text{ g } CuSO_4 \cdot 5H_2O}$ **16 g CuSO₄**	**1 point** is earned for correctly calculating the mass

(c) Equal molar and volume of barium chloride and sodium carbonate solutions are mixed, resulting in the formation of a precipitate.

Note: This is a double replacement (ion exchange) reaction. Chlorine and sodium ions are spectator ions, therefore, are not included in the net equation.

(i) Balanced equation	**1 point** is earned for correct reactants
Ba^{2+} + CO_3^{2-} -----> $BaCO_3$	**2 points are** earned for correct products **1 point** is earned for correctly balancing the equation

(ii) Describe what will occur if the precipitate is dried and a few drops of a dilute hydrochloric acid are added. Explain.

Note: The equation for the reaction described above is as follows:

Bubbles of carbon dioxide gas (CO_2) will form. *or* **Precipitate ($BaCO_3$) will disappear.**	**1 point** is earned for the correct description.

2.   **(8 points)**

The reaction represented below is a reversible reaction.

$$HBr(g) \ + \ NH_3(g) \ <======> \ NH_4Br(s)$$

(a) Predict the sign of the entropy change, ΔS, for the forward reaction. Explain your reasoning.

| **Entropy change will be negative.**
- ΔS

Because:
Two moles of substances form one mole of substance, therefore, entropy is decreasing.
or
Gaseous reactants form solid product, therefore, entropy is decreasing.
Recall: Decreasing entropy = - ΔS | **1 point** is earned for the correct sign of entropy change.

1 point is earned for explanation that is consistent with the sign of entropy change |

(b) Predict the sign of the free energy change, ΔG, when the reaction reaches equilibrium.

| **ΔG = 0**
Zero
Free energy is Zero because the reaction is at equilibrium. | **1 point** is earned for the correct sign of entropy change. |

(c) The forward reaction is spontaneous at low temperatures. When the temperature of the reaction is increased to a high temperature, how would the the sign of ΔG changes. Justify your answer.

Note: ΔG = ΔH - TΔS   (See Reference Materials on pg 339)

Note: Since ΔS is negative (see a) and ΔH is also negative (spontaneous)

ΔG = - ΔH + TΔS   (ΔG sign, therefore, depends on Temperature)

At low temperature, ΔG = - (spontaneous) because TΔS value is smaller than - ΔH value

At high temperature: **ΔG will change from negative (spontaneous) to positive (nonspontaneous)** because	**1 point** is earned for the correct change of ΔG
At a high enough temperature, TΔS value will overcome (be greater than) - ΔH° value	**1 point** is earned for correct justification

(d) Write an expression for calculating the value of the specific temperature referred to in part (c).

Note: ΔG = 0 at equilibrium ΔG° = ΔH° − TΔS° 0 = ΔH° − TΔS° TΔS = ΔH $T = \dfrac{\Delta H}{\Delta S}$	**1 point** is earned for the correct expression

(e) The system is allowed to reach equilibrium at the low temperature described in part (c). Additional solid NH_4Br is added to the reaction vessel. How will the value of the equilibrium constant be affected? Explain.

Adding more $NH_4Br(s)$ will not affect the equilibrium expression. because **a solid has constant concentration, therefore, its concentrations will not be included into equilibrium expression.**	**1 point** is earned for the correct effect **1 point** is earned for correct explanation that is consistent with the effect stated.

Start: Answer all questions on this day before stopping.

Note: NO CALCULATORS may be used for questions on this day.
You may use ONLY the Periodic Table provided on page 337

Note: For all questions, assume that the temperature is 298 K,
the pressure is 1.00 atmosphere and solutions are aqueous
unless otherwise noted.

Questions 1 through 3

$$X \ + \ Y \ \text{---------} > Z$$

The followings are possible rate laws for the hypothetical reaction given above.

(A) Rate = $k[X]$
(B) Rate = $k[X]^2$
(C) Rate = $k[X][Y]$
(D) Rate = $k[X]^2[Y]$
(E) Rate = $k[X]^2[Y]^2$

1. This is the rate law for the first order reaction.

2. This is the rate law for a reaction that is second order with respect to Y.

3. This is the rate law for a third order reaction.

Questions 4 through 7 *refer to the following particles:*

(A) alpha
(B) beta
(C) gamma
(D) X-ray
(E) ultraviolet

4. Radiation having the highest energy.

5. Radiation used in determining the crystal structure of a solid.

6. Radiation that catalyzes the breakdown of the ozone layer.

7. Radiation that exists as a stream of particles that are equivalent to helium nuclei.

---

8. Which of the following is correctly named?

(A) CsCl   cesium (I) chloride
(B) Fe_2O_3 iron (II) oxide
(C) CBr_4 carbon quatrobromide
(D) NO_2 dioxygen mononitride
(E) MnO_2 manganese (IV) oxide

9. Which one of the following electron configurations for the atoms in their ground state is NOT correct?

(A) Ca $1s^2 2s^2 2p^6 3s^2 3p^6 4s^2$
(B) Bi $[Xe]\, 6s^2 4f^{14} 5d^{10} 6p^3$
(C) As $[Ar]\, 4s^2 3d^{10} 4p^3$
(D) Br $[Ar]\, 4s^2 3d^{10} 4p^5$
(E) P $1s^2 2s^2 2p^6 3p^5$

10. At constant temperature and pressure, the heats of formation of $H_2O(g)$, $CO_2(g)$, and $C_2H_6(g)$ (in kilojoules per mole) are as follows:

Species	ΔHf (KJ/mol)
$H_2O(g)$	-251
$CO_2(g)$	-393
$C_2H_6(g)$	-84

If ΔH values are negative for exothermic reactions, what is ΔH for 1 mole of C_2H_6 gas to oxidize to carbon dioxide gas and water vapor (Temperature and pressure are held constant)?

(A) −8730 kJ/mole
(B) −2910 kJ/mole
(C) −1455 kJ/mole
(D) 1455 kJ/mole
(E) 2910 kJ/mole

11. In the periodic table, as the atomic number increases from 3 to 10, what happens to the atomic radius?

(A) It decreases only

(B) It decreases, then increases.

(C) It remains constant.

(D) It increases only.

(E) It increases, and then decreases.

12. When dilute acid was added to a solution of one of the following chemicals, a gas was evolved. This gas is more dense than air and can be poured over a flaming candle to extinguish the flame. The chemical was

(A) household ammonia, NH_3

(B) baking soda, $NaHCO_3$

(C) table salt, NaCl

(D) isopropyl alcohol, C_2H_5OH

(E) vinegar, 5% $HC_2H_3O_2$

13. Acetaldehyde, CH_3CHO, decomposes into methane gas and carbon monoxide gas. This is a second-order reaction (rate is proportional to the concentration of the reactant). The rate of decomposition at 140°C is 0.10 mole / (L · sec) when the concentration of acetaldehyde is 0.010 mole /L. What is the rate of the reaction when the concentration of acetaldehyde is 0.050 mole/L?

(A) 0.50 mole / (L · sec)

(B) 1.00 mole / (L · sec)

(C) 1.50 mole / (L · sec)

(D) 2.00 mole / (L · sec)

(E) 2.50 mole / (L · sec)

14. Which of the following molecules listed below has the largest dipole moment?

(A) Cl_2

(B) HCl

(C) SO_3

(D) NO

(E) N_2

Day 7: Continue

15. Which of the following is a correct Lewis structure for glycine (NH_2CH_2COOH)?

(A) 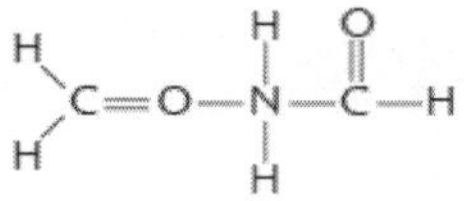

(B) 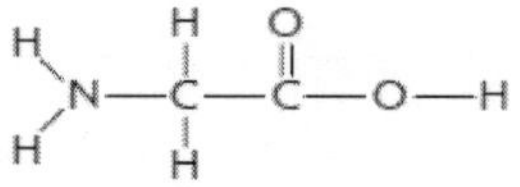

(C) 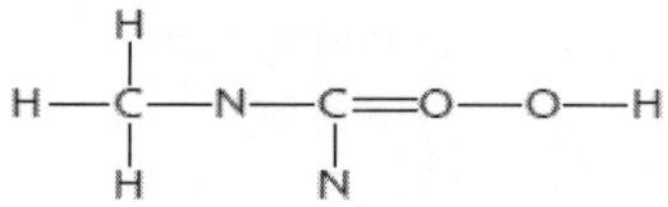

(D) 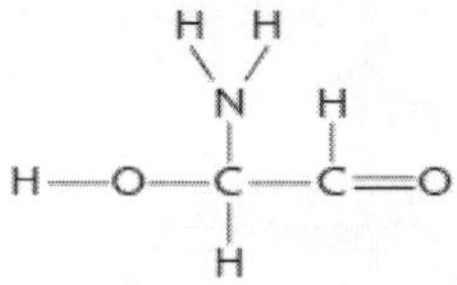

(E) 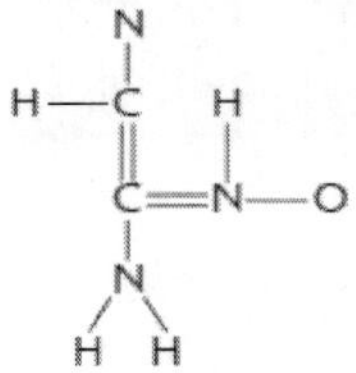

16. $2NO_2Cl(g)$ <=======> $2NO_2(g)$ + $Cl_2(g)$

If the K_c of the reaction is 8.90 at 350°C, what is its K_p?

(A) 0.174
(B) 0.310
(C) 256
(D) 350.
(E) 455

17. The simplest formula for a hydrocarbon that is 20.0 percent hydrogen by mass is

(A) CH

(B) CH_2

(C) CH_3

(D) C_2H_2

(E) C_2H_3

18. The potential energy diagram for the reaction   A + B ----- > C   is shown above.

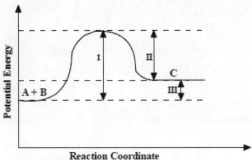

The addition of a catalyst to this reaction would cause a change in which of the indicated energy differences?

(A) I only

(B) II only

(C) III only

(D) I and II only

(E) I, II, and III

19. A gaseous mixture containing 1.5 mol Ne and 4.5 mol NO_2 has a total pressure of 8.0 atm. What is the partial pressure of NO_2?

(A) 1.5 atm

(B) 2.7 atm

(C) 4.5 atm

(D) 6.0 atm

(E) 8.0 atm

20.

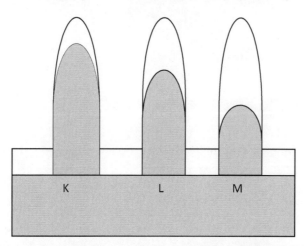

Three manometers are shown in the picture above. One of the manometers had 5 mL of distilled water placed on top of the mercury, another had 5 mL of a 2 m glucose solution placed on top of the mercury, and another had 5 mL of a 2 m NaCl solution placed on top of the mercury.

(A) Manometer K contained the water, manometer L contained the glucose solution, and manometer M contained the NaCl solution.

(B) Manometer K contained the water, manometer L contained the NaCl solution, and manometer M contained the glucose solution.

(C) Manometer K contained the glucose solution, manometer L contained the water, and manometer M contained the NaCl solution.

(D) Manometer K contained the NaCl solution, manometer L contained the glucose solution, and manometer M contained the water.

(E) Manometer K contained the glucose solution, manometer L contained the NaCl solution, and manometer M contained the water.

21. Given $[Cr(NH_3)_6](NO_3)_3$, what is the oxidation number of the Cr?

   (A) 0
   (B) +1
   (C) +2
   (D) +3
   (E) +5

22. $CaCO_3(s) + 2H^+(aq) \text{-----} > Ca^{2+}(aq) + H_2O(l) + CO_2(g)$

If 150 grams of $CaCO_3(g)$ were consumed, what was the volume of $CO_2(g)$ at STP?

   (A) 11-liter
   (B) 22-liter
   (C) 34-liter
   (D) 45-liter
   (E) 56-liter

23. $Zn(s) + Cu^{2+} \text{-----} > Zn^{2+} + Cu(s)$

A galvanic cell based on the reaction represented above was constructed from zinc and copper half-cells. The observed voltage was found to be 1.20 volts instead of the standard cell potential, E°, of 1.10 volts. Which of the following could correctly account for this observation?

   (A) The zinc electrode contained more mass than the copper electrode.
   (B) The Zn^{2+} electrolyte was 0.5M $Zn(NO_3)_2$, while the Cu^{2+} electrolyte was 1.0M $Cu(NO_3)_2$.
   (C) The Zn^{2+} solution was colorless while the Cu^{2+} solution was blue.
   (D) The solutions in the half-cells began at different temperatures.
   (E) The salt bridge contained NaBr as the electrolyte.

Day 7: Continue

24. The first part of the decay of plutonium-240 involves three alpha emissions followed by two beta emissions. What nuclide has been formed at this intermediate stage of the decay series?

(A) Radium-228
(B) Radium-224
(C) Actinium-228
(D) Thorium-232
(E) Thorium-228

25. What ions would you find in solution if potassium perchlorate was dissolved in water?

(A) KCl, O_2
(B) K^+, Cl^-, O_2^-
(C) KCl, O_2^-
(D) K^+, ClO_4^-
(E) K^+, Cl^-, O_2^-

Day 7

STOP. Correct your answers and note how many correct **points**

Day 7: Answers and Explanations

Answers: Quick Check

1. **A** 2. **E** 3. **D** 4. **C** 5. **D** 6. **E** 7. **A** 8. **E** 9. **E** 10. **C**

11. **A** 12. **B** 13. **E** 14. **B** 15. **B** 16. **B** 17. **C** 18. **D** 19. **D** 20. **D**

21. **D** 22. **C** 23. **B** 24. **E** 25. **D**

Answers and Explanations

Questions 1 through 3:   Rate Law, Order of reactions

1. **A**   *Recall:* In first Order reactions, the sum of all exponents of reactants in the rate law equation must add up to 1.

   Note: in Choice A equation: rate = $k[X]^1$ Sum of exponents is **1**

2. **E**   *Recall:* A reaction is second order in respect to a specified reactant if the exponent of the reactant is a 2 in the rate law equation.

   Note: In Choice E equation: rate = $k[X]^2[Y]^2$ exponent of Y is **2**.

3. **D**   *Recall:* In Third Order reactions, the sum of all exponents of reactants in the rate law equation must add up to 3.

   Note: In Choice D equation: rate = $k[X]^2[B]^1$ Sum of exponents is **3**

Questions 4 through 7:   Nuclear particles behavior and properties

4. **C**   *Recall:* Gamma has the highest energy of all radiations.

5. **D.**   *Note:* This is a fact about another use of X-ray
   When focused on a solid, X-ray produces diffraction pattern that can revealed the crystalline structure of the solid.

6. **E**   *Note:* Ozone, O_3, which is found in the upper atmosphere, can be broken down by chlorine (Cl_2). UV light, which is also found in upper atmosphere, catalyzes this reaction.

7. **A**   *Recall:* Symbol for an alpha particle is ^4_2He

8. E **Formula writing, naming**

Note: Formulas for all other choices are incorrectly named. Correct names for these formulas are given below

CsCl: Cesium chloride   CBr$_4$: Carbon tetrabromide
Fe$_2$O$_3$: Iron (III) oxide   NO$_2$: Nitrogen dioxide or

9. E **Atomic Structure, Electron configuration, quantum numbers**

Recall that a ground state configuration is correctly written for an atom when the followings are the case:

. The available sublevels for the atom are correctly represented
. The sublevels are filled in order from lowest energy to highest energy (1s 2s 2p 3s 3p 4s 3d 4p 5s 4d.....)
. Each sublevel has the correct number of electrons it should have according to certain rules
. The sum of electrons in the configuration is equal to the atomic number (or number of protons) of the atom

Note: The ground state configuration $1s^2 2s^2 2p^6 3p^5$ given for P (15 electrons) is incorrect because one of the available sublevels (3s) is missing in the configuration

10. C **Thermodynamic, Enthalpy change calculation, Heat of formation**

Recognize that $\Delta H°$ for this reaction can be calculated using the equation

$$\Delta H° = \sum \Delta Hf°_{products} - \sum \Delta Hf°_{reactants}$$

Step 1: Write a balance equation for the reaction to determine the correct moles of reactants and products.
$$2C_2H_6(g) + 7O_2(g) \ -----> \ 4CO_2(g) + 6H_2O(g)$$

Step 2: Substitute values from the Table in ΔH equation
$$\Delta H° = \sum \Delta Hf°_{products} - \sum \Delta Hf°_{reactants}$$
$$\Delta H° = [4(-393) + 6(-251)] - 2(-84)$$
$$\Delta H° = -1572 - 1506 + 168$$
$$\Delta H° = -3078 \text{ kJ for 2 moles of } C_2H_6$$

Step 3: Adjust the calculated KJ for 1 mole of C$_2$H$_6$:
- 2910 KJ / 2 mol = **−1455 kJ/mol**

Day 7: Answers and Explanations

11. A **Periodic Trend, atomic structure,**

Recall: Atomic radius decreases from Left to right (Increasing atomic number) due to the increase in nuclear charge (number of protons)

12. B **Reaction of acids, property of gases**
Recognize that based on the properties of the gas described in the question, the gas is likely carbon dioxide, CO_2.

Determine: Based on its formula, $NaHCO_3$ (of all the choices listed) is likely to react with an acid to produce CO_2

Note: The net ionic equation for this reaction is:

$$H^+ \quad + \quad HCO^- \text{ ------> } \quad CO_2 \quad + \quad H_2O$$

13. E **Rate law, rate constant, rate calculation, writing equation**

Step 1: Write the correct reaction equation based on info given:

$$CH_3CHO(g) \text{ ------> } CH_4(g) + CO(g)$$

Step 2: Write the rate law based on information given and the equation

$$\text{rate} = k[CH_3CHO]^2 \qquad \text{as stated, rate is } 2^{nd} \text{ order and depends on } [CH_3CHO]$$

Step 3: Determine k (rate-specific constant) at the old concentration

$$k = \frac{\text{rate}}{[CH_3CHO]} = \frac{0.10 \text{ mole} \cdot L^{-1}sec^{-1}}{(0.010 \text{ mole } L^{-1})^2}$$

$$k = 1.0 \times 10^3 \, L \cdot mole^{-1} \, sec^{-1}$$

Step 4: Determine rate at the new $[CH_3CHO]$

$$\text{rate} = k[CH_3CHO]^2 = \left(\frac{1.0 \times 10^3 \, L}{\text{mole} \cdot \text{sec}}\right) \times \left(\frac{0.050 \text{ mole}}{L}\right)^2$$

$$\text{rate} = \frac{2.5 \times 10^1 \text{ mole}}{L \cdot \text{sec}} \quad \text{or} \quad \textbf{2.5 mol / (L} \cdot \textbf{sec)}$$

14. B **Dipole moments, molecular polarity, molecular structures**
Recall: Dipole moment refers to degree of polarity of a molecule. The more polar the molecule, the higher its dipole moment.
Note: HCl is the most polar (biggest difference in electronegativity values) of the five choices given.
N_2 and Cl_2 are nonpolar. Their dipole moments are zero.

15. B **Lewis structures, organic compounds, condensed formula**
Note: Structure B is the only one matches the condensed formula

16. E **Gas equilibrium constant calculation, moles in reaction**
Recognize that based on information given, this gas equilibrium problem can be solved using the equation
$$K_p = K_c \times (RT)^{\Delta n}.$$

Step 1: Convert $350°C$ to Kelvin (Temp in all gas laws must be in Kelvin)
$$K = °C + 273$$
$$K = 350°C + 273 = 623\ K$$

Step 2: Determine Δn (difference in moles of products to reactants)

$$\textbf{2}\ NO_2Cl(g) \ <\text{--------}> \ \textbf{2}\ NO_2(g) + \textbf{1}\ Cl_2(g)$$

Δn = **3** moles of products - **2** moles of reactants = **1**

Step 3: Substitute factors into equation and solve for K_p
$$K_P = K_c \times (RT)^{\Delta n} \qquad (R = 0.0821\ L.atm.mol^{-1}.K^{-1})$$
$$K_p = 8.90 \times (0.0821 \times 623)^1 = \textbf{455.}$$

17. C **Percent composition by mass**

Recognize that the quickest way to determining the answer to this problem is to divide the mass of H in each formula by the molar mass of the formula, and see which one is equal to $1/5^{th}$ or 20%.

Note: in CH_3 $\dfrac{\text{mass of H}}{\text{mass of } CH_3} = \dfrac{3}{15} = \dfrac{1}{5} = 20\%\ H$

18. D *Note:* I and II are measurements of the activation energy.

Recall: A catalyst lowers activation energies of a reaction.

19 **D**   **Partial pressure – mole fraction calculation**
Recognize that based on information given, the equation below can be used to setup and solve the problem for P_{NO_2}

$$P_{NO_2} = \left(\frac{\text{mole of } NO_2}{\text{Total mole}} \right) \times P_{total}$$

$$P_{NO_2} = \left(\frac{4.5 \text{ mol}}{6.0 \text{ mol}} \right) \times 8.0 \text{ atm} = \mathbf{6.0 \text{ atm}}$$

20. **D**   **Number of dissolved particles – Vapor pressure relationship**
Recognize that based on the diagram and information given, each substance that is placed on top of the mercury creates vapor pressure (VP) that pushes down on the mercury in the manometer.

Note: Since the volume (ml) and molality (m) of the substances in all three manometers are equal, the difference in the push on mercury (as represented by the diagram) is dependent upon the amount of vapor pressure created by each substance.

Lowest mercury level (M) = Greatest push = Highest VP substance

Highest mercury level (K) = Least push = Lowest VP substance

Determine highest VP substance (in M)
M has **water** : because it is pure and produces **no dissolved** particles.

Determine lowest VP substance (in K)
K has **NaCl**: Because it is ionic and produces **2 dissolved particles** ($1Na^+$ and $1Cl^-$)

L (intermediate VP) has **glucose** because it is molecular, and produces **1 dissolved** particle

Day 7: Answers and Explanations

21. **D** **Oxidation numbers in a formula**

Recall: Total charge in a neutral formula must equal 0

Note the followings about the given formula: $[Cr(NH_3)_6](NO_3)_3$

NH_3 is neutral : Total Charge of 6 NH_3 = 0

NO_3 - ion = -1: Total charge of 3 NO_3^- = -3

Cr must have a total positive charge of **+ 3** for all charges to equal 0

Note: Since there is just 1 Cr; Oxidation # of Cr = **+3**

22. **C** **Mass–Volume calculation**

Step 1: Determine moles of 150 g $CaCO_3$ consumed

$$\text{moles } CaCO_3 = \frac{\text{mass}}{\text{molar mass}} = \frac{150\text{ g}}{100\text{ g.mol}^{-1}} = \mathit{1.50\ moles}$$

Step 2: Determine volume of CO_2 through mole proportion in the balanced equation

$$\text{Volume} = 1.5\text{ mol } CaCO_3 \times \frac{1\text{ mol } CO_2}{1\text{ mol } CaCO_3} \times \frac{22.4\text{ L}}{1\text{ mol } CO_2}$$

Volume of CO_2 = **34 L**

23. B   Change in voltage, Nernst equation, electrochemistry

Recognize that most of the choices given can be eliminated based on the fact that the information given for these choices will not affect voltage.

Eliminate Choices A, C and E because based on reasoning, mass, color, nor type of salt bridge will not affect voltage.

Eliminate Choice D because both half-cells containing the solutions are in the same area, therefore, the temperature of the solutions should be about the same.

Note: Choice B is left as the correct answer. This can be proven by considering $[Zn^{2+}]$ and $[Cu^{2+}]$ in Nernst equation.

$$E = E^0 \ \frac{RT}{nF} \ \ln Q \qquad Recall: \ Q = \frac{[products]^m}{[reactants]^n} = \frac{[Zn^{2+}]}{[Cu^{2+}]}$$

According to above equations, voltage depends on [ ]

24. E   Nuclear decay series, nuclear particles

Step 1: Write the symbols of emitted particles in the order given

alpha	alpha	alpha	beta	beta
^4_2He	^4_2He	^4_2He	$^0_{-1}e$	$^0_{-1}e$

Step 2: Write the symbol for plutonium – 240

$$^{240}_{94}Pu$$

Step 3: Subtract the sum of the top (mass) # of emitted particles from 240 : $240 - \mathbf{12} = 228$

Subtract the sum of the bottom (charge) # of emitted particles from 94 : $94 - \mathbf{4} = 90$

Note: 90 is the atomic number. The nuclide is Thorium-228

25. D   Composition of a chemical compound, solution, cation and anion

Note: Potassium perchlorate is an ionic compound with the formula $KClO_4$.

Recall: When an ionic compound is placed in water, it dissolves to produce cation (K+) and anion (ClO_4-)

START: Answer all questions on this day before stopping.

Note: You may use a calculator for questions on this day.
You may use any of the reference material provided on pg 337-340

CLEARLY SHOW THE METHOD USED AND THE STEPS INVOLVED IN ARRIVING
AT YOUR ANSWERS. It is to your advantage to do this, since you may obtain
partial credit if you do and you will receive little or no credit if you do not.
Attention should be paid to significant figures.

---

1.   **(10 points)**

The reaction $2NO_2(g) + Cl_2(g) \longrightarrow 2NO_2Cl(g)$
was studied at 20°C and the following data were obtained:

Experiment	Initial $[NO_2]$ (mole/L)	Initial $[Cl_2]$ (mole/L)	Initial Rate increase of NO_2Cl (mole/(L · sec))
1	0.100	0.005	1.35×10^{-7}
2	0.100	0.010	2.70×10^{-7}
3	0.200	0.010	5.40×10^{-7}

(a) Write the rate law for the reaction.

(b) What is the overall order for the reaction? Explain.

(c) Calculate the rate-specific constant, *k*, including the correct units.

(d) In Experiment 3, what is the initial rate of decrease of $[Cl_2]$?

(e) Based on the equation given for this reaction:
  (i) Propose a mechanism for the reaction that is consistent with the
       rate law expression you found in part (a)

  (ii) Which is the rate determining step in the proposed mechanism?

---

2.   **(10 points)**

The setup below shows the electrolysis of water that is at 25°C and 1 atm.

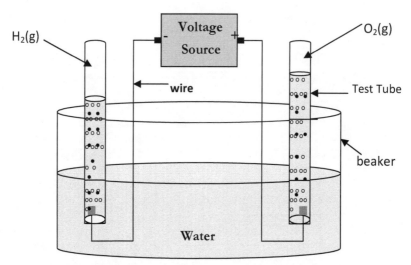

The electrolysis process was allowed to proceed for 4.37 minutes while the voltage source supplies a constant 1.213 amperes of current.

(a) Write a balance equation for the decomposition of water during the electrolysis process.

(b) Write a balance half-reaction equation for the reaction at the cathode.

(c) Calculate the amount of electrical charge, in coulombs, that passes through the solution during the time period mentioned.

(d) The half-reaction that occurs at the anode is:
$$2H_2O(l) \ ---> \ O_2(g) \ + \ 4H^+(aq) \ + \ 4e^-$$
   (i) Calculate the number of moles of $O_2(g)$ produced at the anode.

   (ii) Calculate the volume, in liters, of $O_2(g)$ produced during the electrolysis process.

   (iii) Explain why the volume of $H_2(g)$ collected is different from the volume of $O_2(g)$ collected during the same time.

(e) Identify another substance, including its phase, which is also collected in both test tubes along with $O_2(g)$ and $H_2(g)$.

Day 8

STOP. Correct your answers and note how many correct **points**

Day 8 Question 2: Space for Work and Answers

_____

_____

_____

_____

_____

_____

_____

_____

_____

_____

_____

_____

_____

_____

_____

_____

_____

_____

_____

_____

_____

_____

_____

_____

_____

_____

1.   **(10 points)**

The reaction $2NO_2(g) + Cl_2(g) \longrightarrow 2NO_2Cl(g)$ was studied at 20°C and the following data were obtained:

(a) Write the rate law for the reaction.

Note: Based on equation given, rate expression will be as follows:

$$rate = k[NO_2]^n[Cl_2]^m$$

n = order with respect to $[NO_2]$
m = order with respect to $[Cl_2]$
n and m need to be determined

*Determine order **m** by setting up rate ratio between experiment 2 and 1 since $[NO_2]$ is constant. Substitute data for both experiments from table into rate expression above.* $\dfrac{rate2}{rate1} = \dfrac{k\,(0.100M)^n\,(0.010\,M)^m}{k\,(0.100\,M)^n\,(0.0050\,M)^m} = \dfrac{2.70\times10^{-7}\,mole/(L\cdot sec)}{1.35\times10^{-7}\,mole/(L\cdot sec)}$ $2^m = 2$ $m = 1$	**1 point** is earned for calculating **m**
*Determine order **n** by setting up rate ratio between experiment 3 and 2 since $[Cl_2]$ is constant. Substitute data for both experiments from table into rate expression above.* $\dfrac{rate\,3}{rate2} = \dfrac{k\,(0.200\,M)^n\,(0.010\,M)^m}{k\,(0.100M)^n\,(0.010\,M)^m} = \dfrac{5.40\times10^{-7}\,mole/(L\cdot sec)}{2.70\times10^{-7}\,mole/(L\cdot sec)}$ $2^n = 2$ $n = 1$	**1 point** is earned for calculating **n**
Write rate law by substituting m and n into rate expression: $rate = k[NO_2]^1[Cl_2]^1 = k[NO_2][Cl_2]$	**1 point** is earned for the correct rate law

(b) What is the overall order for the reaction? Explain.

Recall: Overall order of a reaction is the sum of all the orders.

2 **Overall order of a reaction is the sum of all the orders:** $m + n = 1 + 1 = 2$	**1 point** is earned for the correct sum with explanation.

(c) Calculate the rate-specific constant, k, including the correct units.

Note: Since the rate was determined in part (a), k can be determine by substituting data from **one** of the experiments into the rate law, and solve for k

Rearrange rate law for k rate $= k[NO_2][Cl_2]$ $k = \dfrac{rate}{[NO_2][Cl_2]}$ *Substitute data for experiment 1, and solve for k* $k = \dfrac{1.35 \times 10^{-7} \text{ mole/(L} \cdot \text{sec)}}{(0.100 \text{ mole/L)} (0.005 \text{ mol/L})}$ $k = \mathbf{2.7 \times 10^{-4} \text{ L / (mole} \cdot \text{sec)}}$	**1 point** is earned for correctly calculating the k value.
Note: Since temperature is the same for all three experiments, and the reaction is first order with respect to both reactants, data from any of the three experiments can be used to calculate k. The value for k will be the same	**1 point** is earned for the correct unit

(d) In Experiment 3, what is the initial rate of decrease of $[Cl_2]$?

> Note: The initial rate of decrease of a reactant is proportional to the initial rate of increase of the products.

Write rate change equation based on the equation given	
$$2NO_2(g) + Cl_2(g) \longrightarrow 2NO_2Cl(g)$$	
$$\frac{-\,d\,[Cl_2]}{dt} = \frac{1}{2}\frac{d[NO_2Cl]}{dt}$$ *Note:* - sign indicates that the change of Cl_2 is in opposite direction (decreasing) in respect to the direction of change of NO_2Cl (increasing). *Note:* ½ indicates that moles of Cl_2 is half that of NO_2Cl in the balanced equation. They are at a 1 : 2 ratio.	**1 point** is earned for the correct setup to calculate initial rate of decrease of Cl_2
Substitute rate for experiment 3 and solve for [Cl₂]	**1 point** is earned for answer that is consistent with the setup.
$$-\,[Cl_2] = \frac{5.40 \times 10^{-7}\ \text{mol} / (\text{L} \cdot \text{sec})}{2}$$	
$$[Cl_2] = -\,2.7 \times 10^{-7}\ \text{mol} / (\text{L} \cdot \text{sec})$$	

(e) Based on the equation given for this reaction:

  (i) Propose mechanisms for the reaction that is consistent with the
      rate law expression you found in part (a).

  Note: The sum of the steps of the mechanism must equal the balanced
         equation.

         The sum of the mechanism must be consistent with the
         experimentally-determined rate law.

Propose mechanisms (steps) and determine the sum of the equations	
Step 1: $NO_2(g)$ + $Cl_2(g)$ ----- > $NO_2Cl(g)$ + ~~Cl(g)~~	**1 point** is earned for the correct mechanisms
Step 2: ~~Cl(g)~~ + $NO_2(g)$ ----- > $NO_2Cl(g)$	
Sum: **$2NO_2(g)$ + $Cl_2(g)$** ----- > **$2NO_2Cl(g)$**	
Note: The sum of the mechanisms is the same as the equation	
Note: The rate law for the rate-determining step is consistent with the experimentally-determined rate law:	
rate = $k[NO_2][Cl_2]$ for both	

(ii) Which is the rate determining step in the proposed mechanism?

Step 1	**1 point** is earned for mentioning step 1
or	
$NO_2(g)$ + $Cl_2(g)$ ----- > $NO_2Cl(g)$ + $Cl(g)$	
is the slow rate determining step	

2.   **(10 points)**

The setup below shows the electrolysis of water that is at 25°C and 1 atm.

The electrolysis process was allowed to proceed for 4.37 minutes while the voltage source supplies a constant 1.213 amperes of current.

a) Write a balance equation for the decomposition of water during the electrolysis process.

$2H_2O(l)$ ------------> $O_2(g)$ + $2H_2(g)$	**1 point** is earned for a correct balanced equation

b) Write a balance half-reaction equation for the reaction at the cathode.

   Recall: Reduction (gaining of electrons) occurs at the cathode.

   The half-reaction must represent reduction.

$2H_2O(l)$ + $2e^-$ ------> $H_2(g)$ + $2OH^-(aq)$	**1 point** is earned for the correct and balanced half-reaction equation

c) Calculate the amount of electrical charge, in coulombs, that passes through the solution during the time period mentioned.

   Recall: 1 ampere   = 1 coulomb/sec

   1.213 amperes = 1.213 coulomb/sec

Set up using factor-labeling electrical charge = 4.37 min $\times \dfrac{60 \text{ sec}}{1 \text{ min}} \times \dfrac{1.213 \text{ coul}}{\text{sec}}$	**1 point** is earned for setup
electrical charge = 318 coulombs	**1 point** is earned for the correct answer

103

d) The half-reaction that occurs at the anode is:

$$2H_2O \ (l) \ ----> \ O_2 \ (g) \ + \ 4H^+ \ (aq) \ + \ 4e^-$$

(i) Calculate the number of moles of O_2 (g) produced at the anode.

Note: 1 mole of e- = 96500 coulombs (see Reference Materials pg 340)

Set up using factor-labeling involving mole ratio mole of O_2(g) = **318 coul** x $\dfrac{\textbf{1 mol e}^-}{\textbf{96500 coul}}$ x $\dfrac{\textbf{1 mol } O_2}{\textbf{4 mol e}^-}$ **moles of O_2(g) = 8.24 x 10^{-4} moles O_2**	**1 point** is earned for setup **1 point** for correct moles of O_2

(ii) Calculate the volume, in milliliters, of O_2(g) produced during the electrolysis process.

Note: Since temperature (25°C) and pressure (1 atm) are known, use the ideal gas law equation to set up and solve.

$$PV_{O_2} \ = \ n_{O_2} RT$$

Note: T must be in Kelvin
25°C + 273 = 298 K

n = moles of O_2 (see (i))
R = gas constant

Rearrange ideal gas law equation $V_{O_2} = \dfrac{n_{O_2} RT}{P}$ *Substitute values into equation and solve* $V_{O_2} = \dfrac{(8.24 \ \times \ 10^{-4} \text{ mol}) \ (0.0821 \frac{L.atm}{mol.K}) \ (298 \text{ K})}{1 \text{ atm}}$ **V_{O_2} = 0.0202 L = 20 mL**	**1 point** for setup using ideal gas equation **1 point** for the correct volume of O_2

(iii) Explain why the volume of $H_2(g)$ collected is different from the volume of $O_2(g)$ collected during the same time.

Note: The balanced equation for the reaction

$$2H_2O(l) \text{ -----------} > O_2(g) \quad + \quad 2H_2(g)$$

The volume of $O_2(g)$ produced is less than that of the $H_2(g)$ because, according to the balanced equation, **2 moles of H_2 gas are produced to only 1 mole of O_2 gas**	**1 point** for explanation that includes mole ratio of O_2 to H_2

e) Identify another substance, including its phase, which is also collected in both test tubes along with $O_2(g)$ and $H_2(g)$.

H_2O (g) **Water vapor**	**1 point** for the correct answer

START: Answer all questions on this day before stopping.

Note: NO CALCULATORS should be used for questions on this day.
You may use any of the Reference Materials provided on Pg 337-340

---

1. For each of the following three reactions, write a balanced equation for
the reaction in part (i) and answer the question about the reaction in part
(ii). In part (i), coefficients should be in terms of lowest whole numbers.
Assume that solutions are aqueous unless otherwise indicated. Represent
substances in solutions as ions if the substances are extensively ionized.
Omit formulas for any ions or molecules that are unchanged by the reaction.
(15 points)

(a) Methanol and acetic acid are mixed and then gently warmed.

> (i) Balanced equation:

(ii) Identify the type of organic reaction that is taking place?

_____

_____

_____

(b) Solid potassium carbonate is added to 2 *M* sulfuric acid.

> (i) Balanced equation:

(ii) How many molecules of the acid will react with 69 grams of the
potassium carbonate.

_____

_____

_____

(c) Potassium hydroxide is added to a solution of iron (III) sulfate.

> (i) Balanced equation:

(ii) What type of chemical bonding is or are present in a formula unit
of iron (III) sulfate.

_____

_____

_____

Your responses to question 2 will be scored on the basis of the accuracy and relevance of the information cited. Explanations should be clear and well organized. Examples and equations may be included in your responses where appropriate. Specific answers are preferable to broad, diffuse responses. (**8 points**)

2. The first three ionization energies (I_1, I_2, and I_3) for magnesium and argon are given in the following table:

Atom	I_1 (KJ/mol)	I_2 (KJ/mol)	I_3 (KJ/mol)
Mg	738	1,450	7730
Ar	1520	2665	3945

(a) Write the complete electron configurations for magnesium and argon.

(b) Draw the Lewis diagrams for Mg and Ar.

(c) Based on the data table information:
   (i) State one similarity found in ionization energies of both atoms.

   (ii) Explain why the difference between the 2nd and 3rd ionization energy of Mg is much greater than the difference between the 2nd and 3rd ionization energy of Ar.

(d) If chlorine gas is passed into separate containers of heated magnesium and heated argon, explain what compounds (if any) might be formed, and explain your answer in terms of the electron configurations of these two elements.

(e) An unknown element, Y, has the following three ionization energies:

Atom	I_1 (KJ/mol)	I_2 (KJ/mol)	I_3 (KJ/mol)
Y	496	4560	6912

On the basis of the ionization energies given, what is the formula and name of the compound produced when chlorine reacts with element Y. Explain your reasoning.

Day 9

STOP. Correct your answers and note how many correct **points**

Day 9 Question 2: Space for Work and Answers

_____

_____

_____

_____

_____

_____

_____

_____

_____

_____

_____

_____

_____

_____

_____

_____

_____

_____

_____

_____

_____

_____

_____

1.   **(15 points)**
   (a) Methanol and acetic acid are mixed and then gently warmed.

   Note: This is an esterification reaction
   Recall: In esterification, an ester and water are produced by
   reacting an organic acid with alcohol

(i) Balanced equation	**1 point** is earned for correct reactants
CH_3OH + CH_3COOH ----- > CH_3COOCH_3 + H_2O *methanol acetic acid ester water*	**2 points are** earned for correct products **1 point** is earned for correctly balancing the equation

   (ii) Identify the type of organic reaction that is taking place?

esterification	**1 point** is earned for the correct structure of the ester

   (b) Solid potassium carbonate is added to 2 *M* sulfuric acid.

(i) Balanced equation	**1 point** is earned for correct reactants
K_2CO_3 + $2H^+$ ------- > CO_2 + H_2O + $2K^+$	**2 points are** earned for correct products **1 point** is earned for correctly balancing the equation

(ii) How many molecules of the acid will react with 27.6 grams of the potassium carbonate.

Recall: 1 mole = 6.02×10^{23} molecules

Determine moles of K_2CO_3 in 69 g 69g K_2CO_3 x $\dfrac{1 \text{ mole } K_2CO_3}{138 \text{ g } K_2CO_3}$ = 0.5 mol K_2CO_3 Setup proportion to calculate number of molecules 0.5 mol K_2CO_3 x $\dfrac{2 \text{ mol } H^+}{1 \text{ mol } K_2CO_3}$ x $\dfrac{6.02 \times 10^{23} \text{ molecules}}{1 \text{ mole}}$ **6.02×10^{23} molecules**	**1 point** is earned for correctly calculating the number of molecules

(c) A pellet of sodium hydroxide is added to a solution of iron (III) sulfate.

Note: This is a double replacement (ion-exchange) reaction
Note: Sodium and sulfate ions are both spectator ions. Therefore, they are not included in the equation.

(i) Balanced equation **$3OH^-$ + Fe^{3+} -----> $Fe(OH)_3$**	**1 point** is earned for correct reactants
	2 points are earned for correct products
	1 point is earned for correctly balancing the equation

(ii) What type of chemical bonding is or are present in a formula unit of iron (III) sulfate.

Ionic and Covalent bonding or **Ionic and polar** bonding	**1 point** is earned for the correct bond types

Day 9: Answers and Scoring Guidelines

2. **(8 points)**

The first three ionization energies (I_1, I_2, and I_3) for magnesium and Argon are given in the following table:

(a) Write the complete electron configurations for magnesium and argon.

Mg **$1s^2 2s^2 2p^6 3s^2$** Ar **$1s^2 2s^2 2p^6 3s^2 3p^6$**	**1 point** is earned for the correct configurations for both Mg and Ar.

(b) Draw the Lewis electron-dot diagrams for Mg and Ar.

Recall: Lewis electron-dot diagram shows symbol of atom and dots equal to the number of valance electrons

Mg : **: $\ddot{\underset{\cdot\cdot}{Ar}}$:**	**1 point** is earned for the correct Lewis electron-dots for both Mg and Ar.

(c) Based on the data table information:

(i) State one similarity found in ionization energies for both atoms.

Recall: Ionization energy is the energy to remove the most loosely bound electron from an atom

Energy to remove the 1st through 3rd electrons increases steadily. **The first ionization energy is the lowest.** **The third ionization energy is the highest.**	**1 point** is earned for any one correct similarity

(ii) Explain why the difference between the 2nd and 3rd ionization energies of Mg is much greater than the difference between the 2nd and 3rd ionization energies of Ar. Include both Mg and Ar.

In magnesium, the 3rd ionization energy is over 5 times as much as the 2nd ionization because: **the 3rd electron to be removed from Mg is located in the second energy level (closer to the nucleus) while the 2nd electron to be removed is located in the third energy level (farther from the nucleus)** In argon, the energy difference is only twice as much because **both the 3rd and 2nd electrons to be removed are located in the same (third) energy level.**	**1 point** is earned for the correct explanation

(d) If chlorine gas is passed into separate containers of heated magnesium and heated argon, explain what compounds (if any) might be formed, and explain your answer in terms of the electron configurations of these two elements.

$MgCl_2$, magnesium chloride	**1 point** is earned for the correct compound
Mg will react with chlorine because **Mg only has two valance electrons, and will readily give them up** to chlorine to form a stable octet valance configuration. Ar will not react (no product will form) with chlorine because **argon already has a complete valance shell configuration and is stable.**	**1 point** is earned for correct explanation that includes Mg and Ar.

(e) An unknown element, Y, has the following three ionization energies:

Atom	I_1 (KJ/mol)	I_2 (KJ/mol)	I_3 (KJ/mol)
Y	496	4560	6912

On the basis of the ionization energies given, what is the formula and name of the compound produced when chlorine reacts with element Y. Explain your reasoning.

NaCl , sodium chloride	**1 point** is earned for stating NaCl
Element Y is likely sodium for the following reasons: The I_1 of Y is much smaller than the I_1 of Mg indicating that the 1st electron of Y is located farther from the nucleus than the 1st electron of Mg. Y must be an element that is bigger than Mg. **Na is bigger than Mg.** The I_3 of Y is less than twice the I_2 of Y indicating that both the 2nd and 3rd electrons are located in the same energy level. This is the case with most alkali metals. *Note:* If Y was Ca, its I_3 would be much more greater than its I_2 since the 3rd electron would be in an energy level that is closer to the nucleus than that of the 2nd electron.	**1 point** is earned for correct explanation

Start: Answer all questions on this day before stopping.

Note: **NO CALCULATORS may be used for questions on this day.**
You may use ONLY the Periodic Table provided on page 337

Note: For all questions, assume that the temperature is 298 K,
the pressure is 1.00 atmosphere and solutions are aqueous
unless otherwise noted.

For Questions 1 through 5, consider the following system at equilibrium:

$$2N_2O(g) \quad < ===== > \quad 2N_2(g) \quad + \quad O_2(g) \quad \Delta H = \quad +163 \text{ KJ}$$

and select from the following choices:

        (A) to the right
        (B) to the left
        (C) neither
        (D) in both directions
        (E) cannot be determined from information provided

1. In which direction will the system move in order to reestablish
   equilibrium if N_2O is added?

2. In which direction will the system move in order to reestablish
   equilibrium if O_2 is removed?

3. In which direction will the system move in order to reestablish
   equilibrium if the volume is decreased?

4. In which direction will the system move in order to reestablish
   equilibrium if the temperature is raised?

5. In which direction will the system move in order to reestablish
   equilibrium if a catalyst is added?

For questions **6 through 8** refer to the following configurations.

(A) $1s^2 2s^2 2p^6$

(B) $1s^2 2s^2 2p^6 3s^2$

(C) $1s^2 2s^2 2p^6 3s^2 3p^4$

(D) $1s^2 2s^2 2p^6 3s^2 3p^6$

(E) $1s^2 2s^2 2p^6 3s^2 3p^6 4s^2$

6. The configuration of an atom of a paramagnetic element.

7. The ground state configuration for both a potassium ion and a chloride ion.

8. An atom that has this ground state electron configuration will have the smallest radius of those listed.

Questions 9 through 12 refer to the following solutions.

(A) 250 mL of 0.50 M KNO_3 (molar mass = 101)

(B) 400 mL of 0.10 M $Al(NO_3)_3$ (molar mass = 213)

(C) 500 mL of 0.20 M NH_4NO_3 (molar mass = 80)

(D) 300 mL of 0.30 M $Pb(NO_3)_2$ (molar mass = 170)

(E) 200 mL of 0.10 M $Ni(NO_3)_2$ (molar mass = 183)

9. Is an appropriate reagent for a Beer's Law experiment.

10. Forms a precipitate when 0.50 moles of solid NaCl is added.

11. Has the highest boiling point.

12. Has the highest $[NO_3^-]$.

13. Given a molecule with the general formula AB_2, which one of the following would be the most useful in determining whether the molecule was bent or linear?

   (A) ionization energies
   (B) electron affinities
   (C) bond energies
   (D) electronegativities
   (E) dipole moments

14. The radioactive decay of $_{8}^{19}O$ to $_{9}^{19}F$ occurs by the process of

   (A) beta emission
   (B) alpha emission
   (C) positron emission
   (D) electron capture
   (E) neutron capture

15. Which of the following statements about the energy diagram below is incorrect?

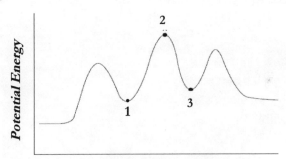

Reaction coordinate

   (A) The overall reaction is endothermic.
   (B) The reaction has two intermediates.
   (C) Point 2 represents a transition state.
   (D) Raising the energy of point 3 decreases the equilibrium concentration of product.
   (E) Raising the energy of point 2 decreases the rate of product formation.

16. In expanding from 5.00 to 6.00 liters at a constant pressure of 2.00 atmospheres, a gas absorbs 505.64 joules of energy (101.32 joules = 1 liter · atm). The change in energy, ΔE, for the gas is

   (A) 50.66 J
   (B) 101.32 J
   (C) 303.00 J
   (D) 505.64 J
   (E) 606.00 J

17. $2\,NH_3 \;\text{-------->}\; NH_4^+ \;+\; NH_2^-$
   In the reaction NH_4^+ acts as

   (A) a catalyst
   (B) both an acid and a base
   (C) the conjugate acid of NH_3
   (D) the reducing agent
   (E) the oxidizing agent

18. A molecule in which the central atom exhibits sp^2 hybrid orbitals has which of the following molecular shapes?

   (A) linear
   (B) trigonal planar
   (C) trigonal bipyramidal
   (D) square planar
   (E) tetrahedral

19. If ΔH is positive and ΔS is negative, then ΔG is always

   (A) positive
   (B) negative
   (C) negative at low temperatures; positive at high temperatures
   (D) positive at low temperatures; negative at high temperatures
   (E) cannot be determined from the information provided

20. Silver hydroxide will be LEAST soluble in a solution with a pH of

(A) 3
(B) 5
(C) 7
(D) 9
(E) 11

21. Which of the following is an impossible set of quantum numbers ?

(A) $4, 0, 0, {}^1/_2$

(B) $4, 0, 1, {}^1/_2$

(C) $4, 1, 0, {}^1/_2$

(D) $4, 1, 1, {}^1/_2$

(E) $4, 2, 1, {}^1/_2$

22. A 96-g sample of methane reacts with fluorine gas to produce 96 g of 1-fluoroethane and hydrogen gas. What is the percent yield?

(A) 33%
(B) 66%
(C) 50%
(D) 100%
(E) 300%

23. Liquid A and liquid B form a solution that behaves ideally according to Raoult's law. The vapor pressures of the pure substances A and B are 75 mmHg and 25 mmHg, respectively. What is the vapor pressure over the solution if 1.50 moles of liquid A is added to 3.50 moles of liquid B?

(A) 30.0 mmHg
(B) 40.0 mmHg
(C) 50.0 mmHg
(D) 5.00 mmHg
(E) 100 mmHg

24. When an aqueous solution of potassium chloride is compared with water, the salt solution will have

  (A) a higher boiling point, a lower freezing point, and a lower vapor pressure

  (B) a higher boiling point, a higher freezing point, and a lower vapor pressure

  (C) a higher boiling point, a higher freezing point, and a higher vapor pressure

  (D) a lower boiling point, a lower freezing point, and a lower vapor pressure

  (E) a lower boiling point, a higher freezing point, and a higher vapor pressure

25. What is the mass of oxygen in 148 grams of a calcium hydroxide?

  (A) 16 g
  (B) 24 g
  (C) 32 g
  (D) 48 g
  (E) 64 g

26. $SnO_2(s)$ + $2CO(g)$ ------- > $Sn(s)$ + $2CO_2(g)$

    Which of the following is a correct equilibrium constant expression for the above reaction?

  (A) $K_{eq} = \dfrac{[CO_2]^2}{[CO]^2}$

  (B) $K_{eq} = \dfrac{[Sn]}{[SnO_2]}$

  (C) $K_{eq} = \dfrac{[SnO_2][CO]^2}{[Sn][CO_2]^2}$

  (D) $K_{eq} = \dfrac{[Sn][CO_2]}{[SnO_2][CO]}$

  (E) $K_{eq} = \dfrac{[Sn][CO_2]^2}{[SnO_2][CO]^2}$

27. In the titration of a weak acid of unknown concentration with a standard solution of a strong base, the pH of the resulting solution was monitored as the titration progresses. Which of the following is true for this experiment?

(A) The pH is 7 at the equivalence point.

(B) The pH at the equivalence point depends on the indicator used.

(C) The graph of pH versus volume of base added rises gradually at first and then much more rapidly.

(D) The graph of pH versus volume of base added shows no sharp rise.

(E) The [H+] at the equivalence point equals the ionization constant of the acid.

28. Consider the reaction below.

$$H_2O(g) \text{ ------- } > H_2O(l)$$

Which of the following is true of the values of ΔH, ΔS, and ΔG for the reaction shown above at $25°C$?

	ΔH	ΔS	ΔG
(A)	Positive	Positive	Positive
(B)	Positive	Negative	Negative
(C)	Negative	Positive	Negative
(D)	Negative	Negative	Positive
(E)	Negative	Negative	Negative

Questions 29 through 30 refer to an electrolytic cell that involves the following half-reaction.

$$AuCl_4^- + 3e^- \text{--------} > Au + 4Cl^-$$

29. Which of the following occurs in the reaction?

   (A) Au is oxidized at the anode.
   (B) $AuCl_4^-$ is reduced at the cathode.
   (C) Gold is converted from the -3 oxidation state to the 0 oxidation state.
   (D) Cl^- acts as a reducing agent.
   (E) Cl^- is oxidized at the anode.

30. A steady current of 4.0 amperes is passed though a gold-production cell for 30 minutes. Which of the following is the correct expression for calculating the number of grams of gold produced?
(1 faraday = 96,500 coulombs)

(A) $\dfrac{(4)\,(30)\,(60)}{(197)\,(96,500)\,(3)}$

(B) $\dfrac{(4)\,(30)\,(96,500)}{(197)\,(60)}$

(C) $\dfrac{(4)\,(30)\,(60)\,(197)}{(3)\,(96,500)}$

(D) $\dfrac{(96,500)\,(197)}{(3)\,(4)\,(60)\,(30)}$

(E) $\dfrac{(3)\,(197)}{(4)\,(60)\,(30)\,(96,500)}$

31. Arrange the following ions in order of increasing ionic radius:
    Mg^{2+}, F^-, and O^{2-}

    (A) O^{2-}, F^-, Mg^{2+}

    (B) Mg^{2+}, O^{2-}, F^-

    (C) Mg^{2+}, F^-, O^{2-}

    (D) O^{2-}, Mg^{2+}, F^-

    (E.) F^-, O^{2-}, Mg^{2+}

32. Which of the following pairs of solutions produce a precipitate if mixed?

    (I) $HBr(aq)$ and $Ca(OH)_2(aq)$
    (II) $Pb(NO_3)_2(aq)$ and $LiI(aq)$
    (III) $(NH_4)_3PO_4(aq)$ and $MgCl_2(aq)$

    (A) I only
    (B) II only
    (C) III only
    (D) I and II only
    (E) II and III only

33. Which of the following systems would NOT experience a change in the concentration of the substances present at equilibrium when the volume of the system is changed at constant temperature?

    (A) $SO(g)$ + $NO(g)$ --------> $SO_2(g)$ + $^1/_2 N_2(g)$
    (B) $O_2(g)$ + $2 H_2(g)$ --------> $2 H_2O(g)$
    (C) $N_2(g)$ + $2 O_2(g)$ -- ------> $2 NO_2(g)$
    (D) $N_2O_4(g)$ --------> $2 NO_2(g)$
    (E) $CH_4(g)$ + $2 O_2(g)$ -------> $CO_2(g)$ + $2 H_2O(g)$

34. What number of moles of O_2 is needed to produce 25.5 grams of Al_2O_3 from solid Al? (Molecular weight Al_2O_3 =102 g/mole)

    (A) 0.125 mole
    (B) 0.250 mole
    (C) 0.375 mole
    (D) 0.500 mole
    (E) 1.00 mole

35. Which of the following acids can be oxidized to form a stronger acid?

(A) $H_2C_2O_4$
(B) HNO_2
(C) H_2SO_4
(D) H_3PO_4
(E) $HC_2H_3O_2$

36. In which equation would you expect ΔE and ΔH to be nearly equal?

(A) $2H_2(g) \quad + \quad O_2(g)$ ------- $> \quad 2H_2O(l)$
(B) $C_2H_4(g) \quad + \quad H_2(g)$ ------ $> \quad C_2H_6(g)$
(C) $BrO_3^-(aq) + \quad 5Br^-(aq) \quad + 6H^+(aq)$ ------> $3Br_2(aq) \quad + \quad 3H_2O(l)$
(D) $HCOOH(aq) + \quad Br_2(aq)$ ----- $> \quad 2H^+(aq) \quad + \quad 2Br^-(aq) \quad + \quad CO_2(g)$
(E) $N_2O(g)$ ------ $> \quad N_2(g) \quad + \quad O(g)$

37. Consider diethyl ether and 1-butanol. Which of the following are correct?

(A) Diethyl ether will have the higher boiling point.
(B) 1-butanol will have the higher boiling point.
(C) Because they contain the same number and types of atoms, they will boil at the same temperature.
(D) Because they contain the same number of atoms, but different types of atoms, more information is needed in order to determine which one will boil at a higher temperature.
(E) Because they contain different numbers of atoms, but the same type of atoms, more information is needed in order to determine which one will boil at a higher temperature.

38. Which of the following gases would be expected to have a rate of effusion that is one-third as great as that of hydrogen gas?

(A) Oxygen
(B) Nitrogen
(C) Helium
(D) Water
(E) Carbon dioxide

39. The O—N—O bond angle in the NO_3^- ion is
   (A) 90°
   (B) 105°
   (C) 109°
   (D) 120°
   (E) 180°

40. A student pipetted five 25.00-milliliter samples of acetic acid and transferred each sample to a beaker, diluted it with distilled water, and added a few drops of phenolphthalein to each. Each sample was then titrated with a sodium hydroxide solution to the appearance of the first permanent faint pink color. The following results were obtained.

Solution	Volume of NaOH
First Sample..................	15.33 mL
Second Sample..............	16.35 mL
Third Sample................	16.37 mL
Fourth Sample..............	16.40 mL
Fifth Sample.................	16.38 mL

Which of the following is the most probable explanation for the variation in the student's results?

   (A) More water was added to the first sample.
   (B) More phenolphthalein was added to the first sample.
   (C) The first sample was titrated beyond the end point.
   (D) The pipette was not rinsed with the acetic acid solution.
   (E) The buret was not rinsed with the NaOH solution

41. Given the following standard molar entropies measured at 25°C and 1 atm pressure, calculate $\Delta S°$ in $(J \cdot mol^{-1} \cdot K^{-1})$ for the reaction

$$2Al(s) \ + \ 3MgO(s) \ \text{---------} > \ 3Mg(s) \ + \ Al_2O_3(s)$$

Substances	$S°$ $(J \cdot mol^{-1} \cdot K^{-1})$
Al(s)	28.0
$Al_2O_3(s)$	51.0
Mg(s)	33.0
MgO(s)	27.0

(A) −29.0 J/(mol· K)

(B) −13.0 J/(mol· K)

(C) 13.0 J/(mol· K)

(D) 69.0 J/(mol· K)

(E) 139 J/(mol· K)

42. An unknown substance is placed into a hot flame. The color of the flame is bright red. Which of the following substances is most likely to be the unknown?

(A) $Cu(NO_3)_2$

(B) NaCl

(C) KCl

(D) LiCl

(E) $Na(NO_3)_2$

43. The atomic mass of copper is 63.55. Given that there are only two naturally occurring isotopes of copper, ^{63}Cu and ^{65}Cu, the natural abundance of ^{63}Cu is approximately

(A) 90 %

(B) 72 %

(C) 63 %

(D) 30 %

(E) 10 %

For Questions 44 and 45, use the following information:

A student prepared a 1.00 M acetic acid solution ($HC_2H_3O_2$). The student found the pH of the solution to be 2.00.

44. What is the K_a value for the solution?

   (A) 3.00×10^{-7}
   (B) 2.00×10^{-6}
   (C) 2.00×10^{-5}
   (D) 1.00×10^{-4}
   (E) 1.00×10^{-3}

45. What is the approximate % dissociation of the acetic acid? (Use the 5% rule.)

   (A) 0.050%
   (B) 1.0%
   (C) 1.5%
   (D) 2.0%
   (E) 2.5%

Questions 46 through 50 refer to types of organic compound below.

(A) alcohol
(B) aldehyde
(C) carboxylic acid
(D) ester
(E) ether

46.

$$H-O-\overset{\overset{O}{\|}}{C}-\overset{\overset{O}{\|}}{C}-O-H$$

47.

$$H-\overset{\overset{H}{|}}{\underset{\underset{H}{|}}{C}}-\overset{\overset{H}{|}}{\underset{\underset{H}{|}}{C}}-O-H$$

48.

$$H-\overset{\overset{H}{|}}{\underset{\underset{H}{|}}{C}}-\overset{\overset{H}{|}}{\underset{\underset{H}{|}}{C}}-O-\overset{\overset{H}{|}}{\underset{\underset{H}{|}}{C}}-\overset{\overset{H}{|}}{\underset{\underset{H}{|}}{C}}-H$$

49.

$$H-\overset{\overset{H}{|}}{\underset{\underset{H}{|}}{C}}-\overset{\overset{}{}}{\underset{\underset{O}{\|}}{C}}-H$$

50.

$$H-\overset{\overset{H}{|}}{\underset{\underset{H}{|}}{C}}-\overset{\overset{}{}}{\underset{\underset{O}{\|}}{C}}-O-C_8H_{17}$$

Day 10

STOP. Correct your answers and note how many correct **points**

Answer: Quick Check

1. A	2. A	3. B	4. A	5. C	6. C	7. C	8. A	9. E	10. D
11. A	12. A	13. E	14. A	15. D	16. C	17. B	18. B	19. A	20. E
21. B	22. B	23. B	24. A	25. E	26. A	27. C	28. E	29. B	30. C
31. B	32. E	33. E	34. C	35. B	36. C	37. B	38. D	39. D	40. D
41. C	42. D	43. B	44. D	45. B	46. C	47. A	48. E	49. B	50. D

Answers and Explanations

Questions 1 through 5: Le Chatelier's Principle, equilibrium reactions

1. **A**   *Note:* N_2O in the equation is a reactant.
   Note: To reestablish equilibrium from adding more reactant, the added reactant must be consumed.
   Relate: Speeding up in the forward direction (***shift to the right***) allow the reaction to consume the added reactant.

2. **A**   *Note:* O_2 in the equation is a product
   Note: To reestablish equilibrium from removal of a product, the reaction will make more of that product.
   Relate: Speeding up in the forward direction (***shift to the right***) allows the reaction to produce more of the removed product.

3. **B**   *Note:*   A decrease in volume means pressure is increased on the reaction.
   Recall: To reestablish equilibrium from a pressure increase, more of the substances on the side that has fewer total moles must be produced.
   Note: In the equation, the reactant side has fewer total moles (2)
   Relate: A decrease in volume speeds up the reverse reaction (***shift to the left***) in order to produce more N_2O

4. **A**   *Note:*   The reaction has + ΔH value. This means :
   Forward reaction is endothermic. Heat is absorbed as a reactant.
   Reverse reaction is exothermic.   Heat is released as a product
   $$N_2O_2 \quad + \quad 163\ KJ \ <======> \ 2N_2 + O_2$$

   Recall: To reestablish equilibrium from increased temperature, endothermic (forward) reaction is favored (***Shift to the right***) so the added heat can be consumed.

5. **C**   *Recall:* Addition of a catalyst lowers the activation energies for both the forward and reverse reactions. As a result, both the forward and reverse reactions are increased equally, and there is ***no shift in either direction.***.

Questions 6 through 8: Electron configuration, atomic structure

6. **C**   *Recall:*   The electron configuration of a paramagnetic element must have a sublevel with at least one unpaired e-

   Note: The configuration $1s^2$ $2s^2$ $2p^6$ $3s^2$ $3p^4$

   ↑↓   ↑↓   ↑↓ ↑↓ ↑↓   ↑↓   ↑↓ ↑ ↑

   has **two unpaired** electrons in the 3p sublevel.

7. **D**   *Note:*   Both potassium ion (K+) and chlorine ion (Cl-) have 18 e- . Both have the same configuration $1s^2 2s^2 2p^6 3s^2 3p^6$, which is the same as that of the noble gas element closest to them (Ar)

8. **A**   *Note:*   The atom of this element (Ne) has only 2 electron shells. All of the others have 3 or more shells.

9. **E**   **Solution – Beer's Law relationship**

   Recall: According to Beer's law, absorbency is directly proportional to the concentration of a solution.

   Note: To measure absorbance, a spectrometer is needed. An appropriate reagent must be a colored solution

   Determine: $Ni(NO_3)_2$, which contains a transition metal, is the only colored solution listed.

10. **D**   **Solubility Guideline, precipitate**

   Note: A Precipitate is formed when an insoluble compound is formed from mixing two solutions.

   Note: Mixing NaCl with $Pb(NO_3)_2$ produces **$PbCl_2(s)$**.

   Recall solubility guidelines: Chloride ion is mostly soluble, EXCEPT when it combines with **Pb^{2+}**, Ag^+, or Hg^{2+}

11. A **Boiling point–concentration relationship, van't Hoff factor**

Recall: The degree of boiling point elevation is related to the number of moles of ions in the solution. Solution with the greatest number of moles of ions will have the highest boiling point.

Note: Based on information given, the number of moles of ions in each solution can be calculated using the equation:

Moles of ion = Molarity x Volume x i (van't Hoff factor)

(A) **Moles in KNO_3** = **0.50** x **.250** x **2 ions = .250 moles**

(B) Moles in $Al(NO_3)_3$ = 0.10 x .400 x 4 ions = .160 moles

(C) Moles in NH_4NO_3 = 0.20 x .500 x 2 ions = .200 moles

(D) Moles $AgNO_3$ = 0.30 x .300 x 2 ions = .180 moles

(E) Moles in $Ni(NO_3)_2$ = 0.10 x .200 x 3 ions = .060 moles

Note: Choice A solution has the highest total moles of ions, therefore, highest boiling point

12. A **Ion concentration in solution**

Note: Highest NO_3^- concentration can be calculated for each solution using the equation:

$$[NO_3^{-v}] = M \text{ x moles of } NO_{3-} \text{ ions}$$

(A) **$[NO_3^-]$ in KNO_3** = **0.50** x **1** = **. 50 M**

(B) $[NO_3^-]$ in $Al(NO_3)_3$ = 0.10 x 3 = . 30 M

(C) $[NO_3^-]$ in NH_4NO_3 = 0.20 x 1 = . 20 M

(D) $[NO_3^-]$ in $AgNO_3$ = 0.30 x 1 = . 30 M

(E) $[NO_3^-]$ in $Ni(NO_3)_2$ = 0.10 x 2 = . 20 M

Note: Choice A has highest $[NO_3^-]$

Day 10: Answers and Explanations

13. E **Factors affecting molecular shape**

Note: Shape of AB_2 molecule can be determined if dipole moments of the molecule are known.

If dipole moments cancel out:

B ------- A-------B   **The molecule is linear and nonpolar**

If dipole moments add (net dipole)

A

B   B   **The molecule is bent and polar**

Note: None of the other properties (alone) will be enough to determine the shape of the molecule

14. A **Nuclear decay, emission particles**

Note: The difference between $^{19}_{8}O$ and $^{19}_{9}F$ is $^{0}_{-1}e$ (beta)

Note: Since this is a decay, the answer is beta emission, NOT, electron capture

15. D **Interpreting potential energy diagram**

Note: To determine the incorrect statement, consider each choice and eliminate those that are true of the energy diagram.

Note: **Eliminate Choice A.** True b/c product energy is higher than reactant's

Eliminate Choice B. True b/c Points 1 and 3 represent intermediates

Eliminate Choice C . True b/c the transitional point is measured at the activated complex

Eliminate Choice E. True b/c increasing energy at point 2 will result in a longer reaction pathway, hence, slower rate.

Note: **Choice D is false:** Equilibrium concentration of products depends on the initial concentration of reactants and final concentration of products only.
Therefore, raising energy of intermediate 3 will not affect the equilibrium concentration of the product

16. **C** **Energy change and pressure calculation, thermodynamic**

Recall : Recognize that based on information given, change in energy, ΔE , can be calculated using the First Law of thermodynamics equation below.

$\Delta E = q + w$ *Note:* $w = -(P_{ext} \times \Delta V)$

Rewrite equation, substitute factors into equation, and solve

$\Delta E = q - (P_{ext} \times \Delta V)$ $101.32\ J \cdot L^{-1} \cdot atm^{-1}$

$\Delta E = 505.64\ J - (2.0\ atm \times 1\ L)$ $101.32\ J \cdot L^{-1} \cdot atm^{-1}$

$\Delta E = 505.64\ J - 202.64\ J =$ **303.00 J**

17. **C** **Interpreting reaction equation**

Note: In the reaction, NH_4^+ has 1 more H^+ (proton) than NH_3

Recall: A species in a reaction with one more H^+ than another is the conjugate acid

Note: None of the other choices is true or can be inferred about the reaction based on just the equation given

18. **B** **Molecular shapes-hybridization relationship**

Recall the relationship between electron pairs, electron geometry and hybridization:

Electron pairs	electron geometry	hybridization
2	*linear*	*sp*
3	**trigonal planer**	$\textbf{\textit{sp}}^{\textbf{2}}$
4	tetrahedral	sp^3
5	trigonal bipyramidal	$sp^3 d$
6	octahedral	$sp^3 d^2$

19. **A** **Interpreting Gibb's free energy**

Recall: Free energy $\Delta G = \Delta H - T\Delta S$

Note: Since ΔH is + and ΔS is - as stated in the question, $\Delta G = +\Delta H + T\Delta S = +\Delta G$ (nonspontaneous) regardless of temperature (T)

20. E   Common-ion effect, solubility

Note: Silver hydroxide (AgOH) is a base.

Relate: Its solubility will be hindered the most when placed in a solution with the highest OH- concentration (highest pH)

21. B   Quantum numbers interpretation

Note: The set of numbers listed in the choices represents

n, l, m_l, and m_s, respectively

Recall what each quantum number represents:

$$n = \text{shells} \qquad n \text{ value range:} \quad 1 \text{ to } 7$$
$$l = \text{subshells} \qquad l \text{ value range:} \quad 0 \text{ to } (n-1)$$
$$m_l = \text{orbitals} \qquad m_l \text{ value range:} \quad -l \text{ to } +l$$
$$m_s = \text{spin} \qquad m_s \text{ values:} \quad -\tfrac{1}{2} \text{ or } +\tfrac{1}{2}$$

Note: Based on information above, m_l value should never be greater than l

Note: In Choice B, the m_l value (1) is greater than the l value (0). Therefore, B has the impossible set of quantum numbers.

22. B   Percent yield calculation, equation writing

Step 1: Write a balanced equation for the reaction described.

$$4CH_4 + F_2 \text{ --------> } 2CH_3CH_2F + 3H_2$$

Step 2: Determine theoretical yield of 1-fluoroethane from 96-g CH_4.

$$96 \text{ g } CH_4 \times \frac{1 \text{ mol } CH_4}{16 \text{ g } CH_4} \times \frac{2 \text{ mol } CH_3CH_2F}{4 \text{ mol } CH_4} \times \frac{48 \text{ g } CH_3CH_2F}{1 \text{ mol } CH_3CH_2F} = 144 \text{ g } CH_3CH_2F$$

Step 3: Calculate percent yield

$$\% \text{ yield} = \frac{\text{actual yield}}{\text{theoretical yield}} \times 100$$

$$\% \text{ yield} = \frac{96}{144} = \frac{2}{3} \times 100 = \mathbf{66\%}$$

23. B   Total pressure–mole fraction relationship

Recognize that based on information given, total pressure (P_{total}) can be calculated using mole fraction equation

$$P_{total} = X_A P_A + X_B P_B$$

X = mole fraction
P = partial pressure

Rewrite equation, substitute factors from question, and solve.

$$P_{total} = \left(\frac{mole\ of\ A}{total\ moles} \right) P_A + \left(\frac{mole\ of\ B}{total\ moles} \right) P_B$$

$$P_{total} = \left(\frac{1.50}{5.0} \right) 75\ mm\ Hg + \left(\frac{3.50}{5.0} \right) 25\ mm\ Hg$$

$$P_{total} = \textbf{40.0 mm Hg}$$

24. A   Solution properties

Note: When solute particles (in this question, potassium and chloride ions) are present in water, they interact and interfere with certain physical and chemical properties of water.

Recall: The present of solute in water allows the solution to have: **Higher boiling point, lower freezing point, and lower vapor pressure**

25. E   Percent composition

Step 1:   Write the correct formula for calcium hydroxide: $Ca(OH)_2$

Step 2:   Determine molar mass of $Ca(OH)_2$

Molar mass = 1 Ca + 2 O + 2H

Molar mass = 1(40) + 2(16) + 2(1) = 74 g/mol $Ca(OH)_2$

Step 3:   Determine mass of Oxygen in 148 g $Ca(OH)_2$

$$Mass\ of\ O = 148\ g\ Ca(OH)_2 \times \frac{32\ g\ O}{74\ g\ Ca(OH)_2} = \textbf{64 g O}$$

26. A **Equilibrium expression**

$$Recall: \quad k_{eq} = \frac{[Products]}{[Reactants]} = \frac{[CO_2]^2}{[CO]^2}$$

Note: Solids are not included in the equilibrium expression because they have constant concentrations

The exponents are the coefficients of the substances in the balanced equation.

27. C **Understanding Titration process**

Note: **Choice C** is the only correct statement. This statement will be true for all acid-base titration graphs.

Note: **Choice A** is false because the equivalent point of weak acid – strong base titration occurs at pH above 7.

Choice B is false because pH does not depends on indicator

Choice D is false because a basic salt will be produced, resulting in a sharp increase in pH

Choice E is false because $[H^+]$ is equal to the ionization constant, K_a, at the half-equivalence point; NOT at the equivalence point.

28. E **Phase change – Energy – Entropy – Free energy relationship**

Note the followings about the phase change of water given.

$$H_2O(g) \quad \text{-------} > \quad H_2O(l)$$

Gas to liquid = **Exothermic** (heat is released) ΔH = -

Gas to liquid = **Entropy decreases** (less disorder) ΔS = -

Gas to liquid = **Spontaneously** (occurs by itself ΔG = -
at room temp)

29. B   Half-reaction interpretation

Note the followings about the half-reaction equation:

$$AuCl_4^- + 3e^- \text{--------} > Au + 4Cl^-$$

It represents reduction as written (e- is a reactant).

Gold changes from +3 to 0 (a reduction of oxidation state)

Recall: Reduction occurs at cathode   **Choice B**

Note: Chloride ion does not change its oxidation state. (Eliminate D & E)

30. C   Coulombs law, factor-labeling

Recognize that based on information given, grams of gold produced can be calculated by setting up factor-labeling. When all units are crossed out, what's left is the correct setup.

$$\frac{4.0\ C}{s} \times \frac{30\ min}{1} \times \frac{60\ s}{1\ min} \times \frac{1\ mol\ e^-}{96,500\ C} \times \frac{1\ mol\ Au}{3\ mol\ e^-} \times \frac{197\ g\ Au}{1\ mol\ Au}$$

$$\frac{4.0\ \cancel{C}}{\cancel{s}} \times \frac{30\ \cancel{min}}{1} \times \frac{60\ \cancel{s}}{\cancel{1\ min}} \times \frac{\cancel{1\ mol\ e^-}}{96,500\ \cancel{C}} \times \frac{\cancel{1\ mol\ Au}}{3\ \cancel{mol\ e^-}} \times \frac{197\ g\ Au}{\cancel{1\ mol\ Au}}$$

31. C   Atomic radius – nuclear charge relationship, ionic size comparison

Recall: The size (radius) of atoms depends on factors such as:
Number of electron shells
Number of electrons
Number of protons (nuclear charge)

Note: All of the ions listed are isoelectronic, meaning they have the same number of electrons (10), therefore, same number of electron shells.

Relate: The difference in size of these ions depends mostly on their nuclear charges. The greater the nuclear charge, the smaller the radius. Therefore:

Order of increasing size = Order of decreasing nuclear charge

Smallest radius : Mg^{2+} (+12 nuclear charge)

F^- (+9 nuclear charge)

Largest radius : O^{2-} (+8 nuclear charge)

32. E Completing equation, Solubility rules, precipitate

Recall: Precipitate is formed when an insoluble compound is formed from mixing two solutions.

Determine product for each reaction, then use solubility rules to determine which product is insoluble

(I) HBr + $Ca(OH)_2$ -----> H_2O + $CaBr_2$
(soluble)

(II) $Pb(NO_3)_2$ + LiI ------> $LiNO_3$ + PbI_2
(soluble)   *(insoluble)*

(III) $(NH_4)_3PO_4$ + $MgCl_2$ ----> NH_4Cl + $Mg_3(PO_4)_2$
(soluble)   *(insoluble)*

Note: Both II and III produce insoluble (precipitate) products

33. E Le Chatelier's Principle

Note: All five reactions involve gaseous reactants and products.

Recall: Equilibrium concentration of substances in a gaseous reaction WILL NOT change when the total moles of reactants and products are equal.

Note: Reaction for Choice E is the only one listed with total moles of reactants and products being equal (3 moles on each side).

34. C Equation writing, mass – mole calculation in equation

Step 1: Write a correct balanced equation for the reaction described.
$4Al$ + $3O_2$ -------> $2Al_2O_3$

Step 2: Use factor- labeling to solve by utilizing mole ratio in equation

$$\text{mole of } O_2 = 25.5 \text{ g } Al_2O_3 \times \frac{1 \text{ mol } Al_2O_3}{102 \text{ g } Al_2O_3} \times \frac{3 \text{ mol } O_2}{2 \text{ mol } Al_2O_3}$$

mole of O_2 = **0.375 mol**

35. **B** **Oxidation of acids, acid formulas, acid strength**

Note: When an oxyacid (acid with oxygen) is oxidized, the number of oxygen of the acid increases. The new acid formed is stronger.

Note: When an oxyacid has the maximum number of oxygen that it could have, that acid can't be oxidized any further.
Ex: H_2SO_3 can be oxidized to form H_2SO_4
But
H_2SO_4 can't be oxidized any further.

Note: Of all the acids listed, only HNO_2 (a weaker acid) can be oxidized further (to HNO_3, a stronger acid)

-36. **C** **Enthalpy change/Energy change in equations, thermodynamics**
Recognize that based on information given, the equation
$$\Delta H = \Delta E + P\Delta V \quad \text{(law of thermodynamic)}$$
must be considered in order to correctly determine the reaction in which ΔH and ΔE are nearly equal.

Note: Based on the equation, ΔH and ΔE will be equal only when $P\Delta V$ is equal to zero. This will be the case if ΔV (change in volume) of the system is zero.

Relate: A reaction will have ΔV equal to zero if there are no gaseous substances involve in the reaction.

Note: Choice C is the only reaction of those listed in which there no gaseous substances are involved.

37. **B** **Comparing properties of organic compounds, isomers**
Recognize that one way to choose the correct statement about the boiling points of these two substances is to correctly draw and compare their structures and formulas.

$$C_4H_{10}O$$
diethyl ether

$$C_4H_{10}O$$
1-butanol

Note: Based on the structures and formulas, these two substances are isomers. (Eliminate Choice E)

Note: Based on the structures, diethyl ether is nonpolar (symmetrical) while 1- butanol is polar (asymmetrical).

Recall: Polar substances have higher boiling point than nonpolar.

---

38. D   **Molar mass – rate relationship, comparing rate of gases**

Recall: Rate of effusion of gases is related to their molar masses (M) according to the equation below:

$$\frac{V_1}{V_2} = \sqrt{\frac{M_2}{M_1}}$$

·*Note:* The mass of H_2 = 2 g

Relate: A gas that travels at $^1/_3$ the speed of H_2 must have a molar mass that is 9 times as great as the molar mass of H_2

Note: H_2O has a molar mass of 18 g (9 times as great as 2 g)

39. C   **Bond angle-Molecular shape relationship**

Note that drawing the Lewis diagram for the nitrate ion is one way of determining its shape, as well as the N – O bond angle.

Determine number of electrons available for bonding in NO_3^- , and then draw the Lewis structure for NO_3-

N = 1(5) = 5 e-

O = 3 (6) = 18 e-

-1 =   1 e-

Total e- = 24 e-

Note: The shape of NO_3^- is trigonal planer. Bond angles of this shape is always 120°

40. D   **Titration data interpretation, sources of errors**

Note: Only the NaOH volume for the first sample is, in terms of titration, significantly different from the rest.

Note: The only reasonable explanations is that the pipet that was used to transfer the acetic acid in the first sample was not rinsed with the acid.

Note: All other errors listed will not affect the volume of the titrant (NaOH)

---

41. C   Entropy Change calculation

Step 1: Recall entropy change, ΔS°, equation

$$\Delta S^\circ = \sum {}^\circ S \text{ products} \quad - \sum {}^\circ S \text{ reactants}$$

Step 2: Substitute numbers from table into equation. Be sure to take number of moles of substances in the balanced equation into account .

$$\textbf{3}\,Mg \;+\; Al_2O_3 \qquad \textbf{2}\,Al(s) \;+\; \textbf{3}\,MgO$$

$$\Delta S^\circ = \left[\; \textbf{3}\,(33.0) + 51.0 \right] - \left[\; \textbf{2}\,(28.0) + \textbf{3}\,(27.0) \right]$$

$$\Delta S^\circ = \qquad 150 \qquad - \qquad\qquad 137 \quad = \textbf{13.0 J/(mole.K)}$$

42. D   Flame test

Recall your flame test colors: Lithium always red

43. B   Percent abundance of isotopes, Atomic mass calculation

Note: Since the atomic mass (63.55) is closer to the mass of ^{63}Cu, the percent of ^{63}Cu will be greater than that of ^{65}Cu

Eliminate choice C and D (these choices reflect greater % of ^{65}Cu)

Note: One way to quickly solve this problem is to set up the problem as follows:

Let x = decimal fraction of percent of ^{63}Cu

then $1 - x$ = decimal fraction of percent of ^{65}Cu

Recall: Atomic mass is the sum of the products of decimal fraction x mass number of the isotopes

$$63(x) \;+\; 65(1-x) \;=\; 63.55$$
$$63x \;+\; 65 - 65x \;=\; 63.55$$
$$2x \;=\; 1.45$$
$$x \;=\; .73 \approx \textbf{70\% of } {}^{63}Cu$$

44. D **Equilibrium expression calculation, dissociation**

Recognize that K_a can be determined from equilibrium expression.

Step 1: Write equation for the dissociation of $HC_2H_3O_2(aq)$

$$HC_2H_3O_2 \text{ (aq)} <=====> H^+ \text{(aq)} + C_2H_3O_2^- \text{ (aq)}$$

Step 2: Write equilibrium expression for above equation

$$K_a = \frac{[H^+]\,[C_2H_3O_2^-]}{[HC_2H_3O_2]}$$

Step 3: Determine concentrations:

$[H^+] = $ -log pH $ = $ -log(2) $ = $ .01 M

$[C_2H_3O\text{-}] = [H^+] = $ .01 M   (based on mole ratio of
$\quad\quad\quad\quad\quad\quad\quad\quad\quad$ **1**H^+ : **1**$C_2H_3O_2^-$)

$[HC_2H_3O] = $ 1.0 M (concentration of a weak acid like
$\quad\quad\quad\quad\quad\quad\quad\quad$ acetic stays nearly unchanged b/c
$\quad\quad\quad\quad\quad\quad\quad\quad$ weak acids dissociate very slightly)

Step 4: Substitute [ ] into equation and solve for Ka

$$K_a = \frac{(0.01)\,(0.01)}{1.0} = .0001 = \mathbf{1.0 \times 10^{-4}}$$

45. B   **Percent calculation**

$$\% \text{ dissociation} = \frac{[Part]}{[whole]} \times 100$$

$$\% \text{ dissociation} = \frac{.01 \text{ M}}{1.0 \text{ M}} \times 100 = \mathbf{1.0\,\%}$$

Questions 46 through 50: Organic functional groups
Recall the functional group associated with each class of
organic compound listed as choices

	class	functional group
(A)	alcohol	- OH
(B)	aldehyde	$\overset{O}{\overset{\|\|}{C}} - H$
(C)	carboxylic acid	$\overset{O}{\overset{\|\|}{C}} - OH$
(D)	ester	$- \overset{O}{\overset{\|\|}{C}} - O -$
(E)	ether	$- O -$

46. **C**   *Note:*   Structure given contains a *carboxylic acid* functional group

47. **A**   *Note:*   Structure given contains an *alcohol* functional group

48. **E**   *Note:*   Structure given contains an *ether* functional group

49. **B**   *Note:*   Structure given contains an *aldehyde* functional group

50. **D**   *Note:*   Structure given contains an *ester* functional group

START: Answer all questions on this day before stopping.

Note: You may use a calculator for questions on this day.
You may use any of the reference material provided on pg 337-340

CLEARLY SHOW THE METHOD USED AND THE STEPS INVOLVED IN ARRIVING AT YOUR ANSWERS. It is to your advantage to do this, since you may obtain partial credit if you do and you will receive little or no credit if you do not. Attention should be paid to significant figures.

---

1.   **(10 points)**

Hypochlorous acid, HOCl, is a weak acid that ionizes in water, as represented by the equation below:

$$HOCl(aq) \quad <====> \quad H^+(aq) \quad + \quad OCl^-(aq)$$

$$K_a = 2.9 \times 10^{-8}$$

(a) Calculate the $[H^+]$ in a HOCl solution that has a pH of 5.24.

(b) Using information provided above:

   (i)   Write the equilibrium expression (K_a) for the ionization of HOCl in   water.

   (ii) Calculate the concentration of HOCl(aq) in a HOCl solution that has $[H^+]$ equal to 2.4×10^{-5} M.

(c) A solution of $Ba(OH)_2$ is titrated into a solution of HOCl.

   (i) Calculate the volume of 0.200 M $Ba(OH)_2(aq)$ needed to reach the equivalence point when titrated into a 75.0 mL sample of 0.150 M HOCl(aq).

   (ii) Write the equilibrium expression, K_b, for the titration reaction that occurs.

   (iii) Calculate K_b of OCl^-

   (iv) Calculate the pH at the equivalence point.

(d) $HClO_3$ is a stronger acid than HOCl. Account for this fact in terms of molecular structure.

                                        147

2.   **(10 points)**
Electrical current is passed through a 1.0*M* solution of HCl(*aq*) by means
of two nonreactive electrodes immersed into the solution, with the
electrodes connected to opposing terminals of a voltage source.

(a) (i) Sketch an electrolytic diagram to show process described above.
   (ii) Labels the anode and cathode on your diagram
   (iii) Write the half-reaction occurring at each electrode on your diagram
   (iv) Indicate direction of electron flow on your diagram.

(b) 4.5 amperes of current is applied to the reaction for 20 minutes.

   i) How many Coulombs pass through the cell during that time?

   ii) How many moles of electrons pass through the cell during that
      time ?

   iii) If the system is at STP, how much volume of hydrogen gas is
       produced during that time?

(c) What happens to the pH of the solution as current passes through it
   within the cell?

Day 11 Question 2: Space for Work and Answers

1. Hypochlorous acid, HOCl, is a weak acid that ionizes in water, as shown in the equation below

$$HOCl(aq) \quad <====> \quad H^+(aq) \quad + \quad OCl^-(aq)$$
$$K_a = 2.9 \times 10^{-8}$$

(a) Calculate the $[H^+]$ in a HOCl solution that has a pH of 5.24.

   Recall: pH $= -\log [H^+]$

$[H^+] = 10^{-pH}$ $[H^+] = 10^{-5.24} = 5.75 \times 10^{-6}$	**1 point** is earned for correctly calculating the $[H^+]$

(b) Using information provided above:

   (i) Write the equilibrium expression (K_a) for the ionization of HOCl in water.

   Recall: $K_a = \dfrac{[Products]}{[Reactants]}$

$K_a = \dfrac{[H^+][OCl^-]}{[HOCl]}$	**1 point** is earned for the correct equilibrium expression

   (ii) Calculate the concentration of HOCl(*aq*) in a HOCl solution that has $[H^+]$ equal to 2.4×10^{-5} M.

   Note: $[OCl^-] = [H^+]$ because they are at 1 : 1 ratio in the equation.

$[HOCl] = \dfrac{[H^+][OCl^-]}{K_a}$ $[HOCl] = \dfrac{(2.4 \times 10^{-5} \text{ M})(2.4 \times 10^{-5})}{2.9 \times 10^{-8}}$ $[HOCl] = = 2.0 \times 10^{-2}$ M	**1 point** is earned for the correct setup to calculate [HOCl] **1 point** is earned for [HOCl] that is consistent with the setup

(c) A solution of $Ba(OH)_2$ is titrated into a solution of HOCl.

(i) Calculate the volume of 0.200 M $Ba(OH)_2(aq)$ needed to reach the equivalence point when titrated into a 75.0 mL sample of 0.150 M $HOCl(aq)$.

Recall: (moles of OH^-)(M_b) (V_b) = (moles of H^+) (M_a) (V_a)

Note: $Ba(OH)_2$ contains 2 moles of OH^-
             HOCl   contains 1 mole of H^+

Substitute values from question into equation and solve for volume of $Ba(OH)_2$ (V_b)
 	
(moles of OH^-)(M_b) (V_b) = (moles of H^+) (M_a) (V_a)
 	
    (2) (0.200 M) V_b = (1) (0.150 M) (0.075 L)
 	
          V_b =   **0.0281 L $Ba(OH)_2$**
	1 point is earned for the correct volume

(ii) Write the equilibrium expression, K_b, for the titration reaction that occurs.

    Note: $OCl^- + H_2O ------ > HOCl + OH^-$

$$K_b = \frac{[HOCl]\ [OH^-]}{[OCl^-]}$$	**1 point** is earned for the correct expression

(iii) Calculate k_b of OCl^-

    Recall:

    $K_w = K_b \times k_a$

$$K_b = \frac{K_w}{K_a} = \frac{1.0 \times 10^{-14}}{2.9 \times 10^{-8}} = \mathbf{3.4 \times 10^{-7}}$$	**1 point** is earned for the correct K_b

(iv) Calculate the pH at the equivalence point.

> *Note:* Once [OH⁻] is known, pH can be calculated.

> *Note:* [OH⁻] can be calculated by substituting values from the question and calculations (i – iii) into the k_b equation

Calculate [OCl⁻]	**1 point** is earned for setup that leads to calculation of [OH⁻] or [H⁺]
$$[OCl^-] = \frac{\text{moles of OCl}^-}{\text{Total volume}} = \frac{\text{Molarity} \times \text{Volume}}{(V_a + V_b)}$$	
$$[OCl^-] = \frac{(0.150 \text{ mol·L}^{-1})(0.075 \text{ L})}{(0.075 \text{ L} + 0.0281 \text{ L})} = 0.109 \text{ M}$$	
Determine concentrations	
$\quad$ [OH⁻] = X	
$\quad$ [HOCl] = X because they at a 1 : 1 ratio	
Substitute [ ] into k_b expression and solve for X)	
$$K_b = \frac{[HOCl][OH^-]}{[OCl^-]}$$	
$$3.4 \times 10^{-7} = \frac{X^2}{0.100}$$	
$$1.93 \times 10^{-4} = X = [OH^-]$$	
Calculate pOH	**1 point** is earned for correctly calculating the pH
$\text{pOH} = -\log[OH^-] = -\log(1.93 \times 10^{-4}) = 3.72$	
Calculate pH	
$\mathbf{pH} = 14 - \text{pOH} = 14 - 3.71 = \mathbf{10.28}$	

(d) $HClO_3$ is a stronger acid than HOCl. Account for this fact in terms of molecular structure.

> *Note:* In both HOCl and $HClO_3$, H – O bond must be broken for the acids to ionize.
>
> The weaker the H – O bond, the easier it is for the acid to ionize, and the stronger the acid.

$HClO_3$ is a stronger acid than HOCl because the H – O bond in $HClO_3$ is weaker than the H – O bond in HOCl. This is due to the fact that the additional O atoms that are bonded to the central Cl atom in $HClO_3$ weakens its H – O bond.	**1 point** is earned for the correct explanation.

2. Electrical current is passed through a 1.0M solution of HCl(aq) by means of two nonreactive electrodes immersed into the solution, with the electrodes connected to opposing terminals of a voltage source.
(8 points)
(a) (i) Sketch and label the diagram of the electrolytic cell, (ii) labels for anode and cathode, (iii) write half- reaction occurring at each electrode, and (iv) direction of electron flow.

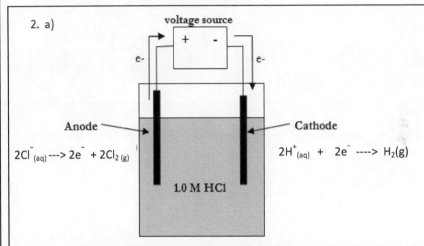

2. a)

voltage source

e-   e-

Anode

$2Cl^-_{(aq)} \text{---}> 2e^- + 2Cl_{2\,(g)}$

Cathode

$2H^+_{(aq)} + 2e^- \text{----}> H_2(g)$

1.0 M HCl

Your diagram will vary greatly from the one above. Points are based on the followings:

(i) A correctly sketched diagram must have: **one cell (beaker), a voltage source, two bars connected to the positive and negative ends of the voltage source and submerged in HCl solution.**	**1 point** for a correct diagram
(ii) Metal bar connected to + is labeled **"Anode"** and Metal bar connected to – is labeled **"Cathode"**	**1 point** for correctly labeled anode and cathode
(iii) Half-reaction at + electrode: $2Cl^-(aq) \text{--}> 2e^- + 2Cl_2(g)$ and Half-reaction at - electrode $2H^+(aq) + 2e^- \text{--}> H_2(g)$	**1 point** for correct and balanced half-reactions at + and - electrodes
(iv) **Direction of e$^-$** is shown from bar at + to bar at –	**1 point** for correct direction of e-

(b) 4.5 amperes of current is applied to the reaction for 20 minutes.

(i) How many Coulombs pass through the cell during that time?

Note: 4.5 amp $= 4.5$ coulomb/sec (1 amp = 1 coulomb/sec)

20 minutes $= 1.2 \times 10^3$ sec

Note: $I = \dfrac{q}{t}$ (see Reference Materials pg 340)

Charge (q) $=$ time (t) $\times$ current (I) Charge (q) $= 1.2 \times 10^3$ sec $\times \dfrac{4.5 \text{ coulombs}}{\text{sec}}$ Charge (q) $= \mathbf{5.4 \times 10^3}$ **coulombs**	**1 point** is earned for the correct charge

(ii) How many moles of electrons pass through the cell during that time?

Note: 1 mole of e - $= 96500$ coulombs (Faraday's constant)

moles of e⁻ $=$ charge $\times$ Faraday's constant moles of e⁻ $= 5.4 \times 10^3$ coulombs $\times \dfrac{1 \text{ mole e}^-}{96500 \text{ coulombs}}$ moles of e⁻ $= \mathbf{5.6 \times 10^{-2}}$ **mol**	**1 point** is earned for correct moles of e⁻

iii) If the system is at STP, how much volume of hydrogen gas is produced during that time?

Recall: 1 mole of gas $= 22.4$ L at STP

Determine moles of H_2 using mole proportion in the half-reaction equation: $\quad 2H^+ + 2e^- \text{------}> H_2$ 5.6×10^{-2} mol e- $\times \dfrac{1 \text{ mole } H_2}{2 \text{ moles e}^-} = \mathbf{0.028 \text{ moles } H_2}$	**1 point** is earned for calculating moles of H_2
Calculate volume of H_2 Volume of H_2 $=$ moles of H_2 $\times$ 22.4 L/mol Volume of H_2 $= 0.028$ mol $\times$ 22.4 L/mol $= \mathbf{0.627 \text{ L}}$	**1 point** is earned for correct volume of H_2

(c) What happens to the pH of the HCl solution as current passes through it within the cell? Justify your response with explanation.

Recall: pH is related to H^+ concentration of a solution.

Note: As current passes through the solution, H^+ ion of the HCl solution is converted to H_2.
As a result, $[H^+]$ decreases.

pH increases	**1 point** is earned for indicating that pH increases
pH increases because **the H^+ concentration decreases as the electrolytic processes is taking place.** A decrease in H^+ resulted in an increase in pH	**1 point** is earned for explanation that is consistent with change in pH indicated.

159

START: Answer all questions on this day before stopping.

Note: NO CALCULATORS should be used for questions on this day.
You may use any of the Reference Materials provided on pg 337-340

---

1. For each of the following three reactions, write a balanced equation for the reaction in part (i) and answer the question about the reaction in part (ii). In part (i), coefficients should be in terms of lowest whole numbers. Assume that solutions are aqueous unless otherwise indicated. Represent substances in solutions as ions if the substances are extensively ionized. Omit formulas for any ions or molecules that are unchanged by the reaction.
(15 points)

(a) Dinitrogen oxide is mixed with water?

(i) Balanced equation:

(ii) Would the pH of the solution that is produced less than 7, equal to 7, or greater than 7. Explain your answer.

_____

_____

_____

(b) Carbon dioxide gas is heated in the presence of solid magnesium oxide.

(i) Balanced equation:

(ii) How many grams of magnesium oxide must completely react with 11 grams of the carbon dioxide?

_____

_____

_____

(c) Small pieces of aluminum are added to a solution of copper(II) sulfate.

(i) Balanced equation:

(ii) Write the correct oxidation and reduction-half equations for the reaction that occurs.

_____

_____

_____

Day 12: Continue

Your responses to question 2 will be scored on the basis of the accuracy and relevance of the information cited. Explanations should be clear and well organized. Examples and equations may be included in your responses where appropriate. Specific answers are preferable to broad, diffuse responses. **(8 points)**

2. Use your knowledge of redox and electrochemistry to answer the following questions.

(a) What is the function of a salt bridge in a galvanic cell, and why is it necessary in order for the cell to work?

(b) Explain why, when a piece of nickel is placed in hydrochloric acid, a reaction occurs, but when a piece of copper wire is placed in hydrchloric acid, no reaction occurs.

(c) Cu^{2+} + $Pb(s)$ -----> $Cu(s)$ + Pb^{2+}

(i) Give the standard cell potential for the reaction above.

(ii) What happens to the cell potential in (i) when $[Pb^{2+}]$ is increased?

(iii) What is the value of $\Delta G°$ for the cell?

Day 12

STOP. Correct your answers and note how many correct **points**

Day 12 Question 2: Space for Work and Answers

Day 12: Answers and Scoring Guidelines

(see important scoring guideline information on on pg i)

---

1.   **(15 points)**

(a) Dinitrogen oxide is mixed with water?

> *Recall:* Nonmetal oxide combines with water to produce an acid.

> *Note:* The acid (HNO_3) formed is left in an ionized form because nitric acid is a strong acid. Strong acids ionize completely.

(i) Balanced equation	**1 point** is earned for correct reactants
N_2O_5 + H_2O -------> $2H^+$ + $2NO_3^-$ *nonmetal oxide* *water* *acid*	**2 points are** earned for correct products **1 point** is earned for correctly balancing the equation

(ii) Would the pH of the solution that is produced less than 7, equal to 7, or greater than 7. Explain your answer.

The pH would be less than 7 because an acidic solution is formed.	**1 point** is earned for the correct pH with explanation

(b) Carbon dioxide gas is heated in the presence of solid magnesium oxide.

> *Note:* This is a combination reaction in which a salt is formed from a basic and an acid anhydrides.

(i) Balanced equation	**1 point** is earned for correct reactants
CO_2 + MgO ------> $MgCO_3$ *Basic anhydride* *Acid anhydride* *Salt*	**2 points are** earned for correct products **1 point** is earned for correctly balancing the equation

164   Copyright © 2012 E3 Scholastic Publishing. All Rights Reserved

(ii) How many grams of magnesium oxide must completely react with 11 grams of the carbon dioxide?

Determine moles of CO_2 in 11 g. 11 g CO_2 x $\dfrac{1 \text{ mole } CO_2}{44 \text{ g } CO_2}$ = 0.25 mol CO_2 *Determine moles of MgO based on proportion* 0.25 mol CO_2 x $\dfrac{1 \text{ mol MgO}}{1 \text{ mol } CO_2}$ = 0.25 mol MgO *Calculate grams of MgO* 0.25 mol MgO x $\dfrac{40 \text{ g MgO}}{1 \text{ mol MgO}}$ = **10 g MgO**	**1 point** is earned for correctly calculating the grams of magnesium oxide

(c) Small pieces of aluminum are added to a solution of copper(II) sulfate.

> *Note: This is a single replacement redox reaction*
> *Note: Sulfate ions is unchanged in the reaction. Therefore, it is not included in the equation.*

(i) Balanced equation	
  2 Al + 3 Cu^{2+} -----> 2 Al^{3+} + 3 Cu	**1 point** is earned for correct reactants
	2 points are earned for correct products
	1 point is earned for correctly balancing the equation

(ii) Write the correct oxidation and reduction half equations for the reaction that occurs.

Oxidation-half: **Al ------> Al^{3+} + $3e^-$** *Reduction-half:* **Cu^{2+} + $2e^-$ ----> Cu**	**1 point** is earned for the correct oxidation and reduction half equations

    165

2. Use your knowledge of redox and electrochemistry to answer the following questions. **(8 points)**

(a) What is the function of a salt bridge in a galvanic cell, and why is it necessary in order for the cell work?

Recall: A salt bridge connects the two compartments of a galvanic cell

A salt bridge **allows anions (-) and cations (+) to flow** between the two compartments.	**1 point** is earned for correct function
A salt bridge is required for a galvanic cell to work because **the flow of the ions maintains cell neutrality .**	**1 point** is earned for correct explanation.

(b) Explain why, when a piece of nickel is placed in hydrochloric acid, a reaction occurs, but when a piece of copper wire is placed in hydrchloric acid, no reaction occurs.

Recall: Spontaneous redox reaction occurs when potential (E) is +.

A reaction occurs between the nickel (Ni) and HCl solution because the reaction has a positive potential (+E). According to the Table of Reduction Potentials: E_{oxi} Ni ---- > Ni^{2+} + 2e- = + 0.25 V E_{red} 2 H^+ + 2e- ----- > H_2 = 0.00 V E for reaction = **+ 0.25 V**	**1 point** is earned for correctly explaining (or showing) why reaction occurs with Ni
A reaction did not occur between the copper wire (Cu) and the HCl solution because the reaction has a negative potential (-E). E_{oxi} Cu ---- > Cu^{2+} + 2e- = - 0.34 V E_{red} 2 H^+ + 2e- ----- > H_2 = 0.00 V E for reaction = **- 0.34 V**	**1 point** is earned for correctly explaining (or showing) why no reaction occurs with Cu

(c) Cu^{2+} + Pb(s) -----> Cu(s) + Pb^{2+}

(i) Give the standard cell potential for the reaction above.

     Recall: E_{cell} = E_{oxi} + E_{red}

     Note: Use Table of Reduction Potential on pg 338 to get E for each half-reaction. Be sure to reverse the sign for oxidation half.

E_{oxi} Pb ----> Pb^{2+} + $2e^-$ = +0.13 V $\underline{E_{red} \;\;\;\; Cu^{2+} + 2e^- -----> Cu \; = \; +0.34 \, V}$ E_{cell} for reaction = **+0.47 V**	**1 point** is earned for the correct cell potential

(ii) What happens to the cell potential in (i) when $[Pb^{2+}]$ is increased? Explain.

The E_{cell} will decrease because $[Pb^{2+}]$ is a product, and increasing [ ] of a product forces the reaction to shift left (favors the reverse reaction). This decreases the voltage that is produced by the cell.	**1 point** is earned for the correct change in E_{cell} with explanation

(iii) What is the value of $\Delta G°$ for the cell?

     Note: $\Delta G°$ = -nFE   (See Reference Materials on pg 339)

     Note: n = moles of electrons = 2   (see equations in (i))
              F = Faraday's constant = 96500 C/mol (see Reference materials)

$\Delta G°$ = - nFE $\Delta G°$ = -(2) (96500 C/mol)(+0.47 V)	**1 point** is earned for correct setup
$\Delta G°$ = **- 90710 C·V/mol** **- 90710 J/mol or 90.7 KJ/mol**	**1 point** is earned for correctly calculating $\Delta G°$

Day 13: 50 Multiple Choice questions

50 points *Section I Part A and B Practice*

Start: Answer all questions on this day before stopping.

Note: NO CALCULATORS may be used for questions on this day. You may use ONLY the Periodic Table provided on page 337

Note: For all questions, assume that the temperature is 298 K, the pressure is 1.00 atmosphere and solutions are aqueous unless otherwise noted.

Questions 1 through 5 refer to the following set of choices:

(A) Particles vibrate about fixed points.
(B) Particles are ordered and occur within a sea of mobile electrons.
(C) Particles are ionized, disordered and highly energetic.
(D) Particles diffuse rapidly and can dissolve many solutes.
(E) Particles do not translate but lack order.

1. Supercritical fluid

2. Metallic solid

3. Amorphous solid

4. Plasma

5. Crystalline solid

Questions 6 through 7 refer to the following substances

(A) Nitric acid
(B) Sulfur dioxide
(C) Hydrochloric acid
(D) Zinc
(E) Potassium permanganate

6. A strong oxidizing agent that changes color upon reduction.

7. Is known as the oxidizing acid.

8. Is used to galvanize building materials.

9. Is known to cause to acid rain.

Day 13: Continue

Questions 10 through 13 refer to types of reactions below.

(A) Oxidation-reduction
(B) Neutralization
(C) Fusion
(D) Combination
(E) Combustion

Which of the reaction types listed above best describes each of these processes?

10. CO_2 (g) + CaO (s) -----> $CaCO_3$ (s)

11. $2Fe^{3+}$ (aq) + $2I^-$ (aq) -------> $2Fe^{2+}$ (aq) + I_2 (aq)

12. CH_3COOH (aq) + NaOH (aq) ------> CH_3COONa (aq) + H_2O (l)

13. C_3H_8 (g) + $5O_2$ (g) -----> $3CO_2$ (g) + $4H_2O$ (g)

Questions 14 through 16 refer to the following.

(A) Arrhenius acid
(B) Bronsted-Lowry acid
(C) Bronsted-Lowry base
(D) Lewis acid
(E) Lewis base

14. BF_3 in the reaction:

BF_3 + F^- -----> BF_4

15. CN- in the reaction:

Cu^{2+} (aq) + $4CN^-$ (aq) ------> $Cu(CN)_4^{2-}$ (aq)

16. H_2O in the reaction:

$HC_2H_3O_2$ (aq) + H_2O (aq) ------> $C_2H_3O_2^-$ (aq) + H_3O^+ (aq)

17. $AgNO_3$ (aq) + KCl (aq) ------> _____ + _____

What are the missing products?

(A) $AgNO_3$ (aq) + KCl (aq)
(B) $AgCl_2$ (s) + K_2NO_3 (aq)
(C) AgCl (s) + KNO_3 (aq)
(D) Ag^{2+} (aq) + Cl^- (aq) + KNO_3 (aq)
(E) $AgCl_2$ (s) + K^+ (aq) + Cl^- (aq)

18. The Lewis dot structure of which of the following molecules shows only one unshared pair of valence electrons around the central atom?

(A) Br_2
(B) O_2
(C) NH_3
(D) CH_4
(E) SO_3

19. The half-life of ^3H is about 12 years. How much of a 4mg sample will remain after 36 years?

(A) 0.25mg
(B) 0.5mg
(C) 1mg
(D) 2mg
(E) 4mg

20. Arrange the following ionic compounds in order of decreasing lattice energy: KBr, LiF, MgO

(A) KBr > LiF > MgO
(B) MgO > LiF > KBr
(C) KBr > MgO > LiF
(D) MgO > KBr > LiF
(E) LiF > KBr > MgO

21. A 40-gram sample of helium and a 40-gram sample of neon are placed in a sealed container. What is the partial pressure of the neon if the total pressure in the sealed container is 6 atm?

    (A) 1 atm
    (B) 2 atm
    (C) 3 atm
    (D) 4 atm
    (E) 5 atm

22. Which of the following must be true for a reaction that proceeds spontaneously from initial standard state conditions?

    (A) $\Delta G°$ is positive and K_{eq} is greater than 1
    (B) $\Delta G°$ is positive and K_{eq} is less than 1
    (C) $\Delta G°$ is negative and K_{eq} is greater than 1
    (D) $\Delta G°$ is positive and K_{eq} is greater than 1
    (E) $\Delta G°$ is equal to zero and K_{eq} is equal to 1

23. Hydrogen gas and iodine gas are introduced into a cylinder with a movable piston as shown in the following diagram:

Which of the following would cause a decrease in the reaction rate?

        (1) adding neon, holding the volume constant
        (2) increase the volume, holding the temperature constant
        (3) increase the temperature, holding the volume constant
        (4) adding a catalyst

    (A) 1
    (B) 2
    (C) 3
    (D) 1 and 3
    (E) 1, 3 and 4

24. The half-reaction at the anode of a galvanic cells is as follows:

$$Zn(s) \longrightarrow Zn^{2+} + 2e^-$$

What is the maximum charge, in coulombs, that can be delivered by a cell with an anode composed of 6.54 grams of zinc?
(1 faraday = 96500 coulombs)

(A) 4820 coulombs
(B) 9650 coulombs
(C) 19300 coulombs
(D) 38600 coulombs
(D) 48200 coulombs

25. Which of the following are compounds that might reasonably form from combining iron and oxygen?

(X) Fe_2O_3
(Y) Fe_3O_2
(Z) FeO

(A) X only
(B) Y only
(C) Z only
(D) X and Y only
(E) X and Z only

26. What is the molar solubility in water of PbI_2?
(The K_{sp} for PbI_2 is 3.2×10^{-8})

A) 3.2×10^{-8} M
B) 8.0×10^{-8} M
C) $\sqrt{1.6 \times 10^{-8}}$ M
D) $\sqrt[3]{1.6 \times 10^{-8}}$ M
E) 2×10^{-3} M

27. The following data was obtained for the reaction

$$2X + Y \text{ ----------} > 3Z$$

Experiment	X $\left(\dfrac{mole}{liter}\right)$	Y $\left(\dfrac{mole}{liter}\right)$	Rate $\left(\dfrac{mole}{liter \cdot sec}\right)$
1	3.0	1.5	1.8
2	1.5	3.0	0.45
3	1.5	1.5	0.45

What is the proper rate expression?

(A) rate = $k[X][Y]$
(B) rate = $k[Y]^2$
(C) rate = $k[X]$
(D) rate = $k[X]^2[Y]$
(E) rate = $k[X]^2$

28. Which of the following elements is a diamagnetic?

(A) Hydrogen
(B) Carbon
(C) Magnesium
(D) Fluorine
(E) Sulfur

29. A student wishes to prepare a buffer solution with a pH of 5. Which of the following acids would be the best choice for the buffer?

(A) $H_2C_2O_4$ $K_a = 5.9 \times 10^{-2}$
(B) H_3AsO_4 $K_a = 5.0 \times 10^{-3}$
(C) $H_2C_2H_3O_2$ $K_a = 1.8 \times 10^{-5}$
(D) $HOCl$ $K_a = 3.0 \times 10^{-8}$
(E) HCN $K_a = 4.9 \times 10^{-10}$

30. Which of the following expressions is equal to the density of helium gas at STP?

(A) $\dfrac{1}{22.4}$ g/L

(B) $\dfrac{2}{22.4}$ g/L

(C) $\dfrac{1}{4}$ g/L

(D) $\dfrac{4}{22.4}$ g/L

(E) $\dfrac{4}{4}$ g/L

31. What is the name of the branched alkene $CH_3(CH_2)_2C(CH_3)=CHCH_3$?

(A) 3-methyl-2-hexene
(B) 2-methyl-3-hexene
(C) 1-methyl-2,3 diethyl-3-hexene
(D) 1-methyl-2,2 diethyl-3-hexene
(E) 1,3-dimethyl-3-hexene

32. An unknown quantity of methane gas, CH_4, is held in a 2.0 L container at 77°C. The pressure inside the container is 3.0 atm. How many moles of methane must be in the container?

(A) 0.21 mol
(B) 0.95 mol
(C) 1.05 mol
(D) 4.8 mol
(E) 0.5 mol

33. Which of the following gases deviates least from ideal behavior?
    (A) N_2
    (B) SO_2
    (C) Ar
    (D) Ne
    (E) CH_4

34. All of the following can be inferred from the dot diagram below EXCEPT

$$\cdot \overset{\displaystyle \cdot\cdot}{\underset{\displaystyle \cdot\cdot}{\mathbf{X}}} \colon$$

    (A) Element X is a halogen.
    (B) Element X forms an anion with a negative one charge.
    (C) Element X has a valence electron with a possible set of quantum numbers equaling 3, 1, 1, $-\frac{1}{2}$
    (D) Element X is highly electronegative when compared to other elements in its period.
    (E) Element X forms a strong acid.

35. The best explanation for the fact that diamond is extremely hard is that diamond crystals

    (A) are made up of atoms that are intrinsically hard because of their electronic structures
    (B) consist of positive and negative ions that are strongly attracted to each other
    (C) are giant molecules in which each atom forms strong covalent bonds with all of its neighboring atoms
    (D) are formed under extreme conditions of temperature and pressure
    (E) contain orbitals or bands of delocalized electrons that belong not to single atoms but to each crystal as a whole

36. Which correctly lists the particles in order of increasing penetrating power?

(A) Gamma rays < alpha particles < beta particles
(B) Beta particles < alpha particles < gamma rays
(C) Beta particles < gamma rays < alpha particles
(D) Alpha particles < beta particles < gamma rays
(E) Alpha particles < gamma rays < beta particles

37. Given standard free energy change for the following reactions:

$$2C_6H_6(l) + 15O_2(g) ----> 12CO_2(g) + 6H_2O(l) \quad \Delta G° = -6400. \text{ kJ}$$

$$C(s) + O_2(g) ------> CO_2(g) \quad \Delta G° = -400. \text{ kJ}$$

$$H_2(g) + \tfrac{1}{2}O_2(g) ----> H_2O(l) \quad \Delta G° = -250. \text{ kJ}$$

What is the standard free energy change for the reaction below, as calculated from the data above?

$$6C(s) + 3H_2(g) ------ > C_6H_6(l)$$

(A) -250. kJ
(B) -100. kJ
(C) -50. kJ
(D) 50. kJ
(E) 100. kJ

38. Which of the following molecules has the highest bond energy?

(A) N_2
(B) O_2
(C) Cl_2
(D) Br_2
(E) H_2

39. How many asymmetric carbon atoms are present in the following molecule?

$$H_3C - \underset{\underset{H}{|}}{\overset{\overset{OH}{|}}{C}} - \underset{\underset{H}{|}}{\overset{\overset{CH_3}{|}}{C}} - CH_2OH$$

(A) 0
(B) 1
(C) 2
(D) 3
(E) 4

40. Which of the following reactions would most likely produce the titration curve represented below?

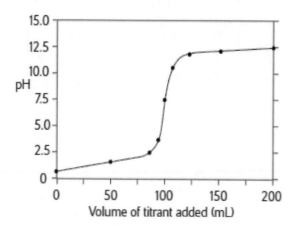

(A) H_2SO_4 + NH_3
(B) KOH + $HC_2H_3O_2$
(C) $HC_7H_5O_2$ + CH_3NH_2
(D) HNO_3 + NaOH
(E) HNO_2 + NaOH

Questions 41 through 42: The phase diagram of an unknown substance is shown below.

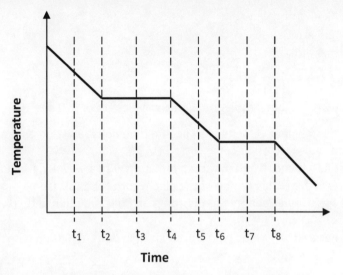

41. The phase diagram above shows the temperature change of a substance that starts of as a gas and heat is removed at constant rate. At which time does the sample contain equal amount of gas and liquid?

   (A) t_1

   (B) t_2

   (C) t_3

   (D) t_5

   (E) t_7

42. Which best describes the potential energy change and the entropy change, ΔS, of the substance from time t_4 to t_5?

   (A) Potential energy increases, and $\Delta S = +$

   (B) Potential energy decreases and $\Delta S = -$

   (C) Potential energy remains the same, and $\Delta S = +$

   (D) Potential energy remains the same, and $\Delta S = -$

   (E) Potential energy remains the same, and $\Delta S = 0$

43. What is the osmotic pressure of 0.100 M NaCl that is at 27°C?

(A) 0.22 atm
(B) 0.44 atm
(C) 2.5 atm
(D) 4.9 atm
(E) 9.8 atm

44. Electromagnetic radiation with a wavelength of 320 nm

(A) has a higher velocity in a vacuum than does radiation with a wavelength of 400 nm.
(B) has a higher frequency than radiation with a wavelength 200 nm.
(C) is in the visible region of the electromagnetic spectrum.
(D) has a lower energy per photon than does radiation with a wavelength of 100 nm.
(E) has a slower velocity in a vacuum than does radiation with a wavelength of 400 nm.

45. Which of the following unbalanced equation demonstrates aluminum hydroxide's amphoteric properties?

(1) $Al(OH)_3 (aq)$ + $H_2O(l)$ ---- > $Al(s)$ + $O_2(g)$ + $H_2O(l)$
(2) $Al(OH)_3 (s)$ ------ > $Al(s)$ + $H_2O(g)$
(3) $Al(OH)_3(s)$ + $O_2(g)$ -------- > $Al(s)$ + $H_2O(g)$
(4) $Al(OH)_3(s)$ + $NaOH(aq)$ --- > $NaIl(OH)_4(aq)$
(5) $Al(OH)_3(s)$ + $HCl(aq)$ ---- > $AlCl_3(aq)$ + $H_2O(l)$

(A) 1
(B) 2 and 3
(C) 3 and 4
(D) 4 and 5
(E) all

46.   __H_2SO_4 + __$Ca(OH)_2$ ----- > __$CaSO_4$ + __H_2O

When the following equation for the acid base reaction above is balanced and all of the coefficients are reduced to lowest whole-number terms, the coefficient of the H_2O is

(A) 1
(B) 2
(C) 3
(D) 4
(E) 5

47. For the reaction

   $2W(g)$ --------- > $2X(g)$ + $Y(g)$,

the equilibrium constant, K_p, is 8×10^3 at 298K. A mixture of three gases at 298K is placed in a rigid metal cylinder and the initial pressures are $P_X = 1$ atmosphere, $P_Y = 0.8$ atmosphere, and $P_W = 2$ atmosphere. At the instant of mixing, which of the following is true for the reaction as written?

(A) more product will form
(B) more reactant will form
(C) $\Delta S = 0$
(D) $\Delta G° = 0$
(E) $\Delta G° > 0$

48. As a beaker of water is heated over a flame, the temperature increases steadily until it reaches 373 K. At that point, the beaker is left on the open flame, but the temperature remains at 373 K as long as the water remains in the beaker. This is because at 373 K, the energy supplied by the flame

(A) no longer acts to increase the energy of the water molecules.
(B) is completely absorbed by the glass beaker.
(C) is less than the energy lost by the water through electromagnetic radiation.
(D) is dissipated by the water as visible light
(E) is used to overcome the heat of vaporization of the water

49. Consider the chemical reaction equation below:

$$16HCl + 2K_2CrO_7 + C_2H_5OH ----> 4CrCl_3 + 4KCl + 11H_2O + 2CO_2$$

According to the balanced equation above, how many moles of HCl would be necessary to produce 4.0 mol of CO_2, starting with 6.0 mol of K_2CrO_7 and 5.0 mol of C_2H_5OH?

(A) 8
(B) 16
(C) 32
(D) 48
(E) 80

50. Solid iron (II) sulfide reacts with atmospheric oxygen to form iron (II) oxide and sulfur dioxide. Which of the following statements are true about the reaction?

   I. Sulfur is the reducing agent, oxygen is the oxidizing agent.
   II. Sulfur is reduced, oxygen is oxidized.
   III. Sulfur transfers electrons to iron and oxygen.

(A) I only
(B) II only
(C) III only
(D) I and II only
(E) II and III only

Day 13

STOP. Correct your answers and note how many correct **points**

Day 13: Answers and Explanations

Answers : Quick Check

1. **D**	2. **B**	3. **E**	4. **C**	5. **A**	6. **E**	7. **A**	8. **D**	9. **A**	10. **D**
11. **A**	12. **B**	13. **E**	14. **D**	15. **E**	16. **C**	17. **C**	18. **C**	19. **B**	20. **B**
21. **A**	22. **C**	23. **B**	24. **C**	25. **E**	26. **E**	27. **E**	28. **C**	29. **C**	30. **B**
31. **A**	32. **A**	33. **E**	34. **E**	35. **C**	36. **D**	37. **D**	38. **A**	39. **C**	40. **D**
41. **C**	42. **D**	43. **D**	44. **D**	45. **D**	46. **B**	47. **A**	48. **E**	49. **C**	50. **A**

Answers and Explanations

Questions 1 through 5: Phases of matter, particle arrangements

1. **D**   *Recall:* A *supercritical fluid* is a material that has properties of both a liquid and a gas at high temperature and pressure conditions that is above the critical point..

    Note: As a gas, a supercritical fluid can diffuse.

    As a liquid, a supercritical fluid can dissolve other substances.

2. **B**   *Note:*   This a definition of a *metallic* bonding

3. **E**   *Recall:* *Amorphous solids* are noncrystalline solids in which particles (atoms and molecules) are not orderly arranged as it would be in real solids.

    Note: Examples of amorphous solids include gel, glass, and certain polymers like plastic.

4. **C**   *Recall:* *Plasma* , the fourth phase of matter, is achieved by a substance when its gaseous particles are ionized under extreme heat.

    Note: Plasma can diffuse like a liquid, but their properties are unique and unusual because they have ionic charge.

5. **A**   *Recall:* *Crystalline solids* have tightly and geometrically packed particles that does not allow for any movement within the structure. As a result, particles of a crystalline solid can only vibrate around a fixed point.

Questions 6 through 9: Characteristics of common substances

6. **E** *Recall:* An oxidizing agent is also a substance that can be easily reduced.

   Note: Both nitric acid (HNO_3) and potassium permanganate ($KMnO_4$) can be easily reduced.

   Recall: $KMnO_4$ contains a transitional metal (Mn) which has different color depending on its oxidation state.

7. **A** *Recall:* An oxidizing acid reacts with certain metals metal to produce oxides rather than hydrogen gas.

   $$Cu + 4\,H^+ + 2\,NO_3^- \text{-------} > Cu^{2+} + 2\,NO_2 + 2\,H_2O$$

   Note: Of the two acids listed, nitric acid, is the oxidizing acid. Other oxidizing acids includes perchloric acid ($HClO_4$) and Iodic acid (HIO_3)

8. **D** *Note:* Galvanizing is a method of protecting building materials by coating the materials with zinc. The zinc will corrode, (oxidized) instead of the building material.

9. **A** *Recall:* Acid rain is composed of H_2SO_4 (sulfuric acid).

   H_2SO_4 is formed in a two step process:

   Step 1: $SO_2 + O_2 \text{--------} > SO_3$

   Step 2: $SO_3 + H_2O \text{-------} > H_2SO_4$

Questions 10 through 13: Reaction types

10. **D** *Note:* In the reaction shown, two reactants combined to form one product.

11. **A** *Note:* In the reaction shown:
    I^- is oxidized to I_2^0 (oxidation number increases)
    and
    Fe^{3+} is reduced to Fe^{2+} (oxidation number decreases)

12. **B**   *Note:*   In the reaction shown, an acid (CH_3COOH) and a base (NaOH) neutralize each other to form water.

13. **E**   *Note:*   In the reaction shown, C_3H_8 (propane) is burned (combust) in the presence of oxygen.

Question 14 through 16: Acid-base reactions. Identifying species

14. **D**   *Note:* BF_3 (a trivalent compound) does not have octet of electrons. This compound only has six electrons in the valance shell and therefore, is capable of accepting electrons from a Lewis Base.

   Note: In the reaction shown, BF_3 is accepting electrons from F-.

   Recall: An electron acceptor (BF_3) is defined as a Lewis acid.

$$BF_3 \quad + \quad F^- \quad ----> \quad BF_4$$
Lewis acid   *Lewis base*   *has a complete octet*

15. **E**   *Note:*   In the reaction shown, CN^- is donating electrons to Cu^{2+} to form a complex ion.

   Recall: An electron donor (CN-) is defined as a Lewis base.

$$Cu^{2+}(aq) \quad + \quad 4CN^-(aq) ------> Cu(CN)_4^{2-}(aq)$$
Lewis acid   *Lewis base*   *complex ion*

16. **C**   *Note:*   In the reaction, H_3O+ is formed from H_2O. This only occurs because the H_2O accepts a proton (H+) from the $HC_2H_3O_2$.

   Recall: A proton acceptor (H_2O) is defined as a Bronsted-Lowery base.

$$HC_2H_3O_2(aq) \quad + \quad H_2O(aq) ----> C_2H_3O_2^-(aq) + H_3O^+(aq)$$
Bronsted-Lowery acid   *Bronsted-Lowery base*   *conjugate base*   *conjugate acid*

17. C   Completing equation

Note: This is a double replacement (ion-exchange) reaction.

Note: Choice B and C contain the same atoms. However, Choice C is correct because the correct formulas for the products, silver chloride (AgCl) and potassium nitrate (KNO_3), are correctly written.

18. C   Lewis structures of formulas, lone pair electrons

Note: If necessary, draw the Lewis electron-dot structures for all five compounds, and note which has one pair of unshared electrons.

Note: The Lewis structure for NH_3 (ammonia) below has one pair of unshared electrons on the nitrogen.

19. B   Half-life calculation, nuclear decay

Step 1:   Determine number of half-life periods (n) from times.

The number of half-life periods (n) is the number of times the given mass of the radioisotopes decayed in half.

$$n = \frac{\text{length of time}}{\text{half-life}} = \frac{36 \text{ hrs}}{12 \text{ hrs}} = 3$$

Step 2:   Cut 4 mg (original mass) in half as many times as n (3)

½ (**4 mg**) = 2 mg

½ (2 mg) = 1 mg

½ (1 mg) = **0.5 mg**

187

20. B Lattice energy, ionic bond strength comparison

Recall: Lattice energy is defined as the energy needed to separate the ions of an ionic compound.

Note: The stronger the ionic bond, the greater the lattice energy needed to separate the ions

Note: The strength of ionic bond depends on two factors: **The Size of the charges** and **the size (radii) of the ions.**

Consider and compare charges of the ions to determine which has the greatest lattice energy

> **The size of charge:** The greater the charge of the ions, the stronger the bond, the greater the lattice energy.
>
> Of the compounds listed: MgO contains ions (Mg^{2+} and O^{2-}) with the greatest charges.
>
> **MgO**, therefore, has the strongest ionic bond, and also the **highest lattice energy** of the three.

> *Note:* Since the two remaining compounds (LiF and KBr) contain ions of the same charges (+1 and -1), other factor must be considered in order to determine which of the two has a higher lattice energy

Consider and compare the size of the ions to determine which has the smaller radius:

> **The size of ionic radius:** The smaller the radius, the stronger the bond, the greater the lattice energy.
>
> Of the two remaining compounds, the radii of the ions (Li^+ and F^-) in LiF are smaller than the radii of the ions (K^+ and Br^-) in KBr.
>
> **LiF**, therefore, has a stronger ionic bond , and also a **higher lattice energy than KBr**

Order of decreasing lattice energy (LE) , therefore, is:

$$MgO \quad > \quad LiF \quad > \quad KBr$$

highest LE   *lowest LE*

21. A Partial pressure calculation, mole fraction

Step 1: Determine moles of the gases

$$40 \text{ g Ne} \ / \ 20 \text{ g·mol}^{-1} \ = \ 2 \text{ mol Ne}$$

$$40 \text{ g He} \ / \ 4 \text{ g·mol}^{-1} \ = \ 10 \text{ mol He}$$

Step 2: Determine partial pressure of Ne (P_{Ne}) using equation below.

$$P_{Ne} \ = \ \frac{\text{moles of Ne}}{\text{Total moles}} \ \times \ P_{total}$$

$$P_{Ne} \ = \ \frac{2 \text{ moles Ne}}{12 \text{ moles}} \ \times \ 6 \text{ atm}$$

$$P_{Ne} = \ \textbf{1 atm}$$

This problem could have been solved using mental math by realizing that the mass of Ne on the Periodic Table is five times greater than that of He. That means, in a **container of equal masses of the gases,** the ratio of moles of Ne to He will always be 1 : 5, and the total moles of the gases in the container will always be 6 (or a factor of 6).

That means: The partial pressure of Ne will always be 1/6th that of the total pressure. In this problem, 1/6th of 6 atm = **1 atm**

22. C Spontaneous reaction – free energy - K_{eq} relationship

Recall: All spontaneous reactions must have $-\Delta G$ (free energy change)

Recall: In spontaneous reactions, product must be favored.
Therefore:

$$K_{eq} \ = \ \frac{[\text{product}]}{[\text{reactant}]} \ > \ 1$$

Day 13: Answers and Explanations

23. B   Factors affecting rate of gaseous reaction

Note: Increasing volume (condition 2) on gaseous reactions decreases the concentration of the gases (H_2 and I_2).

Relate: A decrease in concentration of reactants decreases reaction rate because the frequency of effective collision will decrease.

Note: 1 will not change rate b/c neon is a non-reactive substance

4 will not change overall rate because both forward and reverse reactions will speed up equally

3 will increase rate because kinetic energy of the particles will increase, leading to increase frequency of effective collisions

24. C   Charge calculation from mole of e- , factor labeling

Recognize that moles of electrons produced from 6.54 g Zn can be determine using factor-labeling by utilizing mole proportion in the half-reaction.

$$\text{Charge} = 6.54 \text{ g Zn} \times \frac{1 \text{ mol Zn}}{65.4 \text{ g Zn}} \times \frac{2 \text{ mol e}^-}{1 \text{ mol Zn}} \times \frac{96500 \text{ coulombs}}{1 \text{ mol e}^-}$$

Charge = **19300 coulombs**

If factor-labeling is not your thing: Do this problem in steps:

Step 1: Determine moles of 6.54 g of Zinc

moles = $6.54 \text{ g} / 65.4 \text{ g·mol}^{-1}$ = 0.100 mol Zn

Step 2: Determine moles of electrons produced from 0.100 mol Zn

1 mol Zn   = 2 mol of e⁻ (according to half-reaction)
0.100 mol Zn = 0.200 mol e⁻

Step 3: Calculate charge of 0.200 moles e⁻

Charge = 0.200 mol e⁻ x 96500 coulomb/e⁻

Charge = **19300 coulombs**

25. E   **Formula writing;   oxidation state of atoms**

Recall: The two common oxidation states of iron are Fe^{3+} and Fe^{2+}.

Determine formulas of iron oxide with these two oxidation states.

$Fe^{3+} O^{2-}$ $\qquad$ Fe_2O_3 iron (III) oxide   (X)

$Fe^{2+} O^{2-}$ $\qquad$ FeO iron (II) oxide   (Z)

26. E   **Molar solubility calculation; dissociation, equilibrium constant**

Recall: Molar solubility is defined as the number of moles of solutes that will dissolve in a 1 liter solution.

Recognize that based on the information given, setting up equilibrium expression and solving for moles of the ions is one way of determining molar solubility of the solute (PbI_2).

Step 1: Write the equation for the dissolving of PbI_2

$PbI_2 (s)$ -------- > $Pb^{2+} (aq)$ + $2I^- (aq)$

Step 2: Write equilibrium expression, K_{sp} , based on step 1 equation

Recall: Solids (constant [ ]) are not included in

K_{sp} = $[Pb^{2+}] [I\text{-}]^2$

Step 3: Assume $[Pb^{2+}]$ = X

$\qquad\qquad$ $[I^-]$ = 2X (since moles of I^- is twice that of Pb^{2+})

Step 4: Substitute factors from step 3 and the K_{sp} given into equilibrium expression written in step 2. Solve for X

K_{sp} $\qquad$ = $[Pb^{2+}] [I\text{-}]^2$

3.2×10^{-8} = $(X) (2X)^2$

3.2×10^{-8} = $4X^3$

$\dfrac{3.2 \times 10^{-8}}{4}$ = X^3

8.0×10^{-9} = X^3

$\mathbf{2.0 \times 10^{-3}}$ = X = $[Pb^{2+}]$ = $[PbI_2]$ Note: mole ratio of Pb^{2+} to PbI_2 is

$\qquad\qquad\qquad\qquad\qquad\qquad\qquad\qquad$ 1 : 1

27. E   Rate law; Order of reaction

Recognize that to determine the correct rate expression, the order of the reaction with respect to X and Y must be determined from information given on the Table.

Step 1: Determine order with respect Y
Compare Rates in Experiment 2 and 3 since [X] is constant.

Note: [Y] is doubled (1.5 to 3.0)
But Rate stayed the same (at 0.45)

Recall: When rate does not change, the order with respect to that reactant is 0. This means that $[Y]^0$ cannot be included in the rate law since the reaction does not depend on [Y].
Eliminate A, B and D: These choices have [Y] in their rate laws.

Step 2: Determine order with respect to X
Compare Rates in Experiment 1 and 3 since [Y] is constant.

Note: [X] is doubled (1.5 to 3.0)
Rate is 4 times greater (0.45 to 1.8)

Recall: When rate is quadrupled as [ ] is doubled, the reaction is 2nd order with respect to that reactant $[X]^2$

Step 3: Write correct rate law based on the two determinations:
Rate = $k\,[X]^2$

28. C   Diamagnetic – electron configuration relationship

Recall: Diamagnetic elements have all of their subshells completed. These elements have a pair of electrons in all of their available sublevels.

Draw orbital notation for each element listed as a choice.

(A) Hydrogen   ↑
$1s^2$

(B) Carbon   ↑↓   ↑↓   ↑ ↑
$1s^2$ $2s^2$ $2p^2$

(C) Magnesium ↑↓ ↑↓ ↑↓ ↑↓ ↑↓ ↑↓   all sublevels
$1s^2$ $2s^2$ $2p^6$ $3s^2$ completely filled (paired)

(D) Fluorine   ↑↓   ↑↓   ↑↓ ↑↓ ↑
$1s^2$ $2s^2$ $2p^5$

(E) Sulfur   ↑↓   ↑↓   ↑↓ ↑↓ ↑↓   ↑↓   ↑↓ ↑ ↑
$1s^2$ $2s^2$ $2p^6$ $3s^2$ $3p^4$

29. C   Buffer solution

Recall: The best buffered solution has pKa = pH

This means that the buffered solution contains equal molar concentrations of the acid and conjugate base.

Note: Without a calculator, you must recognize that pKa for choice C will be the closest to the pH given (5)

30. B   Density ; Molar volume

Recall: Density = $\dfrac{\text{Mass}}{\text{Volume}}$

Note: Molecular mass of helium (He)   = 4 g

Recall: At STP, volume of a mole of gas   = 22.4 L

Determine: Density of He at STP   = $\dfrac{4\text{ g}}{22.4\text{ L}}$

31. A   Hydrocarbon formula naming

Note: You may be able to name the condensed formula given correctly without drawing out its structure.

If you choose to draw before naming, be sure the C atoms, the branch or branches, and the H atoms are all bonded correctly according to the condensed formula

$$CH_3\,(C\,H_2)_2\,C\,(CH_3) = CH\,CH_3$$

Naming the structure:

Note: Methyl is on the 3rd C atom from left: 3-methyl

Note: The Long chain has 6 C atoms:
Double bond in bond position 2 :   2 - hexene

Combine names: 3-methyl , 2-hexene

32. A **Ideal gas law calculation**

Recognize that based on the information given, the ideal gas law equation is needed in order to calculate the number of moles (n).

Step 1: Write the ideal gas law equation

$$n = \frac{PV}{RT}$$

Step 2: Convert $77^\circ C$ to Kelvin

$$K = 77^\circ C + 273 = 350\ K$$

Step 3: Substitute factors into equation and solve for n

$$n = \frac{(3.0)(2.0)}{(0.0821)(350)} = \mathbf{0.21\ mol}$$

33. E **Kinetic molecular theory, ideal gas behavior**

Recall: The lightest of the gases will behave most like (or deviates least from) an ideal gas.

Note the molar mass of each gas given as a choice.

N_2	SO_2	Ar	Ne	**CH_4**
(28 g)	(64g)	(40 g)	(20 g)	**(16 g)**

34. E **Dot diagram interpretation**

Note: The Lewis electron-dot diagram has 7 dots (7 valance e-)

Infer: Element X is a halogen because all halogens have 7 valance electrons **(Eliminate Choice A)**
Halogens form – 1 charge **(Eliminate Choice B)**
Halogens have high electronegativity value **(Eliminate D)**
An Halogen can have a set of quantum numbers of 3,1,1,-½ for its valance shell. This is a quantum number set for a valance e- of a chlorine's atom, . **Eliminate C**

Note: **Choice E** is the only remaining answer. HF is a weak acid.

35. C **Network solid compounds, properties**

Recall: Diamond (C) is a network solid substance formed by repeated units of carbon atoms.

Recall: Network solids contain strong covalent bonding between atoms with the absence of discrete particles. This gives diamond, and other network solids such as silicon dioxide, (SiO_2) and silicon carbide (SiC)their extreme hardness.

36. D Penetrating power comparison, nuclear particles

Recall: Penetrating power refers to the ability of a particle to go through another object.

Note: **alpha particles (^{4}He)** have the least penetrating power because of their large mass (4)

βeta particles (^{0}e) encounter less resistance than alpha because their mass is much smaller.

Gamma radiations (^{0}γ) have the most penetrating power because they have no mass and no charge, so they encounter far less resistance than alpha and beta.

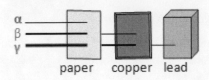

37. D Adding equations

Recognize that to calculate the value of the free energy for the reaction, equations and data from the table must be manipulated to correspond to that of the reaction.

Step 1: Note the reaction and the coefficients of the substances

$$6C(s) + 3H_2(g) ------> C_6H_6(l)$$

Step 2: Manipulate each of the three equations given so that their sums is equal to the reaction above.

Equation 1: Reverse, change sign of ΔG°, and divide everything by 2

$$6 CO_2(g) + H_2O(l) ---> C_6H_6(l) + 7 ½ O_2(g) \quad ΔG° = + 3200 \text{ kJ}$$

Equation 2: Keep equation and sign of Δ G°, multiply everything by 6

$$6C(s) + 6O_2(g) -----> 6CO_2(g) \qquad Δ G° = -2400 \text{ kJ}$$

Equation 3: Keep equation and sign of Δ G°, multiply everything by 3

$$3H_2(g) + 1 ½ O_2(g) ---> 3 H_2O(l) \qquad Δ G° = -750 \text{ kJ}$$

Step 3: Add the three equations and their **Δ G** values.

$$6C(s) + 3H_2(g) ------> C_6H_6(l) \qquad Δ G = 50. \text{ kJ}$$

38. **A** **Comparing Bond energy in formulas**

Recall: Bond energy increases as the number of bonds between atoms increase.

Note the number of bonds between atoms in each of the five diatomics.

N_2	O_2	Cl_2	Br_2	H_2
$N \equiv N$	$O = O$	$Cl - Cl$	$Br - Br$	$H - H$

Note: N_2, with its triple bond, has the most bonding, and therefore, highest bond energy.

39. **C** **Definition of asymmetrical Carbon**

Recall: A carbon atom of a molecule is asymmetrical if it is bonded to four different atoms or groups.

$$H_3C - \underset{\underset{H}{|}}{\overset{\overset{OH}{|}}{C}} - \underset{\underset{H}{|}}{\overset{\overset{CH_3}{|}}{C}} - CH_2OH$$

Note: Each of the **two middle C atoms** is bonded to four different atoms and groups

Note: The other 3 C's are not bonded to four different atoms & groups

40. **D** **Interpreting titration curve, relating curve to acid-base reaction**

Note the following key details about the titration curve given.

The beginning pH is very low: The acid is likely a strong acid

The end pH is very high   : The base is likely a strong base

Relate: The acid is HNO_3 (strong) and the base is NaOH (strong)

41. **C** **Determining phase from phase diagram**

Note: Condensation of the gas to liquid occurs between t_2 and t_4.

Relate: At t_3, a **mixed of gas and liquid** will be present (in equal amount since t_3 is equal distance from t_2 and t_4)

42. D   Phase change , energy and entropy relationship

Note: From time t_4 to t_5, the substance exists as a liquid, and its temperature is decreasing (kinetic energy, KE, is decreasing)

Recall: When KE is changing, **potential energy remains constant**
When KE is decreasing, particles are slowing down, **entropy decreases (- ΔS)**

43. D   Osmotic pressure calculation, solution property

Recognize that based on the information given, osmotic pressure (Π) can be calculated using the equation Π = iMRT

Step 1: Determine van't Hoff factor (i) of NaCl
i for NaCl = **1** Na+   **1** Cl⁻ = **2**

Step 2: Change 27°C temperature (T) to Kelvin
T = 27°C + 273 = 300 K

Step 3: Substitute all factors into osmotic pressure equation and solve

Π = i x M x R   x T

Π = (2)(0.100) (0.0821) (300) = **4.9 atm**

44. D   Frequency, wavelength, and energy Relationship

Recall the following equations that relate wavelength (λ), frequency (v), velocity (v), speed of light (c) and Energy (E).

$v = \lambda v$ $c = \lambda$ $E = hv$ or $E = \dfrac{v}{\lambda}$

Note: Based on these equations and your knowledge of electromagnetic radiation, eliminate some of the choices.

Eliminate A and E because all electromagnetic radiation travel at the same speed (velocity, v) in a vacuum. This is just a fact.
Eliminate B because according to the first equation, the higher the wavelength (λ) , the shorter the frequency (v)
Therefore 320 nm wavelength will have a shorter frequency than a 200 nm wavelength

Eliminate C because the visible light spectrum occurs in the wavelength area of 390 to 750 nm.

Choice D is correct because according to the third equation, the higher the wavelength (λ), the lower the energy (E). Therefore, a 320 wavelength has a lower energy than a 100 nm wavelength.

45. D   Amphoteric species in reactions

Recall that amphoteric is a substance that can act as an acid or a base in a reaction

Note: In equation 4, **Al(OH)₃** acts as **an acid** by combining with the a strong base.

In equation 5, **Al(OH)₃** acts as **a base** to neutralize the acid, HCl.

46. B   Balancing equation

Note: The balance equation for this reaction is

$$H_2SO_4 \ + \ Ca(OH)_2 \ \text{--------} > \ CaSO_4 \ + \ 2H_2O.$$

47. A   Equilibrium constant with pressure

Recognize that based on the choices given, the best way to answer a question like this is to eliminate choices that are clearly false based on equation and information given.

Note the equation: $2W(g) \text{---------} > 2X(g) \ + \ Y(g)$,

***Eliminate* Choice C:** 2 moles of substance are producing 3 moles of substances. Therefore, entropy is increasing ($\Delta S > 0$)

***Eliminate* Choice D:** The reaction is not yet at equilibrium.
Recall: $\Delta G° = 0$ only for a reaction at equilibrium

***Eliminate* Choice E:** The reaction proceed spontaneously as written. Therefore, $\Delta G°$ is negative ($G° < 0$)

Note: Of the remaining choices, A is correct *because K_p* is greater than one. This is the case when reaction proceeds in the forward direction to make more products.

Recall: $\dfrac{[Product]}{[Reactant]}$

48. E   Relating energy to phase change

Recall: 373 K (100°C) is the boiling point of water at standard pressure. At this temperature, energy put into the water is used for increasing potential energy of the molecules in order to overcome the intermolecular forces holding the molecules together.

49. C **Mole – mole calculation in equation**

Recognize that this is a mole ratio problem that is easily solved by setting up factor-labeling using correct mole proportion.

Recognize that K_2CrO_7 and C_2H_5OH will be present in excess, therefore, proportion should be set up between HCl and CO_2 : **16** HCl --- > **2** CO_2

$$\text{moles HCl} = 4.0 \text{ mol } CO_2 \text{ x } \frac{16 \text{ mol HCl}}{2 \text{ mol } CO_2}$$

moles HCl = **32 moles**

Note: Setting up your mole proportion with any of the excess will give you a wrong calculated result for moles of HCl.

50. A **Interpreting redox reaction; writing equation**

Note: One way to determine all true statements about this reaction is to write the *correct equation* to represent the reaction, assign oxidation numbers to species in the reaction, and note oxidation number changes of the substances

Step 1: Write correct equation to represent reaction described.

$$FeS \ + \ O_2 \ ------> \ FeO \ + \ SO_2$$

Step 2: Assign correct oxidation numbers to substances

$$\overset{+2 \ -2}{Fe \ S} \ + \ \overset{0}{O_2} \ ------> \ \overset{+2 \ -2}{Fe \ O} \ + \ \overset{+4 \ -2}{S \ O_2}$$

Step 3: Note and interpret changes in oxidation numbers

S^{2-} --- > S^{4+} **Sulfur** is oxidized, also the **reducing agent**

(because its oxidation number increases)

O_2^{0} --- > O^{2-} **Oxygen** is reduced , also the **oxidizing agent**

(because its oxidation number decreases)

START: Answer all questions on this day before stopping.

Note: You may use a calculator for questions on this day.
You may use any of the reference material provided on pg 337-340

CLEARLY SHOW THE METHOD USED AND THE STEPS INVOLVED IN ARRIVING AT YOUR ANSWERS. It is to your advantage to do this, since you may obtain partial credit if you do and you will receive little or no credit if you do not. Attention should be paid to significant figures.

---

1.   **(10 points)**

The solubility of $Mg(OH)_2$, magnesium hydroxide, is 6.53×10^{-3} g/L at 25°C. Assume that this temperature is maintained for all parts of the question.

(a) Write a balanced equation for the solubility equilibrium.

(b) Based on the equilibrium expression you wrote:

   (i) Write expression for the K_{sp}.

   (ii) Determine the K_{sp} value from the expression in (b).

(c) Calculate the pH of a saturated solution of $Mg(OH)_2$.

(d) If 100 mL of 2.5×10^{-3} M $Mg(NO_3)_2$ solution is added to 100 mL of a 3.5×10^{-4} M NaOH solution:

   (i) What will be the concentration of the magnesium and hydroxide ions in the solution?

   (ii) Will a precipitate of $Mg(OH)_2$ formed in the solution? Justify your response by using your calculated data.

Day 14 Question 1: Space for Work and Answers

2.   **(10 points)**

Substance	Absolute Entropy, S^0 (J/mol · K)	Molecular Weight (g)
$C_6H_{12}O_6(s)$	212	180
$O_2(g)$	205	32
$CO_2(g)$	213	44
$H_2O(l)$	70.0	18

Energy is released when glucose is oxidized in the following reaction, which is a metabolism reaction that takes place in the body.

$$C_6H_{12}O_6(s) \ + \ 6O_2(g) \ ------> \ 6CO_2(g) \ + \ 6H_2O(l)$$

The standard enthalpy change, ΔH°, for the reaction is - 2,801 KJ at 298 K.

(a) Calculate the standard entropy change , ΔS°, for the oxidation of glucose.

(b) Calculate the standard free energy change, ΔG°, for the reaction at 298K.

(c) At which temperature, if any, would the spontaneity of this reaction change. Justify your answer with an explanation.

(d) What is the value of K_{eq} for the reaction?

(e) How much energy is given off by the oxidation of 1.0 grams of glucose, $C_6H_{12}O_6$?

(f) A student conducted a laboratory experiment to determine the standard enthalpy change, ΔH°, for oxidation of glucose. From his data, the student calculated a result that was 11.3 % below the accepted value of ΔH° for glucose. What was the value of the standard enthalpy change from the student's experiment? Assume the experiment was conducted at 298 K.

Day 14

STOP. Correct your answers and note how many correct **points**

Day 14 Question 2: Space for Work and Answers

Day 14: Answers and Scoring Guidelines

(see important scoring guideline information on on pg i)

---

1. The solubility of Mg(OH)$_2$, magnesium hydroxide, is 6.53 x 10^{-3} g/L at 25°C. Assume that this temperature is maintained for all parts of the question.   **(10 points)**

(a) Write a balanced equation for the solubility equilibrium.

Mg(OH)$_2$ (s) < ==== > Mg^{2+} (aq) + 2OH$^-$(aq)	**1 point** for the correct and a balanced equation

(b) Based on the equilibrium expression you wrote:

(i) Write expression for the K_{sp}

Recall: K_{sp} = [Products]

Note: Solids are not included in equilibrium expression of any kind because of their constant concentration

K_{sp} = [Mg^{2+}] [OH$^-$]^2	**1 point** for the correct expression

(ii) Determine the K_{sp} value from the expression in (b).

   Note: In order to calculate K_{sp} value, $[Mg^{2+}]$ and [OH-] must be determined.

Determine the molar solubility (M) of Mg(OH)$_2$ based on information given: M = solubility x molar mass of solute $M = \dfrac{6.53 \times 10^{-3} \text{ g}}{\text{L}} \times \dfrac{1 \text{ mol}}{58 \text{ g}}$ **M = 1.12 x 10^{-4} M**	**1 point** is earned for calculating molar solubility of Mg(OH)2

Determine concentration of substances
 	
Let   X = molar solubility M of Mg(OH)^2
      X = $[Mg^{2+}]$ because they are at 1 : 1 ratio
    2X = [OH$^-$]   because they are at 2 : 1 ratio
 	
Re-write K_{sp} expression, substituting X's for [ ]'s, and solve for K_{sp}
 	
K_{sp} = $[Mg^{2+}]$ $[OH^-]^2$
K_{sp} = $(X)(2x)^2$
K_{sp} = $4X^3$
K_{sp} = $4 (1.12 \times 10^{-4} \text{ M})^3$
 	
K_{sp} =   5.62 x 10^{-12}
	1 point is earned for setup to calculate K_{sp}
	
	1 point is earned for the correct K_{sp} value

(c) Calculate the pH of a saturated solution of $Mg(OH)_2$.

> *Note: T*he quickest way to solve this problem is to determine the
> pOH of the solution based on previously calculated values.

Determine the [OH⁻] in the solution $[OH^-] = 2 X = 2(1.12 \times 10^{-4} M) = 2.24 \times 10^{-4} M$ *Determine pOH* $pOH = -\log [OH^-]$ $pOH = -\log (2.24 \times 10^{-4} M) = 3.6$ *Determine pH* $pH = 14 - pOH$ **pH** $= 14 - 3.6 = $ **10.4**	**1 point** is earned for the correct pH value

(d) If 100 mL of 2.5 $\times$ 10^{-3} M $Mg(NO_3)_2$ solution is added to 100 mL of a 3.5 x 10^{-4} M NaOH solution:

   (i) What will be the concentration of the magnesium and hydroxide ions in the solution?

Determine [Mg²⁺] in the Mg(NO₃)₂ solution mole Mg^{2+} = Volume $Mg(NO_3)_2$ x Molarity $Mg(NO_3)_2$ mole Mg^{2+} = .100 L x 2.5 x 10^{-3} mol/L mole Mg^{2+} = 2.5 x 10^{-4} moles $[Mg^{2+}] = \dfrac{mol\ Mg^{2+}}{total\ Volume} = \dfrac{2.5 \times 10^{-4}\ mol}{.200\ L} = $ **1.25 x 10^{-3} M**	**1 point** is earned for the correctly calculating $[Mg^{2+}]$
Determine [OH⁻] in the NaOH solution mole OH^- = Volume NaOH x Molarity NaOH mole OH^- = .100 L x 3.5 x 10^{-4} mol/L mole OH^- = 3.5 x 10^{-5} moles $[OH^-] = \dfrac{mole\ OH^-}{total\ volume} = \dfrac{3.5 \times 10^{-5}\ mol}{.200\ L} = $ **1.75 x 10^{-4} M**	**1 point** is earned for the correctly calculating $[OH^-]$

(ii) Will a precipitate of $Mg(OH)_2$ formed in the solution? Justify your response by using your calculated data.

Recall: For precipitate to form in a solution, the reaction quotient (Q) must be greater than K_{sp}:   Q > Ksp

Determine Q using the calculated concentrations: $Q = [Mg^{2+}][OH^-]^2$ $Q = (1.25 \times 10^{-3}\ M)(1.75 \times 10^{-4}\ M)^2$ **$Q = 3.8 \times 10^{-11}$** *Note:* $\begin{array}{ccc} Q & > & K_{sp} \\ 3.8 \times 10^{-11} & > & 5.62 \times 10^{-12} \end{array}$	**1 point** is earned for correctly calculating Q
Precipitate of $Mg(OH)_2$ will form because **$Q > K_{sp}$** *Note:* Precipitate is formed as a means of removing excess $Mg(OH)_2$ from solution and restore equilibrium.	**1 point** is earned for indicating precipitate of $Mg(OH)_2$ with correct comparison of Q to Ksp

2. **(10 points)**

Energy is released when glucose is oxidized in the following reaction, which is a metabolism reaction that takes place in the body.

$$C_6H_{12}O_6(s) + 6O_2(g) \longrightarrow 6CO_2(g) + 6H_2O(l)$$

The standard enthalpy change, ΔH°, for the reaction is - 2,801 KJ at 298 K.

(a) Calculate the standard entropy change , ΔS°, for the oxidation of glucose.

Recall: $\Delta S^\circ = \sum S^\circ \text{products} - \sum S^\circ \text{reactants}$

Substitute data from table into equation. *Be sure to take all coefficients into account.* $\Delta S^\circ = \sum S^\circ_{products} - \sum S^\circ_{reactants}$ $\Delta S^\circ = [(6)(213) + (6)(70.0)] - [(212) + (6)(205)]$ $\Delta S^\circ = 255$ **J/K**	**1 point** is earned for correctly calculating the ΔS°

(b) Calculate the standard free energy change, ΔG°, for the reaction at 298K.

Note: $\Delta G^\circ = \Delta H^\circ - T\Delta S^\circ$ *(see Reference Materials)*

Convert the calculated ΔS° to KJ (because ΔH is in KJ) 255 J/K = 0 .255 KJ/K *Substitute factors into equation and solve* $\Delta G^\circ = \Delta H^\circ - T\Delta S^\circ$ $\Delta G^\circ = -2801$ KJ $-$ (298 K) (0.255 KJ/K) $\Delta G^\circ = -2880$ **KJ**	**1 point** is earned for setup **1 point** is earned for correctly calculating the ΔG°

(c) At which temperature, if any, would the spontaneity of this reaction change. Justify your answer with an explanation.

Note: The reaction is spontaneous because its $G°$ value is negative (-)

Note: Spontaneity can change:

If $\Delta G°$ changes to Zero: The reaction will be at equilibrium.

If $\Delta G°$ changes to positive: The reaction will become nonspontaneous.

The question is at which temperature would ΔG become zero or +

Note: The reaction in this question has - ΔH and +ΔS

Spontaneity will not change at any temperature. **Reaction will always be spontaneous at any temperature.**	**1 point** is earned for indicating no change
Since $\Delta G° = -\Delta H° - T\Delta S°$ for this reaction, $\Delta G°$ will always be negative (reaction will always be spontaneous) because **at any temperature , TΔS value will always be positive.**	**1 point** is earned for the correct justification

(d) What is the value K_{eq} for the reaction?

Note : $\Delta G° = -2.303\ RT \log K_{eq}$ (See Reference Materials)

$\log K_{eq} = \dfrac{G°}{-2.303\ RT}$	**Note:** ΔG value is converted to J because R (the gas constant) is in Joules.	
$\log K_{eq} = \dfrac{-2\ 880\ 000}{(-2.303)\ (8.31)(298)}$		**1 point** is earned for setup.
$\log K_{eq} = 505$		**1 point** is earned for correctly calculating the K_{eq}
$K_{eq} = 10^{505}$		

(e) How much energy is given off by the oxidation of 1.0 grams of glucose?

Note: $\Delta H°$, the enthalpy change of the reaction, given in the
problem (-2801 KJ) is the amount of energy given off by
oxidation of 1 mole (180 g) of glucose.

Recognize that in this question, you are calculating $\Delta H°$ given off by
just 1.0 g of glucose.

Determine moles of glucose $(C_6H_{12}O_6)$ $1 \text{ g } C_6H_{12}O_6 \ \times \ \dfrac{1 \text{ mole}}{180 \text{ g}} = \textbf{0.00556 moles}$	**1 point** is earned for calculating moles of glucose
Calculate $\Delta H°$ for 1 g based on mole to ΔH ratio in the balanced equation $0.00556 \text{ mol } C_6H_{12}O_6 \ \times \ \dfrac{-2801 \text{ KJ}}{1 \text{ mol } C_6H_{12}O_6} = \textbf{-15.6 KJ}$	**1 point** is earned for correctly calculating the $\Delta H°$ value

(f) A student conducted a laboratory experiment to determine the standard
enthalpy change, $\Delta H°$, for oxidation of glucose. From his data, the student
calculated a result that was 11.3 % below the accepted value of ΔH for
glucose. What was the value of the standard enthalpy change from the
student's experiment? Assume the experiment was conducted at 298 K.

Note: The accepted $\Delta H°$ value glucose = - 2,801 KJ (given in question)

Student error $= (0.113) (- 2,801 \text{ KJ}) = - 316.5 \text{ KJ}$ **Student $\Delta H°$ value** $= - 2,801 \text{ KJ} - (-316.5 \text{KJ}) = \textbf{-2484.5 KJ}$	**1 point** is earned for the correct $\Delta H°$ value

START: Answer all questions on this day before stopping.

Note: NO CALCULATORS should be used for questions on this day.
You may use any of the Reference Materials provided on pg 337-340

1. For each of the following three reactions, write a balanced equation for the reaction in part (i) and answer the question about the reaction in part (ii). In part (i), coefficients should be in terms of lowest whole numbers. Assume that solutions are aqueous unless otherwise indicated. Represent substances in solutions as ions if the substances are extensively ionized. Omit formulas for any ions or molecules that are unchanged by the reaction.
   (15 points)

(a) Solid sodium hydride is added to water

   (i) Balanced equation:

   (ii) If 12 grams of sodium hydride react with water at STP, how many milliliters of the gaseous product will form?

(b) A solution of hydrogen peroxide is heated.

   (i) Balanced equation:

   (ii) Indicate the oxidation numbers of oxygen before and after the reaction.

(c) A copper coil is placed in a silver nitrate solution.

   (i) Balanced equation:

   (ii) Indicate visible changes that would occur in the reaction container as the reaction is proceeding.

Your responses to question 2 will be scored on the basis of the accuracy and relevance of the information cited. Explanations should be clear and well organized. Examples and equations may be included in your responses where appropriate. Specific answers are preferable to broad, diffuse responses. **(8 points)**

2. A student performed a titration of a weak monoprotic acid, HA , with a sodium hydroxide, NaOH, solution.

   (a) On the graph below, sketch an appropriate representation of the titration curve for the experiment. On the curve, label the half-equivalent point and the equivalent point.

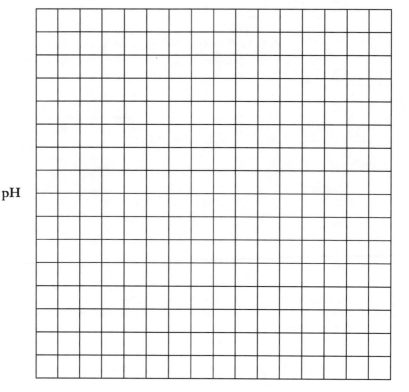

pH

Volume of NaOH (ml)

(b) Discuss at least two ways in which a sketch from the titration of a strong, monoprotic, like HCl will differ from the your sketch in (a)

(c) The student has a choice between the two indicators: methyl red (pH range = 4.8 – 6.0) or phenolphthalein (pH range = 8.2 – 10.0). Which should she choose? Justify your response.

(d) Assume that the acid in this titration was acetic acid, what will be the formula and name of the product (other than water) that is formed during the titration process?

Day 15

STOP. Correct your answers and note how many correct **points**

Day 15 Question 2: Space for Work and Answers

1.   **(15 points)**

(a) Solid sodium hydride is added to water

Recall: Metal hydrides combine with water to produce bases and hydrogen gas.

Note: The base formed (sodium hydroxide) must be in ionized form because strong bases ionize completely.

(i) Balanced equation	**1 point** is earned for correct reactants
NaH + H$_2$O -----> Na$^+$ + OH$^-$ + H$_2$ *metal hydride water base hydrogen gas*	**2 points are** earned for correct products **1 point** is earned for correctly balancing the atoms and charge

(ii) If 12 grams of sodium hydride react, how many milliliters of the gaseous product will form?

| *Determine moles of the gas, H$_2$, produced*

12 g NaH x $\dfrac{\text{1 mole NaH}}{\text{24 g NaH}}$ x $\dfrac{\text{1 mole H}_2}{\text{1 mole NaH}}$ = 0.50 mol H$_2$

Calculate volume of H$_2$ at STP

0.50 mol H$_2$ x $\dfrac{\text{22.4 L}}{\text{1 mol}}$ x $\dfrac{\text{1000 mL}}{\text{1 L}}$ = **11200 mL H$_2$** | **1 point** is earned for correctly calculating the volume of H$_2$. |

(b) A solution of hydrogen peroxide is heated.

Note: This is a decomposition reaction of hydrogen peroxide to water and oxygen.

(i) Balanced equation $2H_2O_2 \quad ------> \quad 2H_2O \ + \ O_2$	**1 point** is earned for correct reactants **2 points are** earned for correct products **1 point** is earned for correctly balancing the equation

(ii) Indicate all oxidation numbers of oxygen before and after the reaction.

Recall: Oxygen has a -1 charge in peroxides.
+2 charge in OF_2
-2 charge in all other compounds

-1 before reaction (in H_2O_2) **-2 after reaction** (in H_2O) **0 after reaction** (in O_2)	**1 point** is earned for correctly listing all oxidation numbers of O

(c) A copper coil is placed in a silver nitrate solution.

  Note: This is a single replacement reaction in which silver ion is reduced to silver metal.

  NO_3^- ion is unchanged, therefore, not included in the equation.

(i) Balanced equation $$Cu + 2Ag^+ ------> Cu^{2+} + 2Ag$$	**1 point** is earned for correct reactants
	2 points are earned for correct products
	1 point is earned for correctly balancing the atoms and charge

(ii) Indicate any visible change that would occur in the reaction container as the reaction is proceeding.

Grayish solid silver will form on the copper coil. **The solution will turn blue as copper ion is formed in the solution.**	**1 point** for listing any change that is typical for this reaction

2.   **(8 points)**
A student performed a titration of a weak monoprotic acid, HA , with a sodium hydroxide, NaOH, solution.

(a) On the graph below, sketch an appropriate representation of the titration curve for the experiment. On the curve, label the half-equivalent point and the equivalent point.

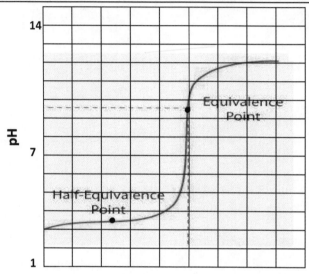

Your diagram will vary a bit from the one above. Points are based on the followings:

The curve starts at pH between 3 to 5 and levels off at the end before 14	**1 point** is earned for a correctly drawn curve
The half-equivalence point is labeled at appropriate point at the beginning of the curve.	**1 point** is earned for correct half-equivalence point
The equivalence point is labeled at a pH between 8 and 12.	**1 point** is earned for correct equivalence point

(b) Discuss at least two ways in which a sketch from the titration of a strong, monoprotic, like HCl will differ from the your sketch in (a)

Note: The curve for the weak acid has equivalent point at a pH that is much higher than 7. **One: A curve for a strong acid like HCl have equivalent point pH right around 7.**	**1 point** is earned for correctly discussing ph around equivalent point
Note: The steepness of the curve around the equivalent point for the weak acid is very short and shows a very small increase in pH due to the high starting pH of the weak acid. **Two: The steepness of a curve around the equivalent point for a strong acid like HCl will be much larger and will show a large increase in pH** due to the low starting pH of a strong acid.	**1 point** is earned for correctly discussing steepness around equivalent point

(c) The student has a choice between the two indicators: methyl red (pH range = 4.8 – 6.0) or phenolphthalein (pH range = 8.2 – 10.0). Which should she choose? Justify your response.

Phenolphthalein Since this is a titration of a weak acid by a strong base, **the equivalent point will be at a pH greater than 7 and the change in pH is gradual**. An indicator that changes color at or above pH 7 will be a good indicator for this titration. Phenolphthalein changes color at a pH range of 8 – 10.	**1 point** is earned for mentioning Phenolphthalein **1 point** is earned for correct justification of indicator that is mentioned

(d) Assume that the acid in this titration was acetic acid, what will be the formula and name of the product (other than water) that is formed during the titration process?

Note the balanced equation for the reaction that will occur during the titration process

$$HC_2H_3O_2 \quad + \quad NaOH \quad \text{-------} > \quad H_2O \quad + \quad NaC_2H_3O_2$$

acetic acid	sodium hydroxide	water	sodium acetate

$NaC_2H_3O_2$ **Sodium acetate**	**1 point** is earned for the correct formula and name.

Start: Answer all questions on this day before stopping.

Note: No calculators may be used for questions on this day.
You may use ONLY the Periodic Table provided on pg 337

Note: For all questions, assume that the temperature is 298 K, the pressure is 1.00 atmosphere and solutions are aqueous unless otherwise noted.

Questions 1 through 5 refer to the following diagram and the accompanying set of choices with regard to the heat being transferred:

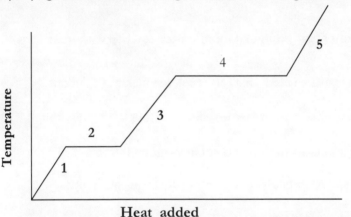

(A) Liquid phase
(B) Increase in average kinetic energy of particles
(C) Decrease in average kinetic energy of particles
(D) Heat of fusion
(E) Heat of vaporization

1. Moving left to right on segment 1 represents this.

2. Segment 2 corresponds to this phase or phase change.

3. Segment 3 corresponds to this phase or phase change

4. Segment 4 corresponds to this phase or phase change.

5. Moving right to left on segment 5 represents this.

Question 6 through 9 refer to atoms for which the occupied atomic orbitals are shown below.

(A) 1s ↑___ 2s ↑↓

(B) 1s ↑↓ 2s ↑↓

(C) 1s ↑↓ 2s ↑↓ 2p ↑___ ↑___ ___

(C) 1s ↑↓ 2s ↑↓ 2p ↑↓ ↑↓ ↑↓

(E) [Ar] 4s ↑↓ 3d ↑↓ ↑___ ↑___ ↑___ ↑___

6. Represents an atom that forms a basic solution when reacted with water.

7. Represents an atom that forms colored aqueous solutions.

8. Represents an atom that readily forms four sp^3 hybrid orbitals.

9. Represents an atom that is not in its ground state.

Questions 10 through 14 refer to the following elements:

(A) Na
(B) Mg
(C) Al
(D) S
(E) Cl

10. Is the heaviest metal

11. Is the most electronegative

12. Has the largest first ionization energy

13. Has the largest jump between second and third ionization energies

14. Has the largest atomic radius

15. Which of the following represents the energy of the single electron in a hydrogen atom when it is in the n = 4 state?

(A) $\dfrac{-2.178 \times 10^{-18}}{2}$ joules

(B) $\dfrac{-2.178 \times 10^{-18}}{4}$ joules

(C) $\dfrac{-2.178 \times 10^{-18}}{8}$ joules

(D) $\dfrac{-2.178 \times 10^{-18}}{16}$ joules

(E) $\dfrac{-2.178 \times 10^{-18}}{64}$ joules

16. A molecule whose central atom has d^2sp^3 hybridization can have which of the following shapes?

          (I) Tetrahedral
          (II) Square pyramidal
          (III) Square planer

(A) I only
(B) III only
(C) I and II only
(D) II and III only
(E) I, II, and III

17. What is the molality of a 10. % (by weight) C_6H_2O (MW = 90.) solution?

(A) 0.012 m
(B) 0.12 m
(C) 1.2 m
(D) 2 m
(E) Not enough information is provided.

18. Which of the following polyatomic ions has the greatest amount of negative charge?

(A) Nitrate
(B) Sulfate
(C) Phosphate
(D) Permanganate
(E) Ammonium

19. Which of the following is the safest and most effective procedure to treat a base spill onto skin?

(A) Dry the affected area with paper towel
(B) Flush the area with a dilute solution of HCl
(C) Flush the affected area with water and then with a dilute NaOH solution
(D) Flush the affected area with water and then with a dilute $NaHCO_3$ solution
(E) Flush the affected area with water and then with a dilute vinegar solution.

20. In solid carbon tetrachloride, the force holding the molecules together is best characterized as

(A) covalent bond
(B) London (dispersion) forces
(C) hydrogen bonds
(D) ionic bonds
(E) molecule-ion attraction

21. Which of the following species *is not* isoelectronic of the others?

    (A) Br^-

    (B) Kr

    (C) Sr^{2+}

    (D) Ga^{3+}

    (E) As^{3-}

22. Which setup is correct for calculating the total amount of Joules that is required to change a 50.0 g piece of ice at -5.00°C to water at 25°C in a calorimeter.

    Physical Constants for Ice and Water are provided below.

    Specific heat(ice)   = 2.10 J/(g°C)

    Specific heat(water) = 4.18 J/(g°C)

    Heat of fusion   = 333 J/g

    Heat of vaporization = 2260 J/g

    (A) Joules = (50 x 333) + (50 x 4.18 x 25)

    (B) Joules = (50 x 333) + (50 x 4.18 x 30)

    (C) Joules = (50 x 2.10 x 5) + (50 x 333) + (50 x 4.18 x 25)

    (D) Joules = (50 x 2.10 x 5) + (50 x 333) + (50 x 4.18 x 30)

    (E) Joules = (50 x 2.10 x 30) + (50 x 333) + (50 x 4.18 x 30)

23. Which of the following pairs of compounds are not a conjugate acid/base pair?

(A) H_3O^+ and H_2O
(B) H_2O and OH^-
(C) NH_3 and NH_2^-
(D) CH_3COOH and CH_3COO^-
(E) H_3PO_4 and PO_4^{3-}

24. In which of the following compounds is the mass ratio of element X to oxygen closest to 2.5 to 1.0? (Molar mass of element X= is 40.0 grams per mole)

(A) XO
(B) XO_2
(C) XO_3
(D) X_2O
(E) X_2O_3

25. Which of the following operations should have a final answer containing four significant figures?

(A) 12.2×13.51
(B) $(62.315)^2$
(C) $0.023 + 1.311$
(D) $1.010 - 11.623$
(E) $64.5 \div 3.2$

26. Which conclusion is based on Rutherford's "gold foil" experiment?

(A) Electrons orbit the nucleus in concentric rings
(B) All neutrons are located in a central nucleus
(C) Most of the mass of an atom is located in a central, dense core
(D) Atoms are composed of positively and negatively charged particles
(E) Alpha particles are attracted to a negative charged plate

27. Excess silver carbonate is added to 500 mL of water and the mixture stirred. Which of the following will cause the equilibrium to shift in the direction that would favor ionization?

    (1) add some $AgNO_3$
    (2) add some NH_3
    (3) add some Na_2CO_3
    (4) add some HNO_3

(A) 1 and 2
(B) 2 and 3
(C) 3 and 4
(D) 1 and 4
(E) 2 and 4

28. The pH of 0.1-molar acetic acid is approximately
(A) 1
(B) 4
(C) 7
(D) 11
(E) 14

29. Given the reaction and rate expression below:

$$W + X \text{-------->} Y + 2Z \quad Rate = k[W][X]$$

What is the relationship between the rates of change in [W], [X], [Y], and [Z]?

(A) Rate = -d[W]/dt = -d[X]/dt = d[Y]/dt = 2d[Z]/dt

(B) Rate = -d[W]/dt = d[X]/dt = -d[Y]/dt = 2d[Z]/dt

(C) Rate = -d[W]/dt = -d[X]/dt = d[Y]/dt = 0.5d[Z]/dt

(D) Rate = d[W]/dt = -d[X]/dt = -d[Y]/dt = 0.5d[Z]/dt

(E) Rate = -2d[W]/dt = -2d[X]/dt = d[Y]/dt = 0.5d[Z]/dt

30.

Time (hours)	% radioisotope remaining
0	100
2	82
4	67
6	50
8	41
10	32
12	25
14	20
...	...
20	10
....	...
40	1

The data table above shows the percentage of a radioisotope remaining every two hour as it decays for a period of 40 hours. Which of the following best describes the order and the half-life of the reaction?

	Order of reaction	Half-life of reaction (in hours)
(A)	Second	6
(B)	Second	20
(C)	First	6
(D)	First	12
(E)	First	20

31. $8CN^- (aq) + 4Ag (s) + O_2 (g) + 2H_2O (l) \longrightarrow$
$$4Ag(CN)_2^-(aq) + 4 OH^- (aq)$$
Which of the following is true regarding the reaction represented above?
(A) The oxidation number of O does not change.
(B) The oxidation number of H changes from -1 to +1.
(C) The oxidation number of Ag changes from zero to -1.
(D) The oxidation number of C is +4 in the cyanide ion.
(E) This oxidation number of N is -3 in the cyanide ion.

32. A radioactive isotope has a half-life of 6.93 years and decays by beta emission. Determine the approximate fraction of the sample that is left undecayed at the end of 11.5 years.

(A) 1%

(B) 5%

(C) 30%

(D) 75%

(E) 99%

33. Which of the following would be spontaneous?

(A) the decomposition of iron(II) oxide to iron metal and oxygen gas

(B) heat transfer from an ice cube to a room maintained at a temperature of 27°C

(C) expansion of a gas to fill the available volume

(D) the decomposition of sodium chloride

(E) freezing of water at 2°C

34. In the reaction

$$2Fe_2O_3 \ + \ 3C \ \text{------>} \ 4Fe \ + \ 3CO_2$$

if 500.g of Fe_2O_3 reacts with 75.0 g of C, how many grams of Fe will be produced?

(A) 56.4g

(B) 75.0g

(C) 316.g

(D) 350.g

(E) 465.g

35. $H_2O(l) \ \text{------->} \ H_2O(s)$

When water freezes at its normal freezing point, 0°C and 1 atm, which of the followings is true for the process shown above?

(A) $\Delta H < 0, \ \Delta S > 0, \ \Delta V > 0$

(B) $\Delta H < 0, \ \Delta S < 0, \ \Delta V > 0$

(C) $\Delta H > 0, \ \Delta S < 0, \ \Delta V < 0$

(D) $\Delta H > 0, \ \Delta S > 0, \ \Delta V > 0$

(E) $\Delta H > 0, \ \Delta S > 0, \ \Delta V < 0$

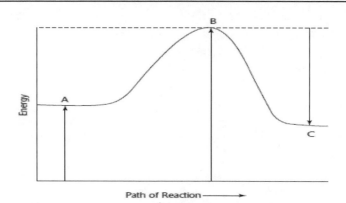

Path of Reaction ⟶

36. Which correctly represents the enthalpy for the reaction?

(A) B − (C − A)
(B) B
(C) C − A
(D) B − C
(E) A − (B − C)

37. 10.0 mL of 1.00 M NaOH will create a solution of pH = 7 when mixed with which of the following (assume the solution is 0.500 M)?
(A) 10.0 mL HNO_3
(B) 10.0 mL CH_3COOH
(C) 5.00 mL HCl
(D) 5.00 mL H_2SO_4
(E) 10.0 mL H_2SO_4

38. When benzene and toluene are mixed together, they form an ideal solution. If benzene has a higher vapor pressure than toluene, the the vapor pressure of a solution that contains an equal number of moles of benzene and toluene will be

(A) higher than the vapor pressure of benzene
(B) equal to the vapor pressure of benzene
(C) lower than the vapor pressure of benzene and higher than the vapor pressure of toluene
(D) equal to the vapor pressure of toluene
(E) lower than the vapor pressure of benzene and higher than the vapor pressure of toluene

39. Which of the following is not a likely product for the decay of iodine-131?

    (A) Antimony-127
    (B) Tellurium-131
    (C) Iodine-131
    (D) Xenon-131
    (E) Cesium-135

40. Which of the following substances will exhibit hydrogen bonding?
    (A) Butane
    (B) Butanone
    (C) Butanol
    (D) Butanoic acid
    (E) Methyl butanoate

Questions 41 through 42

$$BrO_3^- + 5Br^- + 6H^+ \longrightarrow 3 Br_2 + 3H_2O$$

The oxidation of bromide ions by bromate ions in acidic aqueous solution occurs according to the stoichiometry shown above. The experimental rate law of the reaction is:

$$Rate = k\,[BrO_3^-]\,[Br^-]\,[H^+]$$

41. What is the order of the reaction with respect to Br^-?

    (A) 1
    (B) 2
    (C) 3
    (D) 5
    (E) 6

42. According to the rate law for the reaction, an increase in the concentration of hydrogen ion has what effect on this reaction?

    (A) The rate of reaction increases.
    (B) The rate of reaction decreases.
    (C) The value of the equilibrium constant increases.
    (D) The value of the equilibrium constant decreases.
    (E) Neither the rate nor the value of the equilibrium constant is changed.

43. Given the following heat of reaction and the bond energies listed in the accompanying table (measured under standard conditions), calculate the energy of the C=O bond. All numerical values are in kilojoules per mole, and all substances are in the gas phase.

$$CH_3CHO \quad + \quad H_2 \quad \text{--------} > \quad CH_3CH_2OH$$
$$\Delta H° = -71 \text{ kJ/mole}$$

Bond	O − H	C − H	C − C	C − O	H − H
Bond Energy (KJ · mol^{-1})	464	414	347	351	435

(A) 180 KJ
(B) 360 KJ
(C) 723 KJ
(D) 1446 KJ
(E) 2892 KJ

44. Which of the following is not capable of reacting with molecular oxygen?

(A) SO_2
(B) SO_3
(C) NO
(D) N_2O
(E) P_4O_6

45. What is the [H$^+$] of a solution with a pOH of 4.50?

(A) 3.1×10^{-4}
(B) 5.6×10^{-5}
(C) 4.2×10^{-9}
(D) 3.2×10^{-10}
(E) 7.1×10^{-11}

46. Which of the following compounds is least soluble in water?

(A) Sodium propanoate
(B) Propanoic acid
(C) Propanediol
(D) Propanone
(E) Propene

47. Of the following reactions, which involves the largest decrease in entropy?

(A) $MgCO_3(s)$ -------> $MgO(s) + CO_2(g)$
(B) $2NO(g) + O_2(g)$ -----> $2NO_2(g)$
(C) $Pb(NO_3)_3(aq) + 2NaCl(aq)$ ------> $PbCl_2(s) + 2NaNO_3(aq)$
(D) $CH_4(g) + 2O_2(g)$ ------> $CO2(g) + 2 H_2O(l)$
(E) $4 Al(s) + 3O_2(g)$ ------> $2Al_2O_3(s)$

Questions *48* through *50* refer to the following reaction that takes place within an electrochemical cell:

Solid copper reacts with oxygen gas under acidic conditions to produce copper (II) cation and water.

$$Cu^{2+}(aq) \ + \ 2e^- \ \text{------}> \ Cu(s) \qquad E°red = +0.34 \ V$$

$$O_2(g) \ + \ 4H^+(aq) \ + \ 4e^- \ \text{-------}> \ 2H_2O(l) \qquad E°red = +1.23 \ V$$

48. What is the balanced reaction equation?

(A) $2Cu \ + \ O_2 \ \text{------}> \ 2Cu^{2+} \ + \ H_2O$
(B) $Cu \ + \ O_2 \ + \ H^+ \ \text{------}> \ Cu^{2+} \ + \ H_2O$
(C) $2Cu \ + \ O_2 \ + \ 4H^+ \ \text{-----}> \ 2Cu^{2+} \ + \ 2H_2O$
(D) $2Cu \ + \ O_2 \ + \ 2H^+ \ \text{----}> \ 2Cu^{2+} \ + \ H_2O$
(E) $2Cu \ + \ 2O_2 \ + \ 2H^+ \ \text{-----}> \ Cu^{2+} \ + \ 2H_2O$

49. What is the standard cell potential for the reaction?

(A) −0.89 V
(B) +0.89 V
(C) −1.57 V
(D) +1.57 V
(E) +1.23 V

50. What is the standard free energy change for the reaction?
    (Note: $1 J = 1 C·V$, so $1F = \dfrac{96{,}500 \ J}{(V·mol)}$

(A) +610 kJ/mol
(B) −610 kJ/mol
(C) +150 kJ/mol
(D) −340 kJ/mol
(E) +340 kJ/mol

Day 16

STOP. Correct your answers and note how many correct **points**

Day 16: Answers and Explanations

Answers: Quick Check:

1. **B**	2. **D**	3. **A**	4. **E**	5. **C**	6. **B**	7. **E**	8. **C**	9. **A**	10. **C**
11. **E**	12. **A**	13. **B**	14. **A**	15. **D**	16. **D**	17. **C**	18. **C**	19. **E**	20. **B**
21. **D**	22. **C**	23. **E**	24. **A**	25. **C**	26. **C**	27. **E**	28. **B**	29. **C**	30. **C**
31. **E**	32. **C**	33. **C**	34. **D**	35. **C**	36. **D**	37. **E**	38. **C**	39. **E**	40. **D**
41. **A**	42. **A**	43. **C**	44. **B**	45. **D**	46. **E**	47. **E**	48. **C**	49. **B**	50. **D**

Answers and Explanations

Questions 1 through 5: interpreting phase change diagram

1. **B** *Note:* From Left to right of segment 1, temperature is increasing

   Recall: As temperature increases, average kinetic energy increases.

2. **D** *Note:* Melting (solid to liquid) is taking place during segment 2.

   Recall: Fusion is another term for melting.

3. **A** *Note:* The substance exists only as a liquid during segment 3

4. **E** *Note:* Boiling (liquid to gas) is taking place during segment 4.

   Heat of vaporization is measured during boiling.

5. **C** *Note:* From right to left of segment 5, temperature is decreasing

   Recall: As temperature decreases, average kinetic energy decreases.

6. **B** **Relating orbital notation to properties atom**

   Note: The total number of electrons in this configuration is 4.

   The atom is beryllium (Be), an alkaline earth metal.

   Recall: Alkaline earth metals react with water to form bases as represented below.

   $$Be \ + \ H_2O \ ----> \ Be(OH)_2 \ + \ H_2$$
   alkaline earth   water   base

---

7. **E**   *Note:*   The total number of electrons in this configuration is 26. The atom is Fe, a transition metal.

   Recall: Transition metals form colored aqueous solutions

8. **C**   *Note:*   This configuration has 6 electrons. The atom is carbon (C)

   Recall: A carbon atom readily forms four covalent bonds

9. **A**   *Note:*   This configuration has only 1 electron that is occupying a *higher sublevel.*

   Recall: An atom that is not in the ground state (an excited state atom) has electron that had absorbed enough energy to jump to a higher energy level.

10. **C**   **Properties of elements**

   Note: Of the three metals; Na, Mg, and Al, Al has the greatest (heaviest) molecular mass (see Periodic Table)

11. **E**   *Recall:*   Electronegativity values (a measure of atom's ability to attract electrons from another atom during bonding) increases from left to right.

   Note: Of all the elements listed, Cl (a halogen) if the farthest right, hence, the one that is most likely to attract electrons.

12. **A**   *Recall:*   Ionization energy (energy to remove the most loosely bound electron from an atom) decreases from right to left.

   Note: Of all the elements listed, Na (an alkali metal) is the farthest left, hence, the one with the lowest ionization energy.

13. **B**   *Note:*   Of elements listed, Mg is the only atom with two electrons in its valance shell.

   Note: The first and second ionization energies are energies to remove the first and second valance electron, respectively, and form a stable noble gas configuration

   Note: The third ionization energy is, therefore, energy to remove an electron from a stable Mg atom. This energy will be much higher than the second ionization energy since a stable Mg atom (Mg^{2+}) will be unwilling to lose any more electron.

14. **A**   *Note:*   All the elements listed are in the same Period (3).

   Recall: Atomic radius of elements in the same period decreases from left to right due to increase in nuclear charge (number of protons).

   Note: Na is the farthest left of all the listed elements, hence, the one with the largest atomic radius.

15. **D**   **Energy of electron**

   Recall the equation below

$$E_n = \frac{-2.178 \times 10^{-18}}{n^2} \text{ joules}$$

   For n = 4

$$E_n = \frac{-2.178 \times 10^{-18}}{16} \text{ joules}$$

16. D hybrization and molecular shape

Note: A d^2sp^3 hybridized molecule can have different shapes depending on the number of nonbonding electron pairs of the central atom

hybridization	number of unbonded pair	shape
$d^2\,sp^3$	0	Octahedral
$d^2\,sp^3$	1	square pyramidal
$d^2\,sp^3$	2	square planer

Note: d^2sp^3 can never produce a tetrahedral shape molecule.

17. C molality calculation

Assume 100 grams of the solution

Step 1: Determine mass of solvent and solute

mass of solute C_6H_2O = 10% of 100 g = 10 g C_6H_2O

Mass of solvent H_2O = 90% of 100 g = 90 g H_2O

Step 2: Determine moles of solute C_6H_2O

$$\text{moles} = \frac{\text{mass of } C_6H_2O}{\text{molar mass } C_6H_2O} = \frac{10\text{ g}}{90\text{ g/mol}^{-1}} = 0.11\text{ mol}$$

Step 3: Calculate molality (*m*)

$$m = \frac{\text{moles solute}}{\text{Kg solvent}} = \frac{0.11\text{ mol}}{0.090\text{ Kg}} = \mathbf{1.22\ m}$$

18. C Polyatomic ion formulas

Recall the symbols for the polyatomic ions given as choices

(A) Nitrate NO_3^-

(B) Sulfate SO_4^{2-}

(C) Phosphate PO_4^{3-} **(greatest – charge)**

(D) Permanganate MnO_4^-

(E) Ammonium NH_4^+

19. E   **Lab safety**

Recall the following lab safety procedure:
Any spill onto skin should be washed with large amount of water

Note: Since the spill is a base, a dilute acid can also be use to further neutralize the base

Note: A strong acid like HCl should never be used on the skin, no matter how dilute its concentration.

20. B   **Intermolecular forces**

Note: Carbon tetrachloride is a nonpolar substance because its molecules , CCl_4, are symmetrical.

Recall: London (aka dispersion) forces are intermolecular forces that hold nonpolar molecules together in the solid state.

21. D   **Isoelectronic, ion, determining number of electrons**

Recall: Isoelectronic refers to species with the same number of electrons

Determine and compare number of electrons in each particle.

Br^- (36e-)   Kr (36 e-) Sr^{2+} (36 e-)   **Ga^{3+} (28e-)** As^{3-} (36 e-)

Note: All, except Ga^{3+} , have the same number of electrons

22. C   **Thermodynamic, heat calculation**

Note: There are three changes involved in this question.

Temperature change: The ice is warmed from -5°C to 0°C

Joules = mass $_{ice}$ x C_{ice} x ΔT_{ice}

Joules =   50 g   x   2.10 J/g·°C x   5 °C

Phase change : The ice is melted to water at 0°C

Joules = Mass $_{ice}$ x   Hf $_{ice}$

Joules =   50 g   x   333 J/g

Temperature change: The Water is warmed from 0°C to 25°C

Joules = mass $_{water}$ x C_{water} x ΔT_{water}

Joules =   50 g   x   4.18 J/g·°C x   25 °C

Note: Total Joules is the sum from the three changes

Joules   = (50 x 2.10 x 5) + (50 x 333) + (50 x 4.18 x 25)

23. E **Conjugate acid-base pair**

Recall: Formulas of a conjugate acid-base pair differ by just one H.

Note: H_3PO_4 and PO_4^{3-} are the only pair that differs by more than 1 H atom. Therefore, are NOT acid-base pair.

24. A **Percent composition by mass**

Note: The total mass of X must be 2.5 times greater than the total mass of O in the formula

Note: Only in choice A formula, XO, that this is the case

$$\frac{\text{Total mass of X}}{\text{Total mass of O}} = \frac{40\text{ g}}{16\text{ g}} = \frac{2.5}{1}$$

25. C **Significant figures**

Note: You are looking for a choice in which the answer has 4 significant figures

Recall the following rules for determining significant figures

When multiplying or dividing:
Limit or round the answer to the same number of significant figures as the factor with the least number of significant figures.

Eliminate Choice A: Answer will have 3 significant figures
Eliminate Choice B: Answer will have 5 significant figures
Eliminate Choice E: Answer will have 2 significant figures

When adding or subtracting:
Limit or round answer to the same number of decimal places as the factor with the least decimal places.

Eliminate Choice D: Answer will have 5 significant figures

Choice C: 0.023 + 1.311 = 1.334 (4 significant figs)

            3 decimal   *3 decimal*   *3 decimal*
              places   *places*   *places*

26. C **Rutherford Gold Foil experiment, atomic structure**

Recall the following Gold Foil experiment conclusions made by Rutherford
. Atom is mostly unoccupied empty space
. Atom central core is more massive, denser, and smaller
    than the rest of the atom

27. E **Le Chatelier's principle, Solution Equilibrium , dissociation**

Step 1: Write the equilibrium equation to represent the ionization
    reaction described.

$$Ag_2CO_3(s) \; <====== > \; 2Ag^+(aq) \; + \; CO_3^{2-}(aq)$$

Note: The reaction favors ionization when the addition of the listed
    substance **shift the reaction right** (or produces more ions)

Step 2: Use your knowledge of reactions and Le Chatelier's principle
    to indicate what happens to the reaction when each substance
    is added.

    (1) AgNO$_3$ added : ionizes into Ag$^+$:   ↑ [Ag$^+$]   Reaction shifts Left

    (2) **NH$_3$ added:**   forms Ag(NH$_3$)$_2^{2+}$ ↓ [Ag$^+$]   **Reaction shifts Right**

    (3) Na$_2$CO$_3$ added : ionizes into CO$_3^{2-}$: ↑[CO$_3^{2-}$]   Reaction shifts Left

    (4) **HNO$_3$ added : H+ reacts with CO$_3^{2-}$** ↓[CO$_3^{2-}$]   **Reaction shifts Right**

Note: Only the addition of NH$_3$ (2) and HNO$_3$ (4) shift the reaction Right.

28. B **pH – acid concentration relationship**

Note: Acetic is a weak acid.

Where as a strong 0.1 molar acid will have a pH of 1 or 2, a
weak 0.1 molar acid (like acetic) will have a pH higher than
a 2, but less than 7. Choice B (pH 4) is in this range.

29. C **Rate of change, reactant - product relationship**

$$W + X \text{-------} > Y + 2Z$$

Note: W and X are reactants.

Y and Z are products

Relate: The sign for the rate of change will be the same for W and X
The sign for the rate of change will be the same for Y and Z, but opposite that of W and X.
Eliminate Choice B and D because these are not the case.

Note: The mole ratio in the equation is **1W : 1X : 1Y : 2Z**

Relate: The coefficients for rate of change with respect to W, X and Y must be a 1.

The coefficient for rate of change with respect to Z must be ½ or 0.5 since there are twice the number of moles of Z.

Choice C is correct because when all information are considered, the signs for rate of change and the coefficients of substances with respect to each other are all correct.

30. C **Half-life, order of decay reaction, data interpretation**

Note: Half-life of the radioisotope is **6 days** because this is when 50% (½) of it remains.

Recall: All radioactive decay is **First Order** because decay is independent of the initial concentration of the radioisotope.

31. E **Redox reaction interpretation, oxidation numbers**

Note: Oxidation numbers must be correctly assigned to the elements in the equation before the correct statement can be determined.

$$\overset{+2\ -3}{8C\,N^-} + \overset{0}{4Ag} + \overset{0}{O_2} + \overset{+1\ -2}{2H_2O} \text{------} > \overset{+1\ +2\ -3}{4Ag(C\,N)_2^-} + \overset{-2\ +1}{4\,O\,H^-}$$
cyanide ion

Note: Of the statements given as choices, only Choice E (N is -3 in the cyanide ion) is correct

32. **C**   **Half-life, fraction remaining, nuclear decay**

Note: Percent of radioisotope remaining unchanged can be estimated using fraction remaining equation:

$$\text{Fraction remaining} = \left(\frac{1}{2}\right)^n$$

| n = half-life periods |
| n = 11.5 / 6.93 ≈ 2 |

$$\text{Fraction remaining} = \left(\frac{1}{2}\right)^2 = \frac{1}{4} = 25$$

Note: Since all the choices are very far apart, the most reasonable estimated answer is Choice 3 (30%)

33. **C**   **Spontaneity in physical and chemical changes**

Recall: Spontaneous processes occurs when the reaction leads to a state of higher entropy (increase disorder of the system)

Note: In Choice C, expansion of a gas (increase space/volume) is accompanied by increase in entropy because the gas particles can move even more freely (increase disorder)

34. **D**   **Mass – mass calculation in equation, limiting reagent**

Note: To correctly calculated mass of Fe that can be produced, the limiting reagent in the reaction must be identified.

Step 1: Determine mass of C that will react with 500 g of Fe_2O_3 using mass and mole ratios in factor-labeling

$$500 \text{ g } Fe_2O_3 \ \times \ \frac{1 \text{ mole } Fe_2O_3}{160 \text{ g } Fe_2O_3} \ \times \ \frac{3 \text{ mol C}}{2 \text{ mol } Fe_2O_3} \ \times \ \frac{12 \text{ g C}}{1 \text{ mol C}} = \textbf{56 g C}$$

Note: Fe_2O_3 is the limiting reagent in the reaction because:

According to the calculation, all 500 g of the Fe_2O_3 will be completely consumed when only 56 g of the 75 g of C is used up.

Step 2: Calculate mass of Fe using mole ratio of Fe_2O_3 to Fe

$$500 \text{ g } Fe_2O_3 \ \times \ \frac{1 \text{ mol } Fe_2O_3}{160 \text{ g } Fe_2O_3} \ \times \ \frac{4 \text{ mol Fe}}{2 \text{ mol } Fe_2O_3} \ \times \ \frac{56 \text{ g Fe}}{1 \text{ mol Fe}} = \textbf{350 g Fe}$$

35. B   **Enthalpy, entropy, and volume changes of a phase change**

$$H_2O(l) \ \text{-------} \rightarrow \ H_2O(s)$$

Note: The change shown is freezing:

ΔH is – (exothermic) because heat is released as liquid freezes: **$\Delta H < 0$**

ΔS is – ($\downarrow$ entropy) because particles become more organized: **$\Delta S < 0$**

ΔV is + ($\uparrow$ volume) because water expands as it turns to ice: **$\Delta V > 0$**

36. C   **Interpreting potential energy diagram**

Note: A is reactant; C is product

Recall: Enthalpy (ΔH) = $H_{product} - H_{reactant}$

Enthalpy (ΔH) =   **C**   **– A**

37. E   **Acid-base titration, neutralization**

Recall: Acid and abase will produce a neutral solution (pH = 7) when equal moles of H^+ and OH^- are present during the reaction

Note: Only the solution of the acid in Choice E has :

moles of H+   =   mole of OH-

M_a x V_a x # of H^+ = M_b x V_b x # of OH^-
(0.5 M) (10 mL) (2)   =   (1.0 M) (10 mL) (1)

10 moles H^+   =   **10 moles OH**

38. C   **Raoult's law, partial pressure**

Recall: According to Raoult's law, the vapor pressure of an ideal solution is dependent upon the mole fraction of its components.

Note: For a solution with equal moles of two components:

$VP_{solution}$ = ½ $(VP_{benzene})$ + ½ $(VP_{toluene})$

Note: According to question, $VP_{benzene}$ is greater than $VP_{toluene}$.

Assume: $VP_{benzene}$ = 100 kPa

$VP_{toluene}$ = 60 kPa

$VP_{solution}$ = ½ $(VP_{benzene})$ + ½ $(VP_{toluene})$

80   = ½ (100)   + ½ (60)

Note: $VP_{solution}$ (80) is less than $VP_{benzene\,(100)}$ BUT greater $VP_{toluene\,(60)}$

Day 16: Answers and Explanations.

39. E   Nuclear decay

Note: During a nuclear decay, the mass number of the product is either smaller (for alpha decays) or stays the same(for beta, positron or gamma decay)

Note: The masses for choices A – D indicates that these isotopes are possible products of iodine – 131 decay.

Note: Cesium – 135 is not a possible decay product of iodine – 131 because its mass is larger than that of iodine – 131.

40. D   Hydrogen bonding, Functional group of organic compounds

Recall: Hydrogen bonding is formed between molecules that have a hydrogen atom bonded to an atom of high electronegativity and small radius

Note: Of all the choices listed, only butanoic acid contains a COOH (carboxyl) group in which H is bonded to O (a high electronegativity atom)

41. A   Rate law, order of reaction

Recall: The exponent of each substance in the rate law gives the order with respect to that substance.

$$\text{Rate} = k\,[BrO_3^{-}\,]\,[Br^{-}]\,[H^{+}]$$

Note: The exponent of [Br-]in the rate law is 1:
The order with respect to Br- is 1

42. A   Concentration Change – rate change relationship

Note: Since H+ is a reactant, Increasing [H^{+}] in the reaction will increase the rate proportionally.

---

43. C   Hess Law, bond energy

Recognize that Hess Law below is essential in solving this problem.

$$\Delta H° = \sum \Delta H°\text{Reactants} + \sum\Delta H°\text{products}$$

Step 1: Draw out structures of substances in the reaction to help in determining which bonds are broken and which bonds are formed.

$$CH_3CHO + H_2 \text{----------} > CH_3\,CH_2\,OH$$

Step 2: Determine which bonds are broken (on the reactant side) and which bonds are formed (on the product side) Use Table given to note their energies.

Broken: C = O   H − H

$H°_{Reactants}$ X KJ/mol   435 KJ/mol

> *Note:* This energies have + values because these bonds are broken (endothermic = +ΔH)

Formed: C − H   C − O   O − H

$H°_{product}$ - 414 KJ/mol   -351 mol/mol   - 464 KJ/mol

> *Note:* These energies have − values because these bonds are formed (exothermic = - ΔH°)

Step 3: Rewrite Hess law equation, substitute factors, and solve for X (energy of C = O bond)

$$\Delta H° = \sum \Delta H°\text{Reactants} + \sum\Delta H°\text{products}$$

-71 = X + 435 + - 1229

X = -71 - 435 + 1229 = **723 KJ/mol**

44. B   **Properties of elements, valance electron, oxidation reaction**

Note: For a molecule to be capable of reacting with oxygen, the + charge of the element (S, N or P) in the formula must be less than the maximum charge the atom can form . This means that the atom CAN BE oxidized further to react with O.

Therefore: The formula that *IS NOT* capable of reacting with oxygen (your answer) must contain S, N, or P with a a **+ charge that is equal to the atom's maximum charge value.** This means the atom CANNOT BE be oxidized further.

Note: **maximum + charge value = Number of valance electrons** In another words, an atom cannot lose more valance electrons than it has.

Determine   Maximum charge value and Charge in formula

	Formula	Maximum charge	Charge in formula
(A)	SO_2	S = +6	S = +4
(B)	SO_3	S = +6	S = +6
(C)	NO	N = +5	N = +2
(D)	N_2O	N = +5	N = +1
(E)	P_4O_6	P = +5	P = +3

Note: SO_3 (in Choice B) is the only formula in which the charge of S is equal to the maximum + charge S can form. S *CANNOT BE* oxidized further in this formula.

45. D.   **pOH and [H+] relationship**

Recall: 14 = pH + pOH

Determine pH

pH = 14 − pOH
pH = 14 − 4.05 = 9.50

Recall: The value of the exponent of the [H+] must be equal to or close to the value of the pH

Note: in Choice D; 3.2×10^{-10} ⟵ close to 9.5

46. E **Solubility – molecular polarity relationship**

Recall: Polarity of a substance determines its solubility in water.

Recall: Polar substances are the most soluble in water.
Nonpolar substances are the least soluble in water.

Recognize that Propene (an alkene) is the only nonpolar listed as a choice, and therefore, the least soluble in water.

Note: The rest are either highly polar (Sodium propanoate and Propanoic acid) or slightly polar (Propanediol and Propanone).

47. E **Entropy change of chemical reactions**

Recall: Entropy measures disorder, randomness , or chaos of a system.

Note: According to the question, you are choosing a reaction (system) in which the products have the largest decrease in entropy (or is becoming most organized or most ordered)

Note: Examples of a system with a decreasing entropy are:
Gas ------- > solid or **2** moles of gas -------- > **1** mole of gas

Determine and *compare* changes in order, eliminate choices as you go.

(A)
$MgCO_3(s)$ ------ > $MgO(s)$ + $CO_2(g)$
solid ----------- > *gas* = *more disorder (eliminate A)*

(B)
2 $NO(g)$ + $1O_2(g)$ --- > **2** $NO_2(g)$
3 moles gas ------- > *2 moles gas* = *more order (keep B)*

(C)
$Pb(NO_3)_3(aq)$ + $2NaCl(aq)$ ---- > $PbCl_2(s)$ + $2 NaNO_3(aq)$
aqueous ---------------- > *solid and aqueous*
= *more order AND the change is greater than B (keep C, eliminate B)*

(D)
$CH_4(g)$ + $2O_2(g)$ ----- > $CO_2(g)$ + $2H_2O(l)$
gas ---------- > gas and liquid = *more order BUT the change is NOT as great as in C (eliminate D)*

(E)
$4 Al(s)$ + $3 O_2(g)$ ------ > $2 Al_2O3(s)$
gas ----------------- > *All solid* = *More order AND the change is greater than in C (keep E, eliminate C)*

Questions 48 through 50: Adding half-reactions, reduction potentials

48. **C** *Note:* **Choice A, B, D and E can all be eliminated** because these equations are not balanced as written.

To proof check if **Choice C** is correct, do the followings:

Step 1: Reverse the copper reaction : $Cu \longrightarrow Cu^{2+} + 2e^-$

Step 2: Increase moles of electrons to 4: $2Cu \longrightarrow 2\,Cu^{2+} + 4e^-$

Step 3: Write the H_2O reaction: $O_2 + 4H^+ + 4e^- \longrightarrow 2H_2O$

Step 3: Add the two equations $\mathbf{2Cu + O_2 + 4H^+ \longrightarrow 2Cu^{2+} + 2H_2O}$

49. **B** *Recognize* that the equation below is needed to calculate standard cell potential for the reaction $E°$ for the

$$E°_{cell} = E°_{oxidation} + E°_{reduction}$$

Determine which half-reaction is oxidation and which is reduction. Be sure to reverse the $E°$ sign for oxidation-half.

Note: In a reaction of a metal with nonmetal, the metal (Cu) will always be oxidized, the nonmetal (O_2) will always be reduced.

Oxidation: $Cu \longrightarrow Cu^{2+} + 2e^-$ $E°_{oxi} = -0.34$ V

Reduction: $O_2 + 4H^+ + 4e^- \longrightarrow 2H_2O$ $E°_{red} = +1.23$

Calculate standard cell potential ($E°_{cell}$) for the reaction

$$E° = E°_{oxidation} + E°_{reduction}$$
$$E° = -0.34 \text{ V} + 1.23 \text{ V} = \mathbf{+0.89 \text{ V}}$$

50. **D** *Recognize* that the equation below is needed to calculate $\Delta G°$
$$\Delta G° = -n\,F\,E°$$

Note: n = 4 (moles of electrons involve in the reaction)

F = 96,500 Joules / $V^{-1} \cdot mol^{-1}$ (given)

Substitute factors into equation and solve for $\Delta G°$ (free energy change)
$$\Delta G° = -n\,F\,E°$$
$$\Delta G° = -4(\,96{,}500 \text{ J/V}^{-1} \cdot mol^{-1})(0.89 \text{ V})$$
$$\Delta G° = -343{,}500 \text{ J/mol} \approx \mathbf{-340 \text{ KJ/mol}}$$

START: Answer all questions on this day before stopping.

Note: You may use a calculator for questions on this day.
You may use any of the reference material provided on pg 337-340

CLEARLY SHOW THE METHOD USED AND THE STEPS INVOLVED IN ARRIVING AT YOUR ANSWERS. It is to your advantage to do this, since you may obtain partial credit if you do and you will receive little or no credit if you do not. Attention should be paid to significant figures.

---

1.   **(10 points)**

Benzoic acid acid dissociates in water according to the reaction below.

$$C_6H_5COOH(aq) \quad + \quad H_2O(l) \quad ----> H_3O^+(aq) + C_6H_5COO^-(aq)$$

$$K_a = 6.17 \times 10^{-5}$$

(a) Write the equilibrium constant expression for the reaction.

(b) Calculate the molar concentration of $C_6H_5COO^-$ in a 0.0100M benzoic acid solution.

(c) What is the pH of the solution in (b) ?

(d) After adding 10.0mL of 5.00×10^{-6} M $Ca(OH)_2$ to 90.0mL of an unknown concentration of benzoic acid, the pH of the solution is 5.26. Calculate each of the following:

(i) The [H+] of the solution after the addition of $Ca(OH)_2$.

(ii) The [OH–] of the solution after the addition of $Ca(OH)_2$.

(ii) Write a balanced neutralization reaction equation for the reaction of benzoic acid with the calcium hydroxide.

(e) State whether the solution at the equivalence point of this titration is acidic, basic, or neutral. Explain your reasoning.

Day 17 Question 1: Space for Work and Answers

2.   **(10 points)**

A student uses spectrophotometer to collect data on the first order decomposition of a colored chemical species, Z, into colorless products.

The molar absorptivity of Z is 5.0×10^3 /(cm·M). The cuvette containing the reaction mixture has a path length of 1.0 cm.

The data table below contains information collected by the student.

[Z] (M)	?	8.00×10^{-5}	6.00×10^{-5}	3.00×10^{-5}
Absorbance	1.20	0.400	0.300	0.150
Time (min.)	0.0	25.0	46.5	?

(a) What is the initial concentration of the colored species?

(b) Based on the information provided on the table, determine the rate constant for the first order reaction. Include all units with your answer.

(c) How many minutes have elapsed from when the absorbance goes from 1.20 to 0.150.

(d) Determine the half-life of the reaction performed by the student.

(e) The student performed more experiments to determine the rate constant at various temperature, T. The student plotted the graph below from data she collected from the experiments.

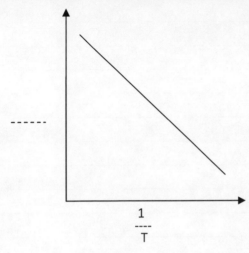

(i) Label the vertical axis of the graph on the dotted line.

(ii) Explain how the student can calculate the activation energy, Ea, for the reaction using information provided by the graph.

Day 17

STOP. Correct your answers and note how many correct **points**

1. **(10 points)**

Benzoic acid acid dissociates in water according to the reaction below.

$$C_6H_5COOH\ (aq)\ +\ H_2O(l)\ ---->\ H_3O^+(aq) + C_6H_5COO^-(aq)$$

$$K_a = 6.17 \times 10^{-5}$$

(a) Write the equilibrium constant , K_a, expression for the reaction.

Recall: $\quad K_a\ =\ \dfrac{[Products]}{[Reactants]}$

Note: Water has a constant concentration. Therefore, it's never included in equilibrium expressions.

$K_a\ =\ \dfrac{[C_6H_5COO^-]\,[H_3O^+]}{[C_6H_5COO]}$	**1 point** is earned for the correct expression

(b) Calculate the molar concentration of $C_6H_5COO^-$ in a 0.010 M benzoic acid solution.

Determine the [ ] of the substances at equilibrium $[C_6H_5COO^-] = X$ mole ratio of $C_6H_5COO^-$ to $[H_3O^+]$ $[H_3O^+]\quad = X$ in the balanced equation is 1 : 1 $[C_6H_5COO^-] = 0.010\ M - X\ \approx 0.010M$ (low dissociation)	**1 point** is earned for substituting concentration into Ka equation
Substitute factors into K_a expression and solve for X $K_a\ =\ \dfrac{[C_6H_5COO^-][H_3O^+]}{[C_6H_5COO]}$ $6.17 \times 10^{-5}\ =\ \dfrac{(X)\,(X)}{0.010\ M}$ $X^2\ =\ 6.17 \times 10^{-7}\ M$ $X\ =\ 7.85 \times 10^{-4}\ M\ =\ [C_6H_5COO^-]$	**1 point** is earned for correctly calculating the $[C_6H_5COO^-]$

(c) What is the pH of the solution in (b) ?

Note: pH $= -\log [H_3O^+]$ (see Reference Materials on Pg 339)

Note: $[H_3O^+]$ $=$ $[C_6H_5COO^-]$ $= 7.85 \times 10^{-4}$ M

pH $= -\log [H_3O^+]$ pH $= -\log (7.85 \times 10^{-4}$ M$)$	**1 point** is earned for setup
pH $= 3.1$	**1 point** is earned for correct pH

(d) After adding 10.0mL of 5.00×10^{-6} M Ca(OH)$_2$ to 90.0mL of an unknown concentration of benzoic acid, the pH of the solution is 5.26. Calculate each of the followings:

(i) The [H$^+$] of the solution after the addition of Ca(OH)$_2$.

Recall: $[H^+] = 10^{-pH}$

$[H^+] = 10^{-pH}$ $[H^+] = 10^{-5.26} = 5.5 \times 10^{-6}$ M	**1 point** is earned for the correct pH

(ii) The [OH$^-$] of the solution after the addition of Ca(OH)$_2$.

Recall: $[H^+] \times [OH^-] = 1.0 \times 10^{-14}$

$[OH^-] = \dfrac{1.0 \times 10^{-14}}{[H^+]} = \dfrac{1.0 \times 10^{-14}}{5.5 \times 10^{-6} \text{ M}}$ $[OH^-] = 1.82 \times 10^{-9}$ M.	**1 point** is earned for setup **1 point** is earned for correct [OH$^-$]

(iii) Write a balanced equation for the reaction of the benzoic acid and calcium hydroxide.

Note: This a double replacement (ion-exchange) neutralization reaction.

Recall: Water and salt are produced in neutralization reactions.

2 C$_6$H$_5$COOH $+$ Ca(OH) $\longrightarrow$ H$_2$O $+$ Ca(C$_6$H$_5$COO)$_2$ *acid* *base* *water* *salt*	**1 point** is earned for correct equation

(e) State whether the solution at the equivalence point of this titration is acidic, basic, or neutral. Explain your reasoning.

The solution at equivalent point will be basic because **calcium benzoate, a basic salt, is formed during the titration.**	**1 point** is earned for stating solution is basic with correct explanation

2. **(10 points)**

A student uses spectrophotometer to collect data on the first order decomposition of a colored chemical species, Z, into colorless products.

The molar absorptivity of Z is 5.0×10^3 /(cm·M). The cuvette containing the reaction mixture has a path length of 1.0 cm.

The data table contains information collected by the student.

(a) What is the initial concentration of the colored species?

> *Recall:* Concentration (c) is related to Absorbance (A), molar absorptivity (a), and path length of cuvette (b) by the equation:
>
> A = abc

$c = \dfrac{A}{ab}$ $c = \dfrac{1.20}{(5.0 \times 10^3 \text{ cm}^{-1}\text{M}^{-1})(1.00 \text{ cm})}$ $c = 2.4 \times 10^{-4}$ M	**1 point** for the correct concentration

(b) Based on the information provided on the table, determine the rate constant for the first order reaction. Include all units with your answer.

Note:

$$\ln \frac{[Z]_{t_1}}{[Z]_{t_0}} = -kt \qquad \text{(see Reference Materials on Pg)}$$

$\ln \dfrac{[8.0 \times 10^{-5}]}{[2.4 \times 10^{-4}]} = -k\,(25 \text{ min})$	**1 point** for setup
$\ln(.333) = -k\,(25 \text{ min})$ $-1.10 = -k\,(25 \text{ min})$ $4.4 \times 10^{-2}\text{min}^{-1} = k$	**1 point** for calculating the rate constant with the correct unit.

(c) How much time had elapsed from when the absorbance goes from 1.20 to 0.150.

Note: Use the same setup and equation as in question (b), except now k is known, and you are solving for t .
Be sure to substitute [Z] that corresponds to the absorbance values mentioned in the question.

$\ln \dfrac{[Z]\,t_4}{[Z]\,t_o} = -kt$	
$\ln \dfrac{[3.0 \times 10^{-5}]}{[2.4 \times 10^{-4}]} = -(4.4 \times 10^{-2})(t)$	1 point for setup
$\ln(.125) = -(4.4 \times 10^{-2})(t)$	
$-2.08 = -(4.4 \times 10^{-2})(t)$	1 point for calculating correct time
47.2 min $= t$	

(d) Determine the half-life of the reaction performed by the student.

Note: Since this is a first order reaction, half-life ($t_{1/2}$) can be calculated with the equation:

$$t_{1/2} = \frac{\ln(^1/_2)}{k} \quad \text{(see reference material pg}$$

$t_{1/2} = \dfrac{0.693}{4.4 \times 10^{-2}}$	1 point for setup
$t_{1/2} = 15.75$ min	1 point for the correct half-life

(e) The student performed more experiments to determine the rate constant at various temperature, T. The student plotted the graph below from data she collected from the experiments.

(i) Label the vertical axis of the graph.

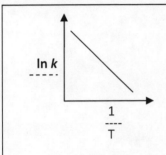

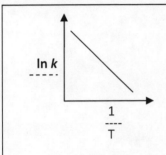	**1 point** for labeling axis **ln k**

(ii) Explain how the student can calculate the activation energy, E_a, for the reaction using information provided by the graph.

Recall: slope = $-\dfrac{E_a}{R}$ where R is the gas constant.

The student should **determine slope of the line.**	**1 point** for mentioning slope must be determined
The student would then **multiply the slope by the gas constant (R)** to get the activation energy (E_a) for the reaction.	**1 point** for explanation that include slope and R

START: Answer all questions on this day before stopping.

Note: **NO CALCULATORS should be used for questions on this day.**
You may use any of the Reference Materials provided on pg 337-340

1. For each of the following three reactions, write a balanced equation for
the reaction in part (i) and answer the question about the reaction in part (ii). In
part (i), coefficients should be in terms of lowest whole numbers. Assume that
solutions are aqueous unless otherwise indicated. Represent substances in
solutions as ions if the substances are extensively ionized. Omit formulas for
any ions or molecules that are unchanged by the reaction.   **(15 points)**

(a) A solution of ammonium thiocyanate is added to a concentrated solution of
iron (III) nitrate.

(i) Balanced equation:

(ii) What is mass of 0. 12 mole of ammonium thiocynate?

(b) Carbon dioxide gas is bubbled through a concentrated solution of
sodium hydroxide.

(i) Balanced equation:

(ii) What happens to the pH of the sodium hydroxide as carbon dioxide is
added to it.

(c) Calcium chloride dihydrate is gently heated in an open test tube.

(i) Balanced equation:

(ii) If 10 grams of calcium chloride dihydrate is heated for 5 minutes,
would the mass of the content of the test tube after heating be greater
than 10 gram, equal to 10 grams, or less than 10 grams. Explain.

Your responses to question 2 will be scored on the basis of the accuracy and relevance of the information cited. Explanations should be clear and well organized. Examples and equations may be included in your responses where appropriate. Specific answers are preferable to broad, diffuse responses.

(8 points)

2. Answer each of the following questions about carbon dioxide and phosphate ion.

(a) Draw a complete Lewis electron-dot diagram for CO_2 and for PO_4^{3-}.

(b) On the basis of your Lewis diagram from part (a), identify the hybridization of the central carbon atom in CO_2 and the central phosphorous atom in PO_4^{3-}.

(c) When carbon dioxide dissolves in water, a small fraction (at equilibrium) of the carbon dioxide reacts with water to form carbonic acid.

 (i) Write out a complete, balanced equation for this reaction and

 (ii) identify the Lewis acid and the Lewis base in the reaction.

(d) Is CO_2 polar? Explain.

Day 18

STOP. Correct your answers and note how many correct **points**

Day 18 Question 2: Space for Work and Answers

(a) A solution of ammonium thiocyanate is added to a solution of iron (III) nitrate.

Note: This reaction involve the formation of a complex ion
Ammonium and nitrate ions are spectator ions

(i) Balanced equation	**1 point** is earned for correct reactants
Fe^{3+} + SCN^- ------ > $Fe(SCN)^{2+}$ *complex ion*	**2 points are** earned for correct products **1 point** is earned for correctly balancing the equation

(ii) What is mass of 0. 12 mole of ammonium thiocynate?

Recall: Mass = moles x molar mass of NH_4SCN

	1 point is earned for the correct grams
Mass = 0.12 mol x 76 g/mol = **9.1 g**	

(b) Carbon dioxide gas is bubbled through a concentrated solution of sodium hydroxide.

Note: This is a neutralization reaction involving a nonmetal oxide
The sodium anion (Na^+) is the spectator ion, therefore, not included in the equation

(i) Balanced equation	**1 point** is earned for correct reactants
CO_2 + 2OH- ------- > CO_3^{2-} + H_2O *nonmetal oxide* *base* *salt* *water*	**2 points are** earned for correct products **1 point** is earned for correctly balancing the equation

Day 18: Answers and Scoring Guidelines

(ii) What happens to the pH of the sodium hydroxide as carbon dioxide is added to it.

The pH of the sodium hydroxide will decrease because carbon dioxide is weakly acidic, and will slowly neutralize the base.	**1 point** is earned for stating pH will decrease

(c) Calcium chloride dihydrate is gently heated in an open test tube.

Recall: Hydrates are ionic substances with attached water molecules. When heated, a hydrate decomposed into the ionic salt and water (which will evaporate out of the test tube)

(i) Balanced equation	**1 point** is earned for correct reactants
	2 points are earned for correct products
$CaCl_2 \cdot 2H_2O$ ----------> $CaCl_2$ + $2H_2O$	**1 point** is earned for correctly balancing the equation

(ii) If 10 grams of calcium chloride dihydrate is heated for 5 minutes, would the mass of the content of the test tube after heating be greater than 10 gram, equal to 10 grams, or less than 10 grams. Explain.

Less than 10 because **the water that evaporated out of the open test tube will account for the missing mass**	**1 point** is earned for stating less than 10 g with correct explanation.

2) 2. Answer each of the following questions about CO_2 and PO_4^{3-} ion
(8 point)

(a) Draw a complete Lewis electron-dot diagram for CO_2 and for PO_4^{3-}

$:\overset{..}{O} = C = \overset{..}{O}:$ carbon dioxide	**1 point** for correct diagram for CO_2
$\left(\begin{array}{c} :\overset{..}{O}: \\ \| \\ :\overset{..}{O} - P - \overset{..}{O}: \\ \| \\ :\overset{..}{O}: \end{array} \right)^{3-}$ phosphate ion	**1 point** for correct diagram for PO_4^{3-}

(b) On the basis of your Lewis diagram from part (a), identify the hybridization of the central carbon atom in CO_2 and the central phosphorous atom in PO_4^{3-}.

In **CO_2** , the **C** atom forms **sp hybrization** *Note:* When drawn correctly, CO_2 has a linear shape, hence, the **sp** hybridization.	**1 point** for stating sp for C
In **PO_4^{3-}**, the **P** atom forms **sp^3** hybridization *Note:* When drawn correctly, PO_4^{3-} has a tetrahedral shape, hence, the **sp^3** hybrization.	**1 point** for stating sp^3 for P

Day 18: Answers and Scoring Guidelines

(c) When carbon dioxide dissolves in water, a small fraction (at equilibrium) of the carbon dioxide reacts with water to form carbonic acid. Write out a complete, balanced equation for this reaction and identify the Lewis acid and the Lewis base in the reaction.

Recall: Lewis base donates electrons in reactions

Lewis acids accept electrons in reactions

CO_2 + H_2O -------> H_2CO_3. **Lewis base: H_2O** The **O** donates a pair of electrons to CO_2 **Lewis acid: CO_2** The **C** accepts the pair of electrons from O	**1 point** for correct Lewis base **1 point** for correct Lewis acid

(d) Is CO_2 polar? Explain.

CO_2 is not polar. The two C = O bonds are polar because of the electronegativity difference between the two nonmetals. However, CO_2 is nonpolar because **the + charges (on C atom) and the – charges (on the O atoms) are evenly and symmetrically distributed.** or **Dipole moments cancel out.**	**1 point** for not polar with correct justification

(e) What is the O-P-O bond angle in PO_4^{3-}?

The bond angle is 109.5 degrees. bond angle is common for sp^3 hybridized (tetrahedral shape) molecules.	**1 point** for correct bond angle

Questions on Days 19 and 20 make up a full AP exam practice.
It is highly recommended that you create an ideal testing conditions, and try to do all the questions on the same day. Follow the time limit allowed for each section, and use only Reference Materials that is allowed for each section.

Once done grading and scoring questions for both days, use the Scoring Worksheet below to determine your AP score. The Scoring Worksheet is based on the new format of determining AP score. The biggest change in scoring is in the multiple choice section. In the past, points were deducted for each incorrect answer, and the total score for this section was based on the number of correct answers minus fraction of a point for each incorrect answer. In the new scoring format, the total score in the multiple choice section is strictly based on the total number of correct answers out of a possible 75.

Practice Exam Scoring Worksheet:

Day 19: Section I: Multiple-Choice

$$\underline{\hspace{3cm}} \quad \times \quad 1.000 \quad = \quad \underline{\hspace{3cm}}$$

number correct   Weighted Section I
(out of 75)   Score

Day 20: Section II: Free Response Part A and B

Question 1: _____ x 1.665 = _____

Question 2: _____ x 1.500 = _____

Question 3: _____ x 1.665 = _____

Question 4: _____ x 0.500 = _____

Question 5: _____ x 1.250 = _____

Question 6: _____ x 1.315 = _____

Sum = _____

Weighted Section II
score

AP score conversion chart:

Composite score range	Practice Exam AP Score
100 – 150	5
81 – 99	4
62 – 80	3
49 – 61	2
0 – 48	1

Composite Score

$$\underline{\hspace{3cm}} \quad + \quad \underline{\hspace{3cm}} \quad = \quad \underline{\hspace{3cm}}$$

Weighted Section I   Weighted Section II   Composite
Score   Score   Score

Section I: Multiple-Choice Questions

Time: 90 minutes

75 questions (75 points)

No calculators allowed
Use ONLY the Periodic Table Provided on page 337.

This section consists of 75 multiple-choice questions. Mark your answers carefully on the answer sheet.

General Instructions

Do not open this booklet until you are told to do so by the proctor. Be sure to write your answers for Section I on the separate answer sheet. Use the test booklet for your scratch work or notes, but remember that no credit will be given for work, notes, or answers written only in the test booklet. After you have selected an answer, blacken thoroughly the corresponding circle on the answer sheet. To change an answer, erase your previous mark completely, and then record your new answer. Mark only one answer for each question.

Example   Sample Answer

Europe is   Ⓐ Ⓑ ● Ⓓ Ⓔ
(A) a country
(B) a state
(C) a continent
(D) a city
(E) an hemisphere

Because it is not expected that all test takers will complete this section, do not spend too much time on difficult questions. Answer first the questions you can answer readily, and then, if you have time, return to the difficult questions later. Don't get stuck on one question. Work quickly but accurately. Use your time effectively. The preceding table on page 337 is provided for your use in answering questions in Section I.

Day 19: Practice Exam Answer Sheet for the Multiple Choice

1. Ⓐ Ⓑ Ⓒ Ⓓ Ⓔ
2. Ⓐ Ⓑ Ⓒ Ⓓ Ⓔ
3. Ⓐ Ⓑ Ⓒ Ⓓ Ⓔ
4. Ⓐ Ⓑ Ⓒ Ⓓ Ⓔ
5. Ⓐ Ⓑ Ⓒ Ⓓ Ⓔ
6. Ⓐ Ⓑ Ⓒ Ⓓ Ⓔ
7. Ⓐ Ⓑ Ⓒ Ⓓ Ⓔ
8. Ⓐ Ⓑ Ⓒ Ⓓ Ⓔ
9. Ⓐ Ⓑ Ⓒ Ⓓ Ⓔ
10. Ⓐ Ⓑ Ⓒ Ⓓ Ⓔ
11. Ⓐ Ⓑ Ⓒ Ⓓ Ⓔ
12. Ⓐ Ⓑ Ⓒ Ⓓ Ⓔ
13. Ⓐ Ⓑ Ⓒ Ⓓ Ⓔ
14. Ⓐ Ⓑ Ⓒ Ⓓ Ⓔ
15. Ⓐ Ⓑ Ⓒ Ⓓ Ⓔ
16. Ⓐ Ⓑ Ⓒ Ⓓ Ⓔ
17. Ⓐ Ⓑ Ⓒ Ⓓ Ⓔ
18. Ⓐ Ⓑ Ⓒ Ⓓ Ⓔ
19. Ⓐ Ⓑ Ⓒ Ⓓ Ⓔ
20. Ⓐ Ⓑ Ⓒ Ⓓ Ⓔ
21. Ⓐ Ⓑ Ⓒ Ⓓ Ⓔ
22. Ⓐ Ⓑ Ⓒ Ⓓ Ⓔ
23. Ⓐ Ⓑ Ⓒ Ⓓ Ⓔ
24. Ⓐ Ⓑ Ⓒ Ⓓ Ⓔ
25. Ⓐ Ⓑ Ⓒ Ⓓ Ⓔ

51. Ⓐ Ⓑ Ⓒ Ⓓ Ⓔ
52. Ⓐ Ⓑ Ⓒ Ⓓ Ⓔ
53. Ⓐ Ⓑ Ⓒ Ⓓ Ⓔ
54. Ⓐ Ⓑ Ⓒ Ⓓ Ⓔ
55. Ⓐ Ⓑ Ⓒ Ⓓ Ⓔ
56. Ⓐ Ⓑ Ⓒ Ⓓ Ⓔ
57. Ⓐ Ⓑ Ⓒ Ⓓ Ⓔ
58. Ⓐ Ⓑ Ⓒ Ⓓ Ⓔ
59. Ⓐ Ⓑ Ⓒ Ⓓ Ⓔ
60. Ⓐ Ⓑ Ⓒ Ⓓ Ⓔ
61. Ⓐ Ⓑ Ⓒ Ⓓ Ⓔ
62. Ⓐ Ⓑ Ⓒ Ⓓ Ⓔ
63. Ⓐ Ⓑ Ⓒ Ⓓ Ⓔ
64. Ⓐ Ⓑ Ⓒ Ⓓ Ⓔ
65. Ⓐ Ⓑ Ⓒ Ⓓ Ⓔ
66. Ⓐ Ⓑ Ⓒ Ⓓ Ⓔ
67. Ⓐ Ⓑ Ⓒ Ⓓ Ⓔ
68. Ⓐ Ⓑ Ⓒ Ⓓ Ⓔ
69. Ⓐ Ⓑ Ⓒ Ⓓ Ⓔ
70. Ⓐ Ⓑ Ⓒ Ⓓ Ⓔ
71. Ⓐ Ⓑ Ⓒ Ⓓ Ⓔ
72. Ⓐ Ⓑ Ⓒ Ⓓ Ⓔ
73. Ⓐ Ⓑ Ⓒ Ⓓ Ⓔ
74. Ⓐ Ⓑ Ⓒ Ⓓ Ⓔ
75. Ⓐ Ⓑ Ⓒ Ⓓ Ⓔ

26. Ⓐ Ⓑ Ⓒ Ⓓ Ⓔ
27. Ⓐ Ⓑ Ⓒ Ⓓ Ⓔ
28. Ⓐ Ⓑ Ⓒ Ⓓ Ⓔ
29. Ⓐ Ⓑ Ⓒ Ⓓ Ⓔ
30. Ⓐ Ⓑ Ⓒ Ⓓ Ⓔ
31. Ⓐ Ⓑ Ⓒ Ⓓ Ⓔ
32. Ⓐ Ⓑ Ⓒ Ⓓ Ⓔ
33. Ⓐ Ⓑ Ⓒ Ⓓ Ⓔ
34. Ⓐ Ⓑ Ⓒ Ⓓ Ⓔ
35. Ⓐ Ⓑ Ⓒ Ⓓ Ⓔ
36. Ⓐ Ⓑ Ⓒ Ⓓ Ⓔ
37. Ⓐ Ⓑ Ⓒ Ⓓ Ⓔ
38. Ⓐ Ⓑ Ⓒ Ⓓ Ⓔ
39. Ⓐ Ⓑ Ⓒ Ⓓ Ⓔ
40. Ⓐ Ⓑ Ⓒ Ⓓ Ⓔ
41. Ⓐ Ⓑ Ⓒ Ⓓ Ⓔ
42. Ⓐ Ⓑ Ⓒ Ⓓ Ⓔ
43. Ⓐ Ⓑ Ⓒ Ⓓ Ⓔ
44. Ⓐ Ⓑ Ⓒ Ⓓ Ⓔ
45. Ⓐ Ⓑ Ⓒ Ⓓ Ⓔ
46. Ⓐ Ⓑ Ⓒ Ⓓ Ⓔ
47. Ⓐ Ⓑ Ⓒ Ⓓ Ⓔ
48. Ⓐ Ⓑ Ⓒ Ⓓ Ⓔ
49. Ⓐ Ⓑ Ⓒ Ⓓ Ⓔ
50. Ⓐ Ⓑ Ⓒ Ⓓ Ⓔ

Questions 1 through 4 refer to the diagram below:
The spontaneous reaction that occurs when the cell operates is given below the diagram.

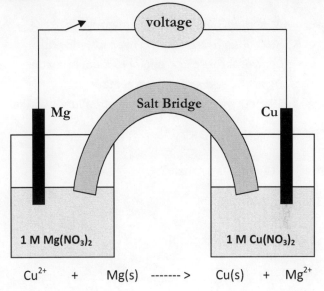

$$Cu^{2+} \quad + \quad Mg(s) \quad \text{------>} \quad Cu(s) \quad + \quad Mg^{2+}$$

(A) Voltage increases.

(B) Voltage decreases.

(C) Voltage becomes zero and remains at zero.

(D) No change in voltage occurs.

(E) Direction of voltage change cannot be predicted without additional information.

Which of the above occurs for each of the following circumstances?

1. A 50-milliliter sample of a 2-molar NaCl solution is added to the right beaker.

2. The salt bridge is removed.

3. 100 mL of water is added to the beaker on the left.

4. Current is allowed to flow for 10 minutes.

Day 19: Practice Exam Section 1

Questions 5 through 8 refer to aqueous solutions containing 1:1 mole ratios of the following pairs of substances. Assume all concentrations are 1 M.

(A) sodium hydroxide and ammonia
(B) sodium hydroxide and hydrochloric acid
(C) hydrobromic acid and potassium bromide
(D) acetic acid and sodium acetate
(E) methylamine and methylammonium chloride

5. A buffer with a pH less than 7

6. A buffer with a pH greater than 7

7. The solution with a pH of 7

8. The solution with the highest pH

Questions 9 through 13 refer to the following list of geometries:

(A) Linear
(B) Bent
(C) Trigonal planar
(D) Tetrahedral
(E) Trigonal bipyramidal

9. Characteristic of four electron pairs, two bonding and two nonbonding

10. Typical of *sp* hybridization

11. Accounts for the nonpolarity of SiF_4

12. Nitrate anion

13. PCl_5

Questions 14 through 17

The choices listed below refer to n, the number of moles of electrons transferred in a reaction

(A) n = 0
(B) n = 1
(C) n = 2
(D) n = 3
(E) n = 4

14. $2Fe^{3+} + Mg \longrightarrow 2Fe^{2+} + Mg^{2+}$
15. $F_2 + 2Br^- \longrightarrow 2F^- + Br_2$
16. $NH_3 + H_2O \longrightarrow NH_4^+ + OH^-$
17. $MnO_4^- + Cr + 2H_2O \longrightarrow MnO_2 + Cr^{3+} + 4OH^-$

Questions 18 through 20 *refer to the phase diagram below*

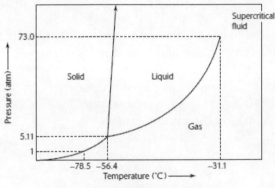

(A) −78.5°C
(B) −56.4°C, 5.11 atm
(C) − 31.1°C, 73.0 atm
(D) 31.1°C
(E) none of the above

18. What does the phase diagram above show to be the normal boiling point of carbon dioxide?

19. Which point represents the critical point?

20. Which point represents the triple point?

21. Which of the following compounds is least likely to form?

    (A) $Na_2Cr_7O_2$
    (B) $LiC_2H_3O_2$
    (C) K_2CN
    (D) $Rb_2C_2O_4$
    (E) HNO_2

22. A hydrocarbon gas with an empirical formula CH_2 has a density of 1.3 grams per liter at 0°C and 1.00 atmosphere. A possible formula for the hydrocarbon is

    (A) CH_2
    (B) C_2H_4
    (C) C_3H_6
    (D) C_4H_8
    (E) C_5H_{10}

23. A sample is confined in a 5-liter container. Which of the following will occur if the temperature of the container is increased?

    I. The kinetic energy of the gas will increase
    II. The pressure of the gas will increase
    III. The density of the gas will increase

    (A) I only
    (B) II only
    (C) I and II only
    (D) I and III only
    (E) I, II, III

24. The AsF_5 molecule has a trigonal bypyramidal structure. Therefore, the hybridization of As orbitals will be

    (A) sp^2
    (B) sp^3
    (C) sp^2d
    (D) sp^3d
    (E) sp^3d^2

25. 1.0 mole of four different compounds containing element X were analyzed and found to contain 36.0 grams, 54.0 grams, 72.0 grams, and 108 grams, respectively. A possible atomic weight of X is

(A) 13.5

(B) 18.0

(C) 25.0

(D) 72.0

(E) 108

26. The proposed steps for a catalyzed reaction between X^{4+} and Z^+ are represented below.

Step 1: X^{4+} + Y^{2+} --------> X^{3+} + Y^{3+}

Step 2: X^{4+} + Y^{3+} ---------> X^{3+} + Y^{4+}

Step 3: Y^{4+} + Z^+ ----------> Z^{3+} + Y^{2+}

The catalyst in this process is

(A) X^{4+}

(B) X^{3+}

(C) Y^{4+}

(D) Y^{2+}

(E) Z^+

27. Pressure cookers are used at high altitudes to cook food faster. Which of the following statements pertaining to this fact is true?

(A) The cooker holds water at a constant pressure at a higher atmosphere, resulting in hotter water

(B) The cooker lowers the pressure on the water causing it to boil at a higher temperature, allowing for hotter water

(C) The cooker raises the pressure on the water causing it to boil at a higher temperature, allowing for hotter water

(D) The cooker forces the water to contain higher concentration of dissolved gases, allowing for hotter water.

(E) The cooker forces the water to maintain constant density, allowing for hotter water

28. The net ionic equation for the reaction that occurs during the titration of chlorous acid with potassium hydroxide is

(A) $H^+ + OH^-$ -----> H_2O
(B) $HClO_2 + K^+ + OH^-$ ------> $KClO_2 + H_2O$
(C) $HClO_2 + OH^-$ --------> $ClO_2^- + H_2O$
(D) $HClO_2 + H_2O$ -------> $ClO_2^- + H_3O^+$
(E) $HClO_2 + KOH$ -------> $K^+ + ClO_2^- + H_2O$

29. A mixture of nitrogen, hydrogen and ammonia gases are in a sealed container and are at equilibrium. Which of the following changes will affect the reaction quotient (Q_c) but not affect the equilibrium constant (K_c)?

    (1) addition of argon to the system
    (2) addition of a catalyst
    (3) decrease the size of the sealed container
    (4) add more hydrogen and nitrogen gases
    (5) increase the temperature

(A) 1 and 2
(B) 2 and 3
(C) 1 and 3
(D) 3 and 4
(E) all of them

30. What is the boiling point of a 2 m solution of NaCl in water? (The boiling point elevation constant, k_f, for water is 0.5°C/m?

(A) 100°C
(B) 101°C
(C) 102°C
(D) 103°C
(E) 104°C

31. You study the following reaction: W + X ---- > ZY + 2Z

You vary the concentration of reactants W and X, and observe the resulting rates:

Experiment	[W] (M)	[X] (M)	Rate (M/s)
1	2.7×10^{-2}	2.7×10^{-2}	4.8×10^{6}
2	2.7×10^{-2}	5.4×10^{-2}	9.6×10^{6}
3	5.4×10^{-2}	2.7×10^{-2}	9.6×10^{6}

At what rate will the reaction occur in the presence of 1.3×10^{-2} M reactant W and 9.2×10^{-3} M reactant X?

(A) $7.9 \times 10^{5} M/s$
(B) $1.2 \times 10^{-4} M/s$
(C) $6.6 \times 10^{9} M/s$
(D) $8.6 \times 10^{7} M/s$
(E) $6.1 \times 10^{7} M/s$

32. Element iodine (I_2) is more soluble in carbon tetrachloride (CCl_4) than it is in water (H_2O). Which of the following statement is the best explanation for this?

(A) I_2 is closer in molecular weight to CCl_4 than it is to H_2O.
(B) The freezing point of I_2 is closer to that of CCl_4 than it is to that of H_2O.
(C) I_2 and CCl_4 are nonpolar molecules, while H_2O is a polar molecule.
(D) The heat of formation of I_2 is closer to that of CCl_4 than it is to that of H_2O.
(E) CCl_4 has a greater molecular weight than does H_2O.

33. If 87.5 percent of a sample of pure Rh-99 decays in 48 days, what is the half life of Rh-99?

    (A) 6 days
    (B) 8 days
    (C) 12 days
    (D) 16 days
    (E) 24 days

34. Which point on the graph below corresponds to activated complex or transitional state?

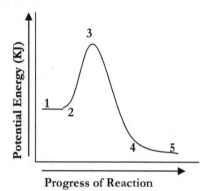

    (A) 1
    (B) 2
    (C) 3
    (D) 4
    (E) 5

35. Each of the following can act as both a Brönsted acid and a Brönsted base EXCEPT

    (A) HSO_3^-
    (B) HPO_4^{2-}
    (C) NH_4^+
    (D) H_2O
    (E) HCO_3^-

36. For a substance that remains a gas under the conditions listed, deviation from the ideal gas law would be most pronounced at

   (A) −100°C and 5 atm
   (B) −100°C and 1.0 atm
   (C) 0°C and 1.0 atm
   (D) 100°C and 1.0 atm
   (E) 100°C and 5.0 atm

37. One of the outermost electrons in a calcium atom in the ground state can be described by which of the following sets of four quantum numbers?

   (A) 4, 2, 0, ½
   (B) 4, 1, 1, ½
   (C) 4, 1, 0, ½
   (D) 4, 0, 1, ½
   (E) 4, 0, 0, ½

38. A 0.25M solution has an [H+] of 4.2×10^{-6} M. What is its pH?

   (A) 5.00
   (B) 5.37
   (C) 6.00
   (D) 6.27
   (E) 7.00

39. A study was made of the effect of the hydroxide concentration on the rate of the reaction

$$I^-(aq) + OCl^-(aq) -----> IO^-(aq) + Cl^-(aq)$$

The experimental rate law of the reaction is determined to be:
$$Rate = k\,[I^-]\,[OCl^-]\,[OH^-]$$

According to the rate law for the reaction, an increase in the concentration of hydroxide ion has what effect on this reaction?

   (A) The rate of reaction increases.
   (B) The rate of reaction decreases.
   (C) The value of the equilibrium constant increases.
   (D) The value of the equilibrium constant decreases.
   (E) Neither the rate nor the value of the equilibrium constant is changed.

40. A chemist analyzed the C – C bond in C_2H_6 and found that it had a bond energy of 350 KJ/mol and a bond length of 1.5 angstroms. If the chemist performed the same analysis on the C – C bond in C_2H_2 how would the results compare?

(A) The bond energies and the lengths for C_2H_2 would be the same as those of C_2H_6

B) The bond energies for C_2H_2 would be smaller, and the bond length would be shorter.

C) The bond energies for C_2H_2 would be greater, and the bond length would be longer.

D) The bond energies for C_2H_2 would be smaller, and the bond length would be longer.

E) The bond energies for C_2H_2 would be greater, and the bond length would be shorter.

41. A 1.0 L sample of an aqueous solution contains 0.10 mol of $BaCl_2$ and 0.10 mol of $Ba_3(PO_4)_2$. What is the minimum number of moles of Na_2SO_4 that must be added to the solution in order to precipitate all of the Ba^{2+} as $BaSO_4(s)$? (Assume that $BaSO_4$ is insoluble.)

(A) 0.10 mol

(B) 0.20 mol

(C) 0.30 mol

(D) 0.40 mol

(E) 0.60 mol

42. Which of the following is a correct representation of the electron configuration for molybdenum?

(A) $1s^2\,2s^2\,2p^6\,3s^2\,3p^6\,4s^2\,3d^{10}\,4p^6\,5s^2\,4d^4$
(B) $[Ar]\,5s^2\,4d^4$
(C) $[Ar]\,5s^1\,4d^5$
(D) $[Kr]\,5s^1\,4d^5$
(E) $[Kr]\,5s^2\,4d^4$

43. For the isoelectronic series S^{2-}, Cl^-, Ar, K^+, and Sc^{3+}, which species requires the least energy to remove an outer electron?

(A) S^{2-}
(B) Cl^-
(C) Ar
(D) K^+
(E) Sc^{3+}

44. The K_{eq} for the following reaction is 0.01

$$X + Y \text{ -------> } 2Z$$

If the concentrations of X and Z are 5.0M and 1.0M, respectively, what must be the approximate concentration of Y in an equilibrium mixture?

(A) 5.0M
(B) 4.0M
(C) 1.0M
(D) 20.M
(E) 0.050M

45. A voltaic cell contains one half-cell with zinc electrode in a Zn^{2+}(aq) solution and a copper electrode in a Cu^{2+}(aq) solution. At standard condition. $E° = 1.10$ V. Which condition below would cause the cell potential to be greater than 1.10 V?

(A) 1.0 M Zn^{2+}(aq), 1.0 M Cu^{2+}(aq)
(B) 5.0 M Zn^{2+}(aq), 5.0 M Cu^{2+}(aq)
(C) 5.0 M Zn^{2+}(aq), 1.0 M Cu^{2+}(aq)
(D) 0.5 M Zn^{2+}(aq), 0.5 M Cu^{2+}(aq)
(E) 0.1 M Zn^{2+}(aq), 1.0 M Cu^{2+}(aq)

46. When subjected to the flame test, a solution that contains Sr^{2+} ions produces the color

(A) yellow
(B) violet
(C) crimson
(D) green
(E) orange

47. Appropriate laboratory procedures include which of the following?

  I. Calibrating a pH probe before using it.
  II. Lubricating glass tubing before inserting it into a stopper.
  III. For accurate results, waiting until warm or hot objects have reached room temperature before weighing them.

(A) I only
(B) II only
(C) I and II only
(D) I and III only
(E) I, II and III

48. Which of the following is the correct name for the compound with formula Ca_3P_2?

(A) Tricalcium diphosphorous
(B) Calcium phosphite
(C) Calcium Phosphate
(D) Calcium diphosphate
(E) Calcium phosphide

49. What number of moles of O_2 is needed to produce 25.5 grams of Al_2O_3 from solid Al? (Molecular weight Al_2O_3 =102)

(A) 0.125 mole
(B) 0.250 mole
(C) 0.375 mole
(D) 0.500 mole
(E) 1.00 mole

50. What is the ideal pKa for an indicator in a titration when the pOH at the equivalence point is 9.8?

(A) 2.1
(B) 4.2
(C) 4.9
(D) 9.8
(E) 10

51. At a temperature of 250K, the molecules of an unknown gas, X, have an average velocity equal to that of HI at 500K. What is the identity of the gas?

(A) SO_2

(B) N_2

(C) NO_2

(D) O_2

(E) HCl

52. Which structure represents an ether?

(A) 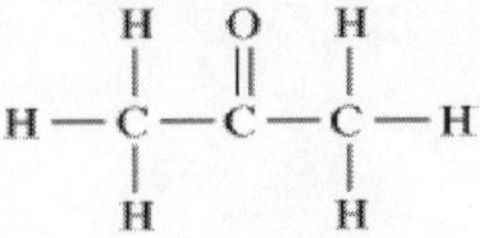
```
      H   O   H
      |   ||  |
  H — C — C — C — H
      |       |
      H       H
```

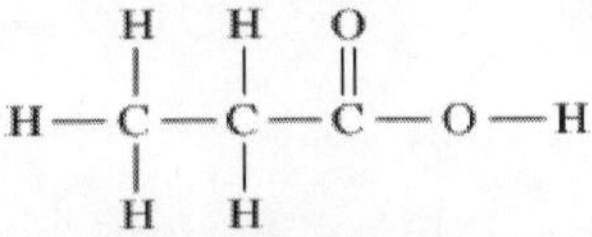

(B)
```
      H   H   O
      |   |   ||
  H — C — C — C — O — H
      |   |
      H   H
```

(C)
```
      H   H   H
      |   |   |
  H — C — C — C — O — H
      |   |   |
      H   H   H
```

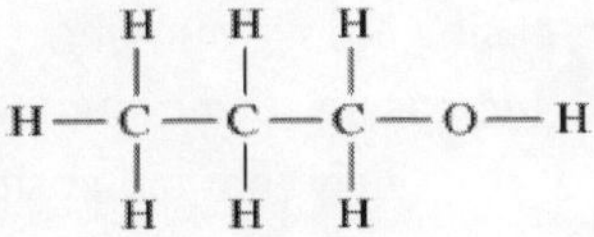

(D) 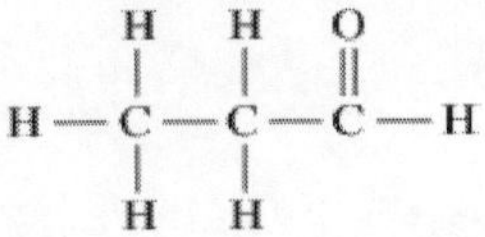
```
      H   H   O
      |   |   ||
  H — C — C — C — H
      |   |
      H   H
```

(E) 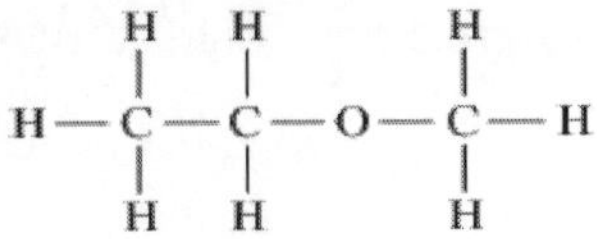
```
      H   H       H
      |   |       |
  H — C — C — O — C — H
      |   |       |
      H   H       H
```

53. Which of the following equations represents the reaction between solid magnesium hydroxide and aqueous hydrochloric acid?

(A) $Mg(OH)_2(s)$ + $2HCl(l)$ ------> $MgCl_2(aq)$ + $H_2O(l)$
(B) $MgOH(s)$ + $HCl(aq)$ -----> $MgCl(aq)$ + $2H_2O(l)$
(C) $Mg(OH)_2(s)$ + $2HCl(aq)$ ----> $MgCl_2(aq)$ + $2H_2O(l)$
(D) $Mg(OH)_2(s)$ + $HCl(aq)$ -----> $MgCl_2(aq)$ + $H_2O(l)$
(E) $MgOH(s)$ + $2HCl(aq)$ ----> $MgCl(aq)$ + $2H_2O(l)$

54. What would be the proper setup to determine the vapor pressure of a solution at 25°C that has 45 grams of $C_6H_{12}O_6$, glucose (MM = 180 g/mol), dissolved in 72 grams of H_2O? The vapor pressure of pure water at 25°C is 23.8 mmHg.

(A) 23.8 – (72/18) + (45/180)
(B) 23.8 – (0.0588)(23.8)
(C) (0.0588 + 23.8) / (72/18)
(D) ((72/18) + (45/180))/23.8
(E) none of the setups are correct

55. A characteristic that is unique to the alkali metals is

(A) their metallic character.
(B) the increase in atomic radius with increasing atomic number.
(C) the decrease in ionization energy with increasing atomic number.
(D) the noble gas electron configuration of the singly charged positive ion.
(E) None of these answer choices are correct.

56. Given the oxidation reaction below:

$CH_3CH_2OH(g)$ + $O_2(g)$ ------> $CO_2(g)$ + $H_2O(g)$

How many moles of O_2 are required to oxidize 1 mole of CH_3CH_2OH?

(A) $^3/_2$ moles
(B) $^5/_2$ moles
(C) 3 moles
(D) $^7/_2$ moles
(E) 4 moles

57. A sulfide of copper is found to contain 20% sulfur. What is the formula of the compound?

(A) CuS

(B) CuS_2

(C) Cu_2S

(D) Cu_2S_2

(E) Cu_4S

For questions 58 and 60 consider the following molecules:

C_2Cl_2 C_2HCl $C_2H_2Cl_2$ C_2HCl_5

58. How many of the molecules contain two pi bonds between the carbon atoms?

(A) 0

(B) 1

(C) 2

(D) 3

(E) 4

59. How many of the molecules contain at least one sigma bond?

(A) 0

(B) 1

(C) 2

(D) 3

(E) 4

60. What is the total number of unshared electron pairs in $C_2H_2Cl_2$?

(A) 0

(B) 3

(C) 6

(D) 8

(E) 12

Day 19: Practice Exam Section 1

61. Which of the following are true about Millikan oil drop experiment?

I. Positively and a negatively charged plates were used to hold oil droplets in the air.

II. X rays were used to charge the oil droplets with electrons

III. This experiment is famous for discovering the density of electrons

(A) I only
(B) I and III only
(C) I and II only
(D) II and III only
(E) I, II, III

62. Which of the following indicators would be the best choice to monitor a change that occurs at pH = 5.0?

(A) Bromophenol blue, p*Ka* = 4.0
(B) Phenolphthalein, p*Ka* = 7.9
(C) Thymol blue, p*K*a = 9.3
(D) Methyl red, p*K*a = 5.1
(E) Methyl orange, p*Ka* = 3.7

63. A yellow precipitate forms when 0.5 M KI(aq) is added to a 0.5 M solution of which of the following ions?

A) $Pb^{2+}(aq)$
B) $Cu^{2+}(aq)$
C) $C_2O_4^{2-}(aq)$
D) $SO_4^{2-}(aq)$
E) $Cl^-(aq)$

64. What is the charge of Zn in $Zn(H_2O)_3(OH)^+$?

(A) 0
(B) +1
(C) +2
(D) +3
(E) +5

65. When lithium chloride is added to a saturated aqueous solution of silver chloride, which of the following precipitate would be expected to appear?

(A) Lithium
(B) Silver
(C) Chlorine
(D) Lithium chloride
(E) Silver chloride

66. 2.0 mol samples of gaseous substances A, B, and C are placed in a one liter container. A and B react according to the following equation:

$$A(g) + B(g) \longleftrightarrow 2C(g)$$

An increase in the temperature of the system would:
(A) Drive the reaction to the right
(B) Drive the reaction to the left
(C) Increase the concentration of all three gaseous substances
(D) Have no effect on the reaction
(E) The effect cannot be determined

67. A Table of three acids and their dissociation constant, K_a, is given below:

Acid	Acid Dissociation Constant, K_a
H_3AsO_4	5×10^{-3}
$H_2AsO_4^-$	8×10^{-8}
$HAsO_4^{2-}$	6×10^{-10}

On the basis of the information on the table below a buffer with a pH = 11 can best be made by using

(A) pure NaH_2AsO_4
(B) H_3AsO_4 + H_2AsO_4-
(C) H_2AsO_4- + AsO_4^{3-}
(D) H_2AsO_4- + $HAsO_4^{2-}$
(E) $HAsO_4^{2-}$ + AsO_4^{3-}

68. Given a molecule with the general formula AB_2, which one of the following would be the most useful in determining whether the molecule was bent or linear?

(A) ionization energies
(B) electron affinities
(C) dipole moments
(D) electronegativities
(E) bond energies

69. Data was obtained for the decomposition of NO_2 according to the following reaction

$$2NO_2(g) \text{ -----> } 2NO(g) + O_2(g)$$

and a plot of $1/[NO_2]$ vs. time produced the following slope.

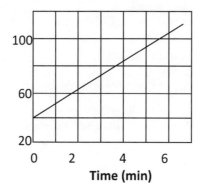

The reaction is

(A) 0 order
(B) 1st order
(C) 2nd order
(D) 3rd order
(E) cannot be determined with information provided

70. If $\Delta H°$ and $\Delta S°$ are both negative, then $\Delta G°$ is

(A) always negative.
(B) always positive.
(C) positive at low temperatures and negative at high temperatures.
(D) negative at low temperatures and positive at high temperatures.
(E) zero.

71. Based on the standard reduction potentials listed below, which is the strongest oxidizing agent?

$$Fe^{2+}(aq) \ + \ 2e^- \ \text{-----}> \ Fe(s) \qquad E°red = -0.44$$

$$Zn^{2+}(aq) \ + \ 2e^- \ \text{-----}> \ Zn(s) \qquad E°red = -0.76$$

$$Mn^{2+}(aq) \ + \ 2e^- \ \text{-----}> \ Mn(s) \qquad E°red = -1.18$$

$$Ni^{2+}(aq) \ + \ 2e^- \ \text{------}> \ Ni(s) \qquad E°red = -0.25$$

$$2H^+(aq) \ + \ 2e^- \ \text{------}> \ H_2(g) \qquad E°red = 0$$

(A) Ni^{2+}
(B) Fe^{2+}
(C) Zn^{2+}
(D) Mn^{2+}
(E) H^+

72. Methane combusts with oxygen to yield carbon dioxide and water vapor:

$$CH_4 \ + \ 2O_2 \ \text{----}> \ CO_2 \ + \ 2H_2O$$

If methane is consumed at 2.79 mole/s, what is the rate of change in the concentrations of carbon dioxide and oxygen?

(A) +2.79 mole/s CO_2 and +5.58mol/s O_2
(B) −2.79 mole/s CO_2 and −5.58mol/s O_2
(C) +5.58 mole/s CO_2 and −5.58mol/s O_2
(D) +2.79 mole/s CO_2 and −2.79mol/s O_2
(E) +2.79 mole/s CO_2 and −5.58mol/s O_2

Questions 73 through 75: Energy is added to a system at a constant rate as shown in the warming curve below.

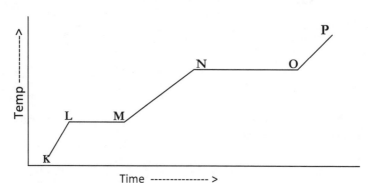

73. Which of the following best represents the energy calculation involving segment MN of the graph?

(A) mass × H_{fus}
(B) mass × c_{vap} × ΔT
(C) mass × H_{vap}
(D) mass × c_{liq} × ΔT
(E) mass × H_{vap} × ΔT

74. Which of the following best represents the energy calculation involving segment NO of the graph?

(A) mass × H_{fus}
(B) mass × c_{vap} × ΔT
(C) mass × H_{vap}
(D) mass × c_{liq} × ΔT
(E) mass × H_{vap} × ΔT

75. Which segments on the curve would be eliminated if the substance sublimes at standard conditions?

(A) LM only
(B) MN only
(C) LM and MN only
(D) LM, MN and NO
(E) NO and OP only

STOP: IF YOU FINISH BEFORE TIME IS CALLED, CHECK YOUR WORK ON THIS SECTION ONLY. DO NOT WORK ON ANY OTHER SECTION IN THE TEST.

Day 19: Practice Exam Section I
Answers

1. A	26. D	51. A
2. C	27. C	52. E
3. A	28. C	53. C
4. B	29. D	54. B
5. D	30. C	55. D
6. E	31. A	56. C
7. B	32. C	57. C
8. A	33. D	58. C
9. B	34. C	59. E
10. A	35. C	60. C
11. D	36. A	61. C
12. C	37. E	62. D
13. E	38. B	63. A
14. C	39. A	64. C
15. C	40. E	65. E
16. A	41. D	66. E
17. D	42. E	67. E
18. E	43. A	68. C
19. C	44. D	69. C
20. B	45. E	70. D
21. C	46. C	71. E
22. B	47. E	72. E
23. C	48. E	73. D
24. D	49. C	74. C
25. B	50. B	75. C

Day 20: Practice Exam
Section II

(Total time—95 minutes)

Section II: 60 points

Part A

Time—55 minutes

YOU MAY USE YOUR CALCULATOR FOR PART A.

YOU MAY USE ANY REFERENCE MATERIALS PROVIDED ON PAGES 337-340

CLEARLY SHOW THE METHOD USED AND THE STEPS INVOLVED IN ARRIVING AT YOUR ANSWERS.

It is to your advantage to do this, since you may obtain partial credit if you do and you will receive little or no credit if you do not. Attention should be paid to significant figures.

Be sure to write all your answers to the questions on the blank pages following each questions.

Answer ALL three questions in this Part.

1.   **(10 points)**
   The equation below shows a reaction between ethylamine and water.

$$C_2H_5NH_2(aq) + H_2O(l) \longrightarrow C_2H_5NH_3^+(aq) + OH^-(aq)$$

The base-dissociation constant, K_b, for the ethylamine ion is 5.6×10^{-4}.

(a) Given a 80.4 mL sample of a 0.500 M solution of ethylamine.

  (i) Write the equilibrium expression for the reaction and calculate the
      OH- ion concentration.

  (ii) Calculate the pOH of the solution.

(b) Calculate the % ionization of the ethylamine in the solution in part (a).

(c) What would be the pH of a solution made by adding 11.4 grams of
    ethylammonium bromide ($C_2H_5NH_3Br$) to 150. ml of a 0.200-molar
    solution of ethylamine?

d) A student adds 0.140 grams of solid silver nitrate to the solution in
    part (a)

  (i) Calculate the concentration of the silver ion in the solution.

  (ii) Will silver hydroxide form as a precipitate? Justify your answer with a
       calculation.   (The value of K_{sp} for silver hydroxide is 1.52×10^{-8})

Day 20 Question 1: Space for Work and Answers

2.   **(10 points)**

In two separate experiments, a sample of an unknown hydrocarbon was burned in air, and a sample of the same hydrocarbon was placed into an organic solvent.

(a) When the hydrocarbon sample was burned in a reaction that went to completion, 2.2 grams of water and 3.6 liters of carbon dioxide were produced under standard conditions. What is the empirical formula of the hydrocarbon?

(b) When 4.05 grams of the unknown hydrocarbon was placed in 100.0 grams of benzene, C_6H_6, the freezing point of the solution was measured to be $1.66°C$. The normal freezing point of benzene is $5.50°C$ and the freezing-point depression constant for benzene is $5.12°C/m$. What is the molecular weight of the unknown hydrocarbon?

(c) What is the molecular formula and the name of the hydrocarbon?

(d) Write the balanced equation for the combustion reaction that took place in (a)

(e) Draw two isomers for the hydrocarbon.

3. The following results were obtained in experiments designed to study the rate of the reaction below: **(10 points)**

$$A + 2B \longrightarrow 2C$$

Experiment	Initial Concentration (mol · L^{-1})		Initial Rate of Disappearance of A (M·sec^{-1})
	A	B	
1	0.05	0.05	3.0 x 10^{-3}
2	0.05	0.10	6.0 x 10^{-3}
3	0.10	0.10	1.2 x 10^{-2}
4	0.20	0.10	2.4 x 10^{-2}

(a) Determine the order of the reaction with respect to each of the reactants, and write the rate law for the reaction.

(b) Calculate the value of the rate constant, k, for the reaction. Include the units.

(c) Another experiment is attempted with [A] and [B] both 0.02 molar, what would be the initial rate of disappearance of A?

(d) The following reaction mechanism was proposed for the reaction above:

$$A + B \longrightarrow C + D$$
$$D + B \longrightarrow C$$

(i) Show that the mechanism is consistent with the balanced reaction.

(ii) Show that the step is the rate determining step, and explain your choice.

STOP
If you finish before time is called, you may check your work on this part only. Do not turn to the other part of the test until you are told to do so.

Day 20 Question 3: Space for Work and Answers

Part B

Time—40 minutes

NO CALCULATORS MAY BE USED FOR PART B.
YOU MAY USE ANY REFERENCE MATERIALS PROVIDED ON
PAGES 337-340

Question 4

For each of the following three reactions, write a balanced equation for the
reaction in part (i) and answer the question about the reaction in part (ii).
In part (i), coefficients should be in terms of lowest whole numbers.

Assume that solutions are aqueous unless otherwise indicated. Represent
substances in solutions as ions if the substances are extensively ionized.
Omit formulas for any ions or molecules that are unchanged by the
reaction.

You may use the empty space at the bottom of the next page for scratch
work, but only equations that are written in the answer boxes and the
answers written in the lines provided will be scored.

Day 20: Practice Exam

Section II Part B

4. **(15 points)**

(a) Boron triiodide is reacted with ammonia

(i) Balanced equation:

(ii) Which species in the reaction is the Lewis acid? Explain.

____

____

____

(b) A piece of calcium carbonate is placed in excess nitric acid

(i) Balanced equation:

(ii) What will be the sign for ΔS° for the reaction? Explain.

____

____

____

(c) Fluorine gas is bubbled through a solution of lithium chloride

(i) Balanced equation:

(ii) Which species will be the reducing agent in the reaction? Justify your answer.

____

____

____

5. Answer all questions in the boxes provided.   **(8 points)**

Seven solid compounds were placed in beakers as shown below.

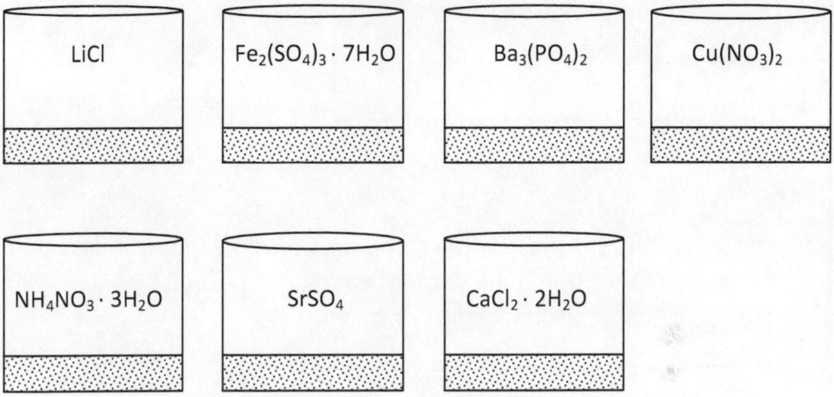

LiCl	$Fe_2(SO_4)_3 \cdot 7H_2O$	$Ba_3(PO_4)_2$	$Cu(NO_3)_2$

$NH_4NO_3 \cdot 3H_2O$	$SrSO_4$	$CaCl_2 \cdot 2H_2O$

An unknown compound is to be identified by students through observations and result of laboratory tests. The observations and test results are listed in order from (a) through (e). Write the formula(s) of compound(s) that should be eliminated in the box following each result.

(a) The unknown compound is white.

(b) The unknown compound dissolves readily in water.

(c) Forms a white precipitate when added to aqueous $AgNO_3$ solution.

(d) When heated, the mass of the compound after heating was less than the mass of the compound before heating.

(e) Below:

(i) Write the formula(s) of the compound(s) that has yet to be eliminated.

(ii) Describe any other test that could be done using only the substances in the beaker to confirm the identity of the unknown. Indicate the result of the test as well as formula of any products that is formed from your testing.

6.   **(7 points)**

Answer the following questions about Lewis structure and shapes of compounds.

a) Draw Lewis structures for

(i) BF_3

(ii) $TiCl_3$

(b) Determine the molecular geometries including all idealized bond angles for ClNO where the N atom is in the center of the molecule.

(c) Classify XeF_4 as polar or nonpolar and explain why.

(d) Describe the orbital hybridization scheme used by the central atom in its sigma bonding for the following molecules. The central atom is underlined. How many pi bonds are contained in each molecule?

(i) XeF_4

(ii) XeF_2

STOP

END OF EXAM

Day 20: Practice Exam
Section II: Scoring Guidelines

1.   **(10 points)**

The equation below shows a reaction between ethylamine and water.

$$C_2H_5NH_2(aq) + H_2O(l) \; ------> \; C_2H_5NH_3^+(aq) + OH^-(aq)$$

The base-dissociation constant, K_b, for the ethylamine ion is 5.6×10^{-4}.

(a) Given a 80.4 mL sample of a 0.500 M solution of ethylamine.

   (i) Write the equilibrium expression for the reaction and calculate the OH- ion concentration.

$$K_b = \frac{[C_2H_5NH_3^+]\,[OH^-]}{[C_2H_5NH_2]}$$	**1 point** is earned for writing the correct equilibrium expression
Concentration at equilibrium $[C_2H_5NH_3^+] = X$ $[OH^-] = X$ $[C_2H_5NH_2] \approx 0.500\ M$ *(low dissociation)*	
$$5.6 \times 10^{-4} = \frac{x^2}{0.500}$$ **X = [OH-] = 0.017 M**	**1 point** is earned for the correct calculation of the [OH-]

   (ii) Calculate the pOH of the solution.

pOH = -log [OH⁻] pOH = -log (0.017 M) = **1.78**	**1 point** is earned for the correct calculation of the pOH

(b) Calculate the % ionization of the ethylamine in the solution in part (a).

% dissociation = $\dfrac{[C_2H_5NH_3^+]}{[C_2H_5NH_2]}$ x 100 **% dissociation** = $\dfrac{0.017\ M}{0.500\ M}$ **x 100** **% dissociation = 3.4 %**	**1 point** is earned for correctly calculating the % dissociation

(c) What would be the pH of a solution made by adding 11.4 grams of ethylammonium bromide ($C_2H_5NH_3Br$) to 150. ml of a 0.200-molar solution of ethylamine?

Write equilibrium equation $$C_2H_5NH_3^+ \quad <=====> \quad H^+ \quad + \quad C_2H_5NH_2$$	
Calculate K_a $$K_a = \frac{[H^+][C_2H_5NH_3^+]}{[C_2H_5NH_2]} = \frac{K_w}{K_b} = \frac{1.0 \times 10^{-14}}{5.6 \times 10^{-4}}$$ $$K_a = 1.8 \times 10^{-11}$$	
Determine initial [ ] of the solutions $[H+] = 0$ $[C_2H_5NH_2] = 0.200$ M $[C_2H_5NH_3^+] = 11.4$ g $C_2H_5NH_3^+ \times \dfrac{1 \text{ mol}}{126 \text{ g}} \times \dfrac{1}{.150 \text{ L}}$ $\mathbf{[C_2H_5NH_3^+] = 0.603}$ M	**1 point** is earned for calculating initial $[C_2H_5NH_3^+]$
Determine final [ ] of the solutions $[H^+] = X$ $[C_2H_5NH_2] = 0.200$ M $+ X \approx 0.200$ M $[C_2H_5NH_3^+] = 0.603$ M $- X \approx 0.603$ M — X will be very small due to low dissociation	
Determine [H+] and pH $$1.8 \times 10^{-11} = \frac{(X)(.200 \text{ M})}{0.603 \text{ M}}$$ $$X = [H^+] = 5.4 \times 10^{-11}$$ $$pH = -\log[5.4 \times 10^{-11}]$$ $$\mathbf{pH = 10.3}$$	**1 point** is earned for calculating $[H+]$ **1 point** is earned for correctly calculating the pH

d) A student adds 0.140 grams of solid silver nitrate to the solution in part (a)

(i) Calculate the concentration of the silver ion in the solution.

$AgNO_3(s) <=====> Ag^+(aq) + NO_3^-(aq)$ $[Ag^+] = \dfrac{0.140 \text{ g } AgNO_3}{0.0804 \text{ L}} \times \dfrac{1 \text{ mol } AgNO_3}{169.9 \text{ g } AgNO_3} \times \dfrac{1 \text{ mol } Ag^+}{1 \text{ mole } AgNO_3}$ $[Ag^+] = 0.010 \text{ M}$	**1 point** earned for correcting calculating $[Ag^+]$

(ii) Will silver hydroxide form as a precipitate? Justify your answer with a calculation. (The value of K_{sp} for silver hydroxide is 1.52×10^{-8})

Precipitate of AgOH will form. $[OH^-] = 0.017 \text{ M}$ (calculation a(i)) $Q = Ag+] [OH^-] = (0.010 \text{ M}) (0.017 \text{ M})$ $Q = 1.74 \times 10^{-4}$ $K_{sp} = 1.52 \times 10^{-8}$ $Q > K_{sp}$	**1 point** earned for stating that precipitate will form **1 point** earned for showing that Q is greater than K_{sp}

Day 20: Practice Exam
Section II: Scoring Guidelines

2. **(10 points)**

In two separate experiments, a sample of an unknown hydrocarbon was burned in air, and a sample of the same hydrocarbon was placed into an organic solvent.

(a) When the hydrocarbon sample was burned in a reaction that went to completion, 2.2 grams of water and 3.6 liters of carbon dioxide were produced under standard conditions. What is the empirical formula of the hydrocarbon?

$$2.2 \text{ g } H_2O \times \frac{1 \text{ mol } H_2O}{18 \text{ g } H_2O} \times \frac{2 \text{ mol } H}{1 \text{ mol } H_2O} = 0.24 \text{ mol } H$$

$$3.6 \text{ L } CO_2 \times \frac{1 \text{ mol } CO_2}{22.4 \text{ L } CO_2} \times \frac{1 \text{ mol } C}{1 \text{ mol } CO_2} = 0.16 \text{ mol } C$$

$$\text{Mole Ratio} = \frac{0.24}{0.16} = \frac{1.5}{1} = \frac{3H}{2C}$$

Empirical Formula = C_2H_3

1 point is earned for calculating moles of H and C.

1 point is earned for correctly calculating the empirical formula.

b) When 4.05 grams of the unknown hydrocarbon was placed in 100.0 grams of benzene, C_6H_6, the freezing point of the solution was measured to be 1.66°C. The normal freezing point of benzene is 5.50°C and the freezing-point depression constant for benzene is 5.12°C/m. What is the molecular weight of the unknown hydrocarbon?

$$T = i \times K_f \times m \quad (i = 1)$$

$$m = \frac{\Delta T}{k_f} = \frac{3.84\,^\circ C}{5.12\,^\circ C/m} = 0.750 \text{ m}$$

moles = molality × kg solvent

moles = 0.750 mol/Kg × 0.100 Kg = **0.0750 moles**

$$\text{Molecular Weight} = \frac{mass}{moles} = \frac{4.05 \text{ g}}{0.0750 \text{ mol}}$$

Molecular Weight = 54.0 g/mol

1 point is earned for calculating moles of the solute.

1 point is earned for correctly calculating the molecular mass.

(c) What is the molecular formula and the name of the hydrocarbon?

$\dfrac{\text{Molecular Weight} \quad 54\,g}{\text{Empirical Mass} \quad 27\,g} = 2$	
Molecular formula = $2(C_2H_3)$	**1 point** is earned for a correct formula
Molecular formula = **C_4H_6**	
Molecular name = **butyne**	**1 point** is earned for a name that is consistent with the formula.

(d) Write the balanced equation for the combustion reaction that took place in (a)

$2C_4H_6 + 11O_2 \ \text{------>} \ 8CO_2 + 6H_2O$	**1 point** is earned for correct reactants and products
	1 point earned for correctly balancing the equation

(e) Draw two isomers for the hydrocarbon.

$\begin{array}{c}\quad\;\; H \;\; H \\ \quad\;\; | \;\;\; | \\ H-C\equiv C-C-C-H \\ \quad\;\quad\; | \;\;\; | \\ \quad\;\quad\; H \;\; H \end{array}$ $\quad$ $\begin{array}{c} H \quad\quad H \\ | \quad\quad | \\ H-C-C\equiv C-C\,\text{-}\,H \\ | \quad\quad | \\ H \quad\quad H \end{array}$ 1-butyne $\quad\quad\quad\quad$ 2-butyne	**1 point** is earned for each correctly drawn structure of butyne isomers.. **(2 points total)**

3.	**(10 points)**

(a) Determine the order of the reaction with respect to each of the reactants, and write the rate law for the reaction.

m = Order with respect to A $\dfrac{\text{Rate 4}}{\text{Rate 3}} = \dfrac{2.4 \times 10^{-2}}{1.2 \times 10^{-2}} = \dfrac{k\,[\,0.20]^m\,[0.10]^n}{k\,[0.10]^m\,[0.10]^n}$ $\quad\quad 2 \;=\; 2^m$ $\quad\quad\quad m = 1$ n = Order with respect to B $\dfrac{\text{Rate 2}}{\text{Rate 1}} = \dfrac{6.0 \times 10^{-3}}{3.0 \times 10^{-3}} = \dfrac{k[\,0.05]^m\,[0.10]^n}{k\,[0.05]^m\,[0.05]^n}$ $\quad\quad 2 \;=\; 2^n$ $\quad\quad\quad n = 1$ **Rate** = k **[A] [B]**	**1 point** is earned for calculating order with respect to A (m) and order with respect to B (n) . **1 point** is earned for the correct rate law.

(b) Calculate the value of the rate constant, k, for the reaction. Include the units.

$k = \dfrac{\text{Rate}}{[A]\,[B]} = \dfrac{(3.0 \times 10^{-3}\ \text{M.sec}^{-1})}{(0.05\ \text{M})\,(0.05\ \text{M})}$ $k = 1.2\ \text{M}^{-1}.\text{sec}^{-1} = 1.2\ \text{L}\,/(\text{mol . sec})$	**1 point** is earned for correctly calculating the rate constant. **1 point** for the correct unit.

(c) If another experiment is attempted with [A] and [B], both at 0.02 molar, what would be the rate initial rate of disappearance of A?

Rate = k[A] [B] **Rate** = $\dfrac{1.2\ \text{L}}{\text{mol.sec}} \times \dfrac{0.02\ \text{mol}}{\text{L}} \times \dfrac{0.02\ \text{mol}}{\text{L}}$ Rate = 4.8×10^{-4} mol /L.sec^{-1} **Rate** = 4.8×10^{-4} **M/sec^{-1}**	**1 point** is earned for setup **1 point** is earned for correctly calculating the rate of disappearance of A **1 point** is earned for the correct unit

(d) The following reaction mechanisms was proposed for the reaction above:

Rxn 1: A + B ----- > C + D
Rxn 2: D + B ----- > C

(i) Show that the mechanism is consistent with the balanced reaction.

Rxn 1: A + B ---- > C + D̶ Rxn 2: D̶ + B ---- > C **A + 2B ---- > 2C**	**1 point** earned for a correctly shown mechanism

(ii) Show that the step is the rate determining step, and explain your choice.

Rxn 1: **A + B ----- > C + D (slow)** Rxn 2: D + B ----- > C (fast)	**1 point** is earned for stating that Rxn 1 is the rate determining step.
Rxn 1 is the rate determining step because its **rate law**, rate = k [A] [B] , **is the same as the experimentally determined rate law.**	**I point** is earned for correctly justifying the answer

Day 20: Practice Exam
Section II: Scoring Guidelines

4.   **(15 points)**
(a) Boron triiodide is reacted with ammonia.

(i) Balanced equation	**1 point** is earned for correct reactants
$BI_3 + NH_3 \longrightarrow I_3BNH_3$	**2 points** are earned for correct products
	1 point is earned for correctly balancing the equation

(ii) Which species in the reaction is the Lewis acid? Explain.

BI_3 is the Lewis acid because The compound has and incomplete octet and **can accept a pair of electrons** from NH_3	**1 point** is earned for the correct choice with explanation.

b) A piece of calcium carbonate is placed in excess nitric acid.

(i) Balanced equation	**1 point** is earned for correct reactants
$2H^+ + CaCO_3 \longrightarrow Ca^{2+} + H_2O + CO_2$	**2 points** are earned for correct products
	1 point is earned for balancing mass and charge

(ii) What will be the sign for $\Delta S°$ for the reaction? Explain.

$\Delta S°$ **will be positive** because **a gaseous product (high entropy) is formed from a solid product (low entropy).**	**1 point** is earned for the correct sign of $\Delta S°$ with correct explanation.

Day 20: Practice Exam
Section II: Scoring Guidelines

(c) Fluorine gas is bubbled through a solution of lithium chloride.

(i) Balanced equation	**1 point** is earned for correct reactants
$$F_2 \ + \ 2\,Cl^- \ ---> \ Cl_2 \ + \ 2\,F^-$$	**2 points** are earned for correct products
	1 point is earned for balancing mass and charge

(ii) Which species will be the reducing agent in the reaction? Explain your answer.

Chlorine is the reducing agent (oxidized substance) because **its oxidation number in the reaction increases from -1 to 0**	**1 point** is earned for the correct answer with an appropriate explanation.

Day 20: Practice Exam
Section II: Scoring Guidelines

5.   **(9 points)**

Seven solid compounds were placed in beakers as shown below.

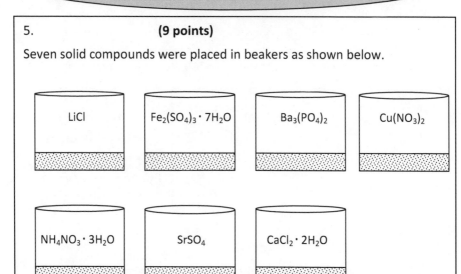

An unknown compound is to be identified by students through observations and results of laboratory tests. The observations and test results obtained by one student are listed in order from (a) through (e). Write the formula(s) of compound(s) that the student should eliminate in the box following each result.

(a) The unknown compound is white.

> *Recall:* Compounds of **transition metals** are generally colored.
> *Note:* Compounds containing a **transition metal** should be eliminated

$Fe_2(SO_4)_3 \cdot 7H_2O$ $Cu(NO_3)_2$	**1 point** is earned for each correct formula **(2 points total)**

(b) The unknown compound dissolves readily in water.

> *Note:* Any Compound containing an insoluble ion should be eliminated

$Ba_3(PO_4)_2$ $SrSO_4$	**1 point** is earned for each correct formula **(2 points total)**

(c) Forms a white precipitate when added to aqueous AgNO₃ solution.

Recall: Ag+ + Cl- ------ > AgCl(s) (a white precipitate)

Note: Eliminate any remaining compound that does not contain Cl- ion.

NH₄NO₃ · 3H₂O	**1 point** for eliminating $NH_4NO_3 \cdot 3H_2O$ or **1 point** for eliminating $Fe_2(SO_4)_3 \cdot 7H_2O$ if it hasn't been previously eliminated.

(d) When heated, the mass of the compound after heating was less than the mass of the compound before heating.

Recall: Hydrates contains water in their crystalline structures. When heated, the water evaporates, leaving behind anhydrous compound that weighs less than the hydrate

Note: Eliminate any remaining compounds that is not a hydrate.

LiCl	**1 point** for eliminating LiCl or **1 point** for eliminating either $Ba_3(PO_4)_2$, $SrSO_4$, or $CuNO_3$ if they have not been previously eliminated

(e) Below:
   (i) Write the formula(s) of the compound(s) that has yet to be eliminated. This is your unknown compound.

$CaCl_2 \cdot 2H_2O$	**1 point** is earned for identifying $CaCl_2 \cdot 2H_2O$ as the unknown

   (ii) Describe any other test that could be done using only the substances in the beaker to further confirm the identity of the unknown.
   Indicate the result of the test as well as formula of any products that are formed from your testing.

Dissolve CaCl$_2$ · 2H$_2$O and **Fe$_2$(SO$_4$)$_3$ · 7H$_2$O** in separate test tubes, **and** then **mix the two solutions.** A white **precipitate of CaSO$_4$** should form.	**1 point** for describing mixing the unknown with a compound that will form a precipitate. **1 point** is earned for correctly identifying the formula of the precipitate

6. **(7 points)**

Answer the following questions about Lewis structures and shapes of compounds.

a) Draw Lewis structures for BF_3 and $TiCl_3$.

(i) BF_3 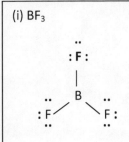	**1 point** is earned for correctly drawing the structure for BF_3
(ii) $TiCl_3$: Cl – Ti – Cl : : Cl :	**1 point** is earned for correctly drawing the structure for $TiCl_3$

b) Determine the molecular geometries including all idealized bond angles for ClNO where the N atom is in the center of the molecule.

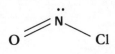 Molecular Geometry = **V-shape** **bent** **angular** Idealize bond angles: **113° – 120°**	**1 point** is earned for correctly stating the geometry and bond angle. Allow point if molecule is correctly drawn without stating the shape.

(c) Classify XeF_4 as polar or nonpolar and explain why.

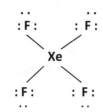

Nonpolar

XeF_4 (Xenon tetrafluoride) has a square planer geometry that allows the **four Xe-F polar bonds (dipole moments) to cancel out.**

1 point is earned for stating that the molecule is nonpolar.

1 point is earned for explanation that is consistent with the type of molecule stated .

(d) Describe the orbital hybridization scheme used by the central atom in its sigma bonding for the following molecules. How many pi bonds are contained in each molecule?

(i) XeF_4 - d^2sp^3 hybridization

no (zero) pi bonds

1 point is earned for correctly identifying hybridization and number of pi bonds in XeF_4

(ii) XeF_2 - dsp^3 hybridization

no (zero) pi bonds

1 point is earned for correctly identifying the hybridization and number of pi bonds in XeF_2

PERIODIC TABLE OF THE ELEMENTS

1	2	3	4	5	6	7	8	9	10	11	12	13	14	15	16	17	18
1 H 1.008																	2 He 4.00
3 Li 6.94	4 Be 9.01											5 B 10.81	6 C 12.01	7 N 14.01	8 O 16.00	9 F 19.00	10 Ne 20.18
11 Na 22.99	12 Mg 24.30											13 Al 26.98	14 Si 28.09	15 P 30.97	16 S 32.06	17 Cl 35.45	18 Ar 39.95
19 K 39.10	20 Ca 40.08	21 Sc 44.96	22 Ti 47.90	23 V 50.94	24 Cr 52.00	25 Mn 54.94	26 Fe 55.85	27 Co 58.93	28 Ni 58.69	29 Cu 63.55	30 Zn 65.39	31 Ga 69.72	32 Ge 72.59	33 As 74.92	34 Se 78.96	35 Br 79.90	36 Kr 83.80
37 Rb 85.47	38 Sr 87.62	39 Y 88.91	40 Zr 91.22	41 Nb 92.91	42 Mo 95.94	43 Tc (98)	44 Ru 101.1	45 Rh 102.91	46 Pd 106.42	47 Ag 107.87	48 Cd 112.41	49 In 114.82	50 Sn 118.71	51 Sb 121.75	52 Te 127.60	53 I 126.91	54 Xe 131.29
55 Cs 132.91	56 Ba 137.33	57 *La 138.91	72 Hf 178.49	73 Ta 180.95	74 W 183.85	75 Re 186.21	76 Os 190.2	77 Ir 192.2	78 Pt 195.08	79 Au 196.97	80 Hg 200.59	81 Tl 204.38	82 Pb 207.2	83 Bi 208.98	84 Po (209)	85 At (210)	86 Rn (222)
87 Fr (223)	88 Ra 226.02	89 †Ac 227.03	104 Rf (261)	105 Db (262)	106 Sg (266)	107 Bh (264)	108 Hs (277)	109 Mt (268)	110 Ds (271)	111 Rg (272)							

*Lanthanide Series

58 Ce 140.12	59 Pr 140.91	60 Nd 144.24	61 Pm (145)	62 Sm 150.4	63 Eu 151.97	64 Gd 157.25	65 Tb 158.93	66 Dy 162.50	67 Ho 164.93	68 Er 167.26	69 Tm 168.93	70 Yb 173.04	71 Lu 174.97

†Actinide Series

90 Th 232.04	91 Pa 231.04	92 U 238.03	93 Np (237)	94 Pu (244)	95 Am (243)	96 Cm (247)	97 Bk (247)	98 Cf (251)	99 Es (252)	100 Fm (257)	101 Md (258)	102 No (259)	103 Lr (262)

STANDARD REDUCTION POTENTIALS IN
AQUEOUS SOLUTIONS AT 25°C

Half-reaction			$E°$(V)
$F_2(g) + 2e^-$	$\rightarrow$	$2F^-$	2.87
$Co^{3+} + e^-$	$\rightarrow$	Co^{2+}	1.82
$Au^{3+} + 3e^-$	$\rightarrow$	$Au(s)$	1.50
$Cl_2(g) + 2e^-$	$\rightarrow$	$2Cl^-$	1.36
$O_2(g) + 4H^+ + 4e^-$	$\rightarrow$	$2H_2O(l)$	1.23
$Br_2(l) + 2e^-$	$\rightarrow$	$2Br^-$	1.07
$2Hg^{2+} + 2e^-$	$\rightarrow$	Hg_2^{2+}	0.92
$Hg^{2+} + 2e^-$	$\rightarrow$	$Hg(l)$	0.85
$Ag^+ + e^-$	$\rightarrow$	$Ag(s)$	0.80
$Hg_2^{2+} + 2e^-$	$\rightarrow$	$2Hg(l)$	0.79
$Fe^{3+} + e^-$	$\rightarrow$	Fe^{2+}	0.77
$I_2(s) + 2e^-$	$\rightarrow$	$2I^-$	0.53
$Cu^+ + e^-$	$\rightarrow$	$Cu(s)$	0.52
$Cu^{2+} + 2e^-$	$\rightarrow$	$Cu(s)$	0.34
$Cu^{2+} + e^-$	$\rightarrow$	Cu^+	0.15
$Sn^{4+} + 2e^-$	$\rightarrow$	Sn^{2+}	0.15
$S(s) + 2H^+ + 2e^-$	$\rightarrow$	$H_2S(g)$	0.14
$2H^+ + 2e^-$	$\rightarrow$	$H_2(g)$	0.00
$Pb^{2+} + 2e^-$	$\rightarrow$	$Pb(s)$	-0.13
$Sn^{2+} + 2e^-$	$\rightarrow$	$Sn(s)$	-0.14
$Ni^{2+} + 2e^-$	$\rightarrow$	$Ni(s)$	-0.25
$Co^{2+} + 2e^-$	$\rightarrow$	$Co(s)$	-0.28
$Cd^{2+} + 2e^-$	$\rightarrow$	$Cd(s)$	-0.40
$Cr^{3+} + e^-$	$\rightarrow$	Cr^{2+}	-0.41
$Fe^{2+} + 2e^-$	$\rightarrow$	$Fe(s)$	-0.44
$Cr^{3+} + 3e^-$	$\rightarrow$	$Cr(s)$	-0.74
$Zn^{2+} + 2e^-$	$\rightarrow$	$Zn(s)$	-0.76
$2H_2O(l) + 2e^-$	$\rightarrow$	$H_2(g) + 2OH^-$	-0.83
$Mn^{2+} + 2e^-$	$\rightarrow$	$Mn(s)$	-1.18
$Al^{3+} + 3e^-$	$\rightarrow$	$Al(s)$	-1.66
$Be^{2+} + 2e^-$	$\rightarrow$	$Be(s)$	-1.70
$Mg^{2+} + 2e^-$	$\rightarrow$	$Mg(s)$	-2.37
$Na^+ + e^-$	$\rightarrow$	$Na(s)$	-2.71
$Ca^{2+} + 2e^-$	$\rightarrow$	$Ca(s)$	-2.87
$Sr^{2+} + 2e^-$	$\rightarrow$	$Sr(s)$	-2.89
$Ba^{2+} + 2e^-$	$\rightarrow$	$Ba(s)$	-2.90
$Rb^+ + e^-$	$\rightarrow$	$Rb(s)$	-2.92
$K^+ + e^-$	$\rightarrow$	$K(s)$	-2.92
$Cs^+ + e^-$	$\rightarrow$	$Cs(s)$	-2.92
$Li^+ + e^-$	$\rightarrow$	$Li(s)$	-3.05

EQUATIONS AND CONSTANTS

ATOMIC STRUCTURE

$$E = hv \qquad c = \lambda v$$

$$\lambda = \frac{h}{mv} \qquad p = mv$$

$$E_n = \frac{-2.178 \times 10^{-18}}{n^2} \text{ joule}$$

EQUILIBRIUM

$$K_a = \frac{[H^+][A^-]}{[HA]}$$

$$K_b = \frac{[OH^-][HB^+]}{[B]}$$

$$K_w = [OH^-][H^+] = 1.0 \times 10^{-14} \text{ @ } 25°C$$
$$= K_a \times K_b$$

$$pH = -\log[H^+], \ pOH = -\log[OH^-]$$
$$14 = pH + pOH$$

$$pH = pK_a + \log\frac{[A^-]}{[HA]}$$

$$pOH = pK_b + \log\frac{[HB^+]}{[B]}$$

$$pK_a = -\log K_a, \ pK_b = -\log K_b$$

$$K_p = K_c(RT)^{\Delta n},$$

where Δn = moles product gas – moles reactant gas

THERMOCHEMISTRY/KINETICS

$$\Delta S° = \sum S° \text{ products} - \sum S° \text{ reactants}$$

$$\Delta H° = \sum \Delta H_f° \text{ products} - \sum \Delta H_f° \text{ reactants}$$

$$\Delta G° = \sum \Delta G_f° \text{ products} - \sum \Delta G_f° \text{ reactants}$$

$$\Delta G° = \Delta H° - T\Delta S°$$
$$= -RT \ln K = -2.303 RT \log K$$
$$= -n\mathcal{F}E°$$

$$\Delta G = \Delta G° + RT \ln Q = \Delta G° + 2.303 RT \log Q$$
$$q = mc\Delta T$$

$$C_p = \frac{\Delta H}{\Delta T}$$

$$\ln[A]_t - \ln[A]_0 = -kt$$

$$\frac{1}{[A]_t} - \frac{1}{[A]_0} = kt$$

$$\ln k = \frac{-E_a}{R}\left(\frac{1}{T}\right) + \ln A$$

E = energy $\qquad v$ = velocity
v = frequency $\qquad n$ = principal quantum number
λ = wavelength $\qquad m$ = mass
p = momentum

Speed of light, $c = 3.0 \times 10^8 \text{ m s}^{-1}$

Planck's constant, $h = 6.63 \times 10^{-34}$ J s

Boltzmann's constant, $k = 1.38 \times 10^{-23}$ J K^{-1}

Avogadro's number $= 6.022 \times 10^{23}$ mol^{-1}

Electron charge, $e = -1.602 \times 10^{-19}$ coulomb

1 electron volt per atom = 96.5 kJ mol^{-1}

Equilibrium Constants
K_a (weak acid)
K_b (weak base)
K_w (water)
K_p (gas pressure)
K_c (molar concentrations)

$S°$ = standard entropy
$H°$ = standard enthalpy
$G°$ = standard free energy
$E°$ = standard reduction potential
T = temperature
n = moles
m = mass
q = heat
c = specific heat capacity
C_p = molar heat capacity at constant pressure
E_a = activation energy
k = rate constant
A = frequency factor

Faraday's constant, $\mathcal{F} = 96,500$ coulombs per mole
of electrons

Gas constant, $R = 8.31$ J mol^{-1} K^{-1}
$= 0.0821$ L atm mol^{-1} K^{-1}
$= 62.4$ L torr mol^{-1} K^{-1}
$= 8.31$ volt coulomb mol^{-1} K^{-1}

GASES, LIQUIDS AND SOLUTIONS

$$PV = nRT$$

$$\left(P + \frac{n^2a}{V^2}\right)(V - nb) = nRT$$

$$P_A = P_{total} \times X_A, \text{where } X_A = \frac{\text{moles A}}{\text{total moles}}$$

$$P_{total} = P_A + P_B + P_C + ...$$

$$n = \frac{m}{M}$$

$$K = {}^\circ C + 273$$

$$\frac{P_1V_1}{T_1} = \frac{P_2V_2}{T_2}$$

$$D = \frac{m}{V}$$

$$u_{rms} = \sqrt{\frac{3kT}{m}} = \sqrt{\frac{3RT}{M}}$$

$$KE \text{ per molecule} = \frac{1}{2}mv^2$$

$$KE \text{ per mole} = \frac{3}{2}RT$$

$$\frac{r_1}{r_2} = \sqrt{\frac{M_2}{M_1}}$$

molarity, M = moles solute per liter solution

molality = moles solute per kilogram solvent

$$\Delta T_f = iK_f \times \text{molality}$$

$$\Delta T_b = iK_b \times \text{molality}$$

$$\pi = iMRT$$

$$A = abc$$

P = pressure
V = volume
T = temperature
n = number of moles
D = density
m = mass
v = velocity

u_{rms} = root-mean-square speed
KE = kinetic energy
r = rate of effusion
M = molar mass
π = osmotic pressure
i = van't Hoff factor
K_f = molal freezing-point depression constant
K_b = molal boiling-point elevation constant
A = absorbance
a = molar absorptivity
b = path length
c = concentration
Q = reaction quotient
I = current (amperes)
q = charge (coulombs)
t = time (seconds)
E° = standard reduction potential
K = equilibrium constant

OXIDATION-REDUCTION; ELECTROCHEMISTRY

$$Q = \frac{[C]^c[D]^d}{[A]^a[B]^b}, \text{ where } a\,A + b\,B \rightarrow c\,C + d\,D$$

$$I = \frac{q}{t}$$

$$E_{cell} = E^\circ_{cell} - \frac{RT}{n\mathscr{F}}\ln Q = E^\circ_{cell} - \frac{0.0592}{n}\log Q \;@\;25^\circ C$$

$$\log K = \frac{nE^\circ}{0.0592}$$

Gas constant, $R = 8.31 \text{ J mol}^{-1}\text{K}^{-1}$
$= 0.0821 \text{ L atm mol}^{-1}\text{K}^{-1}$
$= 62.4 \text{ L torr mol}^{-1}\text{K}^{-1}$
$= 8.31 \text{ volt coulomb mol}^{-1}\text{K}^{-1}$

Boltzmann's constant, $k = 1.38 \times 10^{-23} \text{ J K}^{-1}$

K_f for $H_2O = 1.86 \text{ K kg mol}^{-1}$

K_b for $H_2O = 0.512 \text{ K kg mol}^{-1}$

1 atm = 760 mm Hg
= 760 torr

STP = $0.00\,^\circ C$ and 1.0 atm

Faraday's constant, $\mathscr{F} = 96,500$ coulombs per mole of electrons

Use the grids to plot the number of points you got correct for each question set to better see your progress and improvements in each question category.

You hope to see an upward trend on each graph.

Multiple Choice Questions:

Section I Part A and B Practice

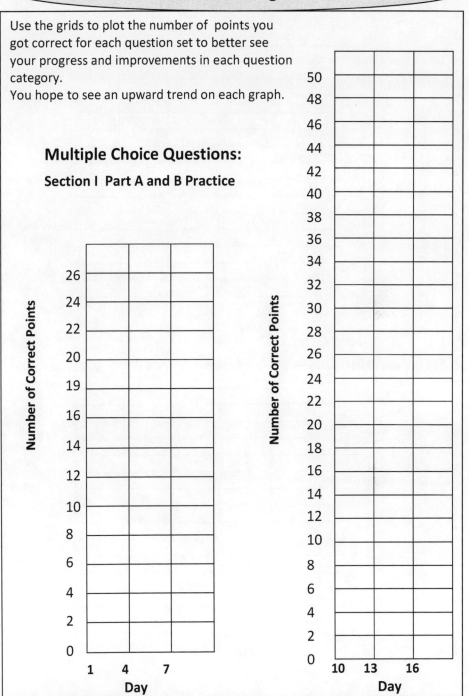

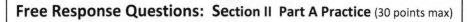

Free Response Questions: Section II Part A Practice (30 points max)

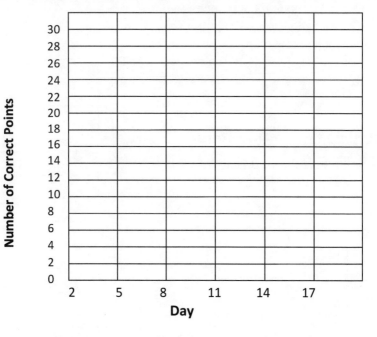

Number of Correct Points

Day

Free Response Questions: Section II Part B Practice (23 points max)

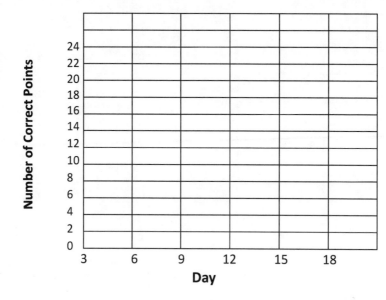

Number of Correct Points

Day

E3 Scholastic Publishing
7 MARNE AVE. NEWBURGH, NY 12550

Surviving Chemistry Books: Ordering Catalog for Schools and Teachers

Our Exam Preps

Questions for Chemistry AP Exam Practice – 2013 $16.64
ISBN: 978-1478324812

Questions for Biology Regents Exam Practice $15.64
ISBN: 978-1469979441

Questions for Regents Chemistry Exam Practice $15.64
ISBN: 978-0983132981

Chemistry Regents Pocket Study Guide (Black Print) $13.82
ISBN: 978-1460970874

Chemistry Regents Pocket Study Guide (Color Print) $19.98
ISBN: 978-1460980620

Our Classroom Materials

Surviving Chemistry Review Book – 2012 Revision* $15.64
ISBN: 978-1478395409

Review Book Student Answer Sheet Booklet $6.99
ISBN: 978-1466319523

Surviving Chemistry Guided Study Book - 2012 Revision* $17.99
ISBN: 978-1478257868

Surviving Chemistry Workbook* $17.99
ISBN: 978-1460942765

Free Answer Booklets (up to 4) with all class-size orders

Cover colors: Each of our book titles is printed in three different cover colors.

Same book title, same great contents, same price, three different cover colors to choose from.

Visit our website **e3chemistry.com** to see all available cover colors for each title.

List Price: Visit our website for list price of each title

Catalog Price: Prices shown are discounted up to 25% from book list price.

Online Prices: Book prices on our website are lower (at a higher discount up to 35%) than our catalog prices.

We encourage schools and teachers to place orders on our website for bigger savings.

Book prices and discounts on other online sites like amazon.com and barnesandnoble.com may be different from our catalog and website prices.

Shipping: 10% shipping and handling charge on all class orders. Shipping discount is available for online orders.

Ordering Methods:

Online: e3chemistry.com

Fax/Phone: (877) 224-0484

Mail: Send Purchase Order to above address

E3 Scholastic Publishing is a Print-On-Demand publisher. Books are printed only when an order is placed.
ALL pre-paid class orders are processed, printed and shipped within a couple of days.
Class-size orders that are not pre-paid may experience significant delays in processing and shipment.
We encourage schools and teachers to prepay for class-size orders to ensure that books are delivered by the time they are needed.

Three convenient ways to Pre-Pay for your class-size orders:
1. Place your order from our website. Save big and pay Securely with a credit card through *PayPal.*
2. Call us to request an online invoice. Just Click and Pay Securely with a credit card through *PayPal* (this is our most convenient method)
3. Send a check for Order Total with your completed Purchase Order form. We also accept pre-payment of *half the order total.* We will invoice you the remaining amount after delivery.

Call or email us with questions or comments at anytime.

345

Made in the USA
San Bernardino, CA
26 October 2012